Marching Orders

Recent Titles in
Contributions in Economics and Economic History

MARCHING ORDERS

The Role of the Military in South
Korea's "Economic Miracle,"
1961–1971

Jon Huer

Contributions in Economics and Economic History,
Number 92

GREENWOOD PRESS
New York • Westport, Connecticut • London

Library of Congress Cataloging-in-Publication Data

Huer, Jon.
  Marching orders : the role of the military in South Korea's
"economic miracle," 1961-1971 / Jon Huer.
     p. cm. — (Contributions in economics and economic history,
ISSN 0084-9235 ; no. 92)
  Bibliography: p.
  Includes index.
  ISBN 0-313-26648-4 (lib. bdg. : alk. paper)
  1. Korea (South)—Economic policy—1960-   2. Korea (South)—
Politics and government—1960-   3. Civil-military relations—Korea
(South) I. Title. II. Series.
HC467.H76   1989
338.9519'5—dc19   88-38381

British Library Cataloguing in Publication Data is available.

Library of Congress Catalog Card Number: 88-38381
ISBN: 0-313-26648-4
ISSN: 0084-9235

First published in 1989

Greenwood Press, Inc.
88 Post Road West, Westport, Connecticut 06881

Printed in the United States of America

The paper used in this book complies with the
Permanent Paper Standard issued by the National
Information Standards Organization (Z39.48-1984).

10 9 8 7 6 5 4 3 2 1

To
Jonathan Blake Huer
and
Marian Elsie Blake

Contents

Tables

Preface

Professor Eric McKitrick, a historian of the old American South, once said of the many arguments for slavery put forward by its defenders that "nothing is more susceptible to oblivion than an argument, however ingenious, that has been discredited by events."[1] We may also say that nothing is easier to retell than a story, however improbable, that has been made credible by events. Such, I believe, is the story of South Korea's so-called "economic miracle."

Because of the very nature of the subject, I have tried to present it as a historical chronicle, with emphasis on narrative continuity, rather than as a detailed technical analysis. For the latter approach, there are many books of superior quality, which I have mentioned where appropriate in the text. My intention is primarily historical and only secondarily socio-logical. Since the subject of Korea's economic development is already well known among the American public, it seems entirely justifiable to keep it as a story.

As a chronicler of events I disclaim any original contribution to the writing of this book. The task has been made easier not only by the events themselves, which contain much that is dramatic, but also by the numerous researchers and writers on the subject of Korean economic development whose works I have freely used in putting together this volume.

Of the many scholars whose writings form the mosaic of this book, I would like to acknowledge my special debt to David Cole, Princeton Lyman, Hahn-been Lee, and Gregory Henderson. On a personal level, my thanks go to Sam Friedman for his insightful comments and to Mary Lou Barker for her editorial suggestions. Both helped make this a much better book than it would otherwise have been. I am also grateful to Suzanne Davidson for her meticulous copyediting; her professionalism is imprinted on every page of this book.

I have followed the conventional spelling format for Korean names (such as in Hahn-been Lee) unless a particular usage (such as in Park Chung Hee) has already been widely adopted.

NOTE

1. Eric McKitrick, "Introductory Essay," *Slavery Defended: The View of the Old South*, Eric McKitrick, ed. (Englewood Cliffs, N.J.: Prentice-Hall, 1963), p. 1.

Introduction

With the spectacle of the Summer Olympics as its crowning achievement, South Korea is emerging on the world scene with a decidedly new and more mature face. The transition has been accompanied by two other events, one within Korea itself and the other within the United States.

Within Korea, democacy returned rather unexpectedly and dramatically. Chun Doo Hwan's military-backed government gave way to a new administration under Roh Tae Woo, elected after bloody student uprisings and against a split opposition that once again had failed to unify its forces. Both these phenomena—student uprisings and fragmented oppostion—have been common sights in modern Korean politics.

Roh is the third leader in the last three decades to have come from the military ranks—after Park Chung Hee, who took over Korea in 1961, and Chun, who succeeded Park after his assassination in 1981. Although he won only one-third of the vote, Roh had enough approval to overcome the split opposition. Because support from the military is a necessary evil in Korean politics, Roh's victory over his civilian opposition was greeted by many with a sigh of relief.

In the United States, the Korean image is being transformed in a way that would have been unthinkable only a few years ago. It has changed from that of a trusted but poor dependent to an economic competitor strong enough to cause the industrial sector considerable discomfort. Often stirred by political pressure and media coverage, many Americans suddenly see Korea as the symbol of all that is troubling America economically, making ''Korea bashing'' a fairly popular thing to do.

The new Korea, both true and imagined, has come a long way from its chaotic postwar economic debris. To most Americans who remember the Korean War (1950-1953), the image of Korea remains almost synonymous with poverty. In fact, many older Americans associate Korea with little else. To them, this emergence of Korea as a new economic and industrial power from Asia is nothing short of astounding.

Consider the following simple facts:

For many years after the war, Korea was one of the world's most backward countries. Prior to 1961, the pivotal year of Park's takeover, Korea's economy was one of the poorest in the world. With its GNP per capita less than $100 per year, Korea stood equivalent to today's Bangladesh. (By contrast, Korea's 1988 GNP per capita, over $3,000, is comparable with that of Italy in the sixties.) Systematically deprived as a colony during the Japanese occupation (1910-1945) and subsequently devastated by the war, Korea had been left with virtually no industrial infrastructure in the postwar period.

Only continuous economic largesse in the form of aid from the United States could keep Korea's fragile existence afloat. Its dependence on American aid was so complete, in fact, that the government's policy for economic development before 1961 consisted almost entirely of extracting as much annual American assistance as possible. An economically successful year was normally one in which Korea, with much handwringing, somehow extracted generous donations from the United States. Korean politicians usually defined their accomplishments by the amount of foreign aid promised from the American government. It was under these circumstances that the image of wretched poverty was naturally associated with South Korea in the American mind.

Prior to 1961, Korea was no better off politically than economically. President Syngman Rhee's autocratic rule (1948-1960), tradition-bound and nationalistic, had come to an abrupt end. Angered by massive election rigging and galvanized by the government's violent reaction to protests, a coalition of university students and citizens proceeded to topple the regime. Rhee, once venerated as founder of Korea's first republic but now discredited, fled to Hawaii, where he died a few years later. The Chang administration that succeeded Rhee's (1960-1961) could do no better, incessantly pressured and badgered by the now-demanding students, who took to the streets whenever they were dissatisfied with government policy. Civil disorder under the new regime replaced the despotism and corruption of the old. Korea became the classic breeding ground of opportunism and inefficiency at every level of society. A sense of hopelessness pervaded the populace. Taught endurance by historical experience and stoicism by Confucian ethics, most Koreans suffered the burden and looked no farther than each day.

On May 16, 1961, the citizens of Seoul awoke to the sound of small arms over the Han River, which, with the Bukak Mountains on the other side, brackets the capital city. They were soon greeted by the news that a small group of military men, led by Major General Park Chung Hee, had taken over the government, placing Prime Minister John Chang and his cabinet under arrest. Seeing the coup as a fait accompli, the entire military establishment joined the junta within days. Thus Korea took its first step toward a new era and within decades would emerge as a cause of America's economic troubles and the symbol of a new Yellow Peril in its charged political passions.

The military junta established the Supreme Council for National Reconstruction as its political and administrative vehicle of authority. To the men of the junta, national reconstruction essentially meant economic reconstruction, and this task could not be accomplished without other changes. The new rulers made no secret of their ambition, which was nothing short of a total transformation of the traditional ways of Korea, especially those elements that they considered nonrational and contrary to progress. The following frenetic decade of 1961-1971, which is the subject of this book, witnessed such sweeping changes as few generations in any society have ever experienced. It was in this decade that Korea's economic "takeoff" was launched and, along with it, a new Korea emerged. Indeed, the present image of Korea—hardworking, disciplined, and almost disturbingly dedicated to high productivity, creating what economist William Overholt called "the most efficient economic machine the world has ever known"—was born in that crucial decade. This awesome transformation from a backward society to one of today's most technologically advanced nations has been described by *Forbes* as "unimaginable to most late-20th-century Westerners."

This book answers the question that naturally arises: How did Korea do it? There are five aspects to the answer, each considered in a separate section of the book.

Part One describes Korea prior to 1961, from its historical legacy to the Rhee and Chang administrations. It outlines the social structure that the military junta inherited.

Part Two analyzes the military establishment in Korea as a crucial factor in the equation, the significance of which is indelibly linked to Korea's economic prosperity. Even today, the military continues to determine the very viability of a democratic, civil government.

Part Three chronicles the "rationalization" of the political sphere prior to economic development. It also describes how the organizational restructuring within the national government became a crucial factor for later developments in the economic sphere.

Part Four deals with the various aspects of economic rationalization: changes in policies and structure, commitment to population control, the ideology of planned economy in a supposedly free market system, and the now-famous New Village Movement as part of its rural policy, which has become something of a model of agricultural development for other emerging nations.

Part Five discusses the role and the possibility of the military in national development. Because of the impressive results of military-civil coalition, Korea may serve as a useful model for other emerging nations.

The appendix presents selected economic figures to demonstrate the magnitude of the changes that took place from 1961 to 1971.

What did take place in that decade is at once historical and intimate in its conception, rational and daring in its execution, and profound and immediate in its consequences. The military men who took over the country and gave their fellow citizens marching orders were no less than founders of a totally new society. With the passage of time, every succeeding generation tends to display progressively less of the virtue of its founding generation. This moral decline has overtaken once industrious, lofty, and purposeful nations such as the United States, the Soviet Union, and Israel. How South Korea will fare in this regard, only time will tell. Just now, it is Korea's finest hour and its drama is still being played out.

What remains inadequate in this story of Korea's economic miracle, I must admit, may be only in its telling.

Part I

KOREA PRIOR TO 1961

1

The Inherited Social Structure

It is essential for our present purpose to reduce the long, often cumbersome history of Korea to three periods: (1) the Traditional Period (from the beginning of Korean history up to 1910); (2) the Transitional Period (1910 to 1961, which includes Japanese rule, the U.S. military government, the Rhee and Chang administrations—the last of which ushered in the military coup d'état); and (3) the Modern Functional Period (1961 to the present). Thus conceived, Korean history will be dealt with in this book only to the extent that it serves to illuminate our present purpose.

1. *The Traditional Period:* The Yi dynasty, the last of the Korean kingdoms, is annexed by Japan in 1910, thus ending the history of independent Korea.
2. *The Transitional Period:* Japanese rule over Korean society through its governor general continues until 1945, the end of World War II; during the rule, the newly modernized Japan attempts western-style reforms on its Korean colony. Following the U.S. military government in Korea, 1945-1948, a native administration is formed by Syngman Rhee, who is Korea's first president. The Rhee administration governs Korea until it falls under massive student protests in 1960. The Chang administration, which succeeds Rhee's, also falls a year later to a military coup.
3. *The Modern Functional Period:* The military takes over. Profound social, political, and economic changes take place in Korea beginning in 1961. The period is the main subject of this book.

The Traditional Period—both as a social structure and as a character type—stretches from the first settlement of the Han people on the Korean peninsula to 1910, the year in which the last king of the Yi dynasty witnessed the forcible annexation of Korea by Japan. Thus

Korea ended its struggle, against the West in general and Japan in particular, to keep the fragile kingdom away from the rush of modern ideas and material and to resist the superpowers for Korean political independence and cultural purity. Economically, Korea at the turn of the century was a backward society with no signs of economic modernization; nor had any rational and efficient habits of mind necessary for modernization developed in its society. Politically, Korea suffered generally from unenlightened and incompetent feudal rulers who had systematically suppressed the inroads of all modern forms of governance and social relations. The government possessed neither plans for Korea's future nor power to implement them. Korea still seemingly maintained a rigid system of social stratification up to the very minute of the annexation; and an overwhelming majority of the Korean population existed in great ignorance and poverty.

The class system in traditional Korea was loosely divided into the ruling ("yangban') and the ruled classes. The yangban class made up the bulk of the officials of the imperial bureaucracy until they were pushed out by the invading Japanese bureaucrats.[1] The yangban aristocrats consisted of two subgroups: the "munkwan" (civilian) and the "mukwan" (military).[2] Following the Confucian tradition of placing a high premium on learning, a career in the bureaucracy as a man of letters (the munkwan) was always preferred, and the men of the sword, the mukwan, occupied positions of more or less secondary importance within the aristocracy. Civilian supremacy over the military, however, was challenged a few times in typical cloak-and-dagger palace maneuvers during the Yi dynasty. At least in formal social relations "class distinctions were extremely severe. Yangban could marry only yangban, and any transgression of this rule was severely punished."[3]

Below the yangban class stood a small group of technicians and professionals called the "jungin" (meaning "middle people"), which consisted mainly of illegitimate yangban children. Their status was something between the yangban above them and the "sangin," or commoner, below. These jungin were the actual workhorses in daily government operations in "medical, astronomical, accounting, legal, geomancy, interpreter, and clerkly or petty official fields."[4] The jungin were selected through public examinations and could advance to a certain rank in the hierarchy but not—at least formally—to the rank of a yangban.

The majority of the people were "sangin" or commoners, to which merchants, soldiers, and artisans belonged. Many of them were also tenant farmers for private landlords or the government. The sangin were generally free men and women, although some artisans were more or less forced to perform certain functions in official courts. Their lifestyle was austere, generally limited to bare subsistence.[5] "Though forming the bulk of the population and bearing most of the burdens of the state, the sangin were actually given no opportunities for education or advancement, and were excluded from even the most minor of the government examinations. Like the members of all other classes their status was hereditary, and they were legally bound to the land they tilled."[6]

At the very bottom of social stratification existed the government and private slaves called the "chunin" (meaning literally "low people"). Until the class was abolished toward the turn of the century, they performed tasks that were considered far inferior to those of the sangin class. The government chunin worked mostly in workshops providing courts and bureaucracy with various manufactured goods and performed a variety of menial tasks for the officials. Private slaves served as household servants and frequently tilled the soil for their masters (their labor being cheaper than that of sangin farmers). Marriages outside of the chunin class were officially forbidden, and those born of slave women were made slaves by decree regardless of the status of the father. This class also included the holders of certain occupations such as actors, witch doctors, "kisaeng" (female court entertainers), and butchers. The latter incidentally were the most degraded of all, forced to follow the family occupation and live segregated.

The four-class social system continued to characterize Korean society in this feudal period until the Japanese annexation in 1910. But the system often provoked violent protests from the oppressed and impoverished peasants. Nineteenth century Korea saw a constant turmoil of peasant revolts and governmental countermeasures; the last of such rounds eventually ushered in a Japanese intervention. In 1812, for example, a combination of bad harvest and other equally harsh social conditions triggered a mass agrarian revolt. The rebels actually controlled several northern provinces, threatening to march to the capital city. The revolt coincided with similar movements throughout the country "against oppression at the hands of the government, the local nobility and the wealthy landlords."[7] But the peasant revolt and other similar attempts failed. In 1862, another peasant movement flared up; it had started as a local incident against a corrupt governor but spread quickly to other parts of the country. That revolt was also quenched by the government. Through this period of chaos, discontent, popular uprisings, and advancing foreign powers, Korea managed to survive as a sovereign state.

The largest perhaps the most significant popular movement singularly reflecting the Korean social conditions, however, was the "Tonghak" revolt that culminated in 1894, which most historians refer to as a genuine native uprising of the nationalist strain.[8] Toward the end of the century, Korea had reached a peak of the traditional form of political tyranny and economic backwardness. While the yangban enjoyed their social, political, and economic privileges, the vast majority of peasants suffered oppression and impoverishment. The newly increasing foreign intrusions on Korea also added fuel to the domestic discontent already fraught with tension and resentment.

Since Korea was forced to open her door to the foreign powers, her foreign trade increased rapidly; from 1877 to 1881 imports increased eight times; and from 1885 to 1891 exports increased four times. The Japanese, Chinese, and British flooded the country with their merchandise. Foreign-made textiles exceeded all other imported goods. The native handicraft industries were ruined. Rice exported by the Japanese merchants in Korea exceeded all other exports, and shortages in the rural areas became acute, leading to social unrest. No native merchants who could compete with the foreign merchants existed, and no industrial revolution as in the Western nations took place in Korea. The country faced bankruptcy by the penetration of foreign merchants, especially Chinese and Japanese.[9]

Tonghak means "eastern learning," so named in opposition to the foreign powers that the peasants associated with "western learning." From its foundation in 1860 the messianic gospel of Tonghak foretold the fall of the Yi dynasty and the establishment of a new kingdom under its principles of humanity. The Tonghak revolt, touched off first in a small southern town, grew into a massive peasant rebellion. As the rebels gained ground, defeating sizable government forces, their demands shifted from reform measures and punishing tyrannical local governors to cutting off all foreign relations, especially with Japan and China. The initial list of their demands, which mirrors the stark conditions of their society at the threshold of modernity, contained the following:

1. Government tolerance and cooperation with Tonghak believers.
2. Punishment of corrupt officials.
3. Punishment of dishonest yangban.
4. Abolition of slavery.
5. Better treatment of the underclass.
6. Provisions allowing widows to marry.
7. Fair taxation.
8. Selection of bureaucrats based on qualification.
9. Punishment of those secretly connected with the Japanese.
10. Governmental resolution of all debts involving farmers.
11. Fair land redistribution.[10]

However, largely due to their very own success in making their demands heard, the Tonghak rebels gradually transformed their essentially reformist and forward-looking cause into extreme isolationism.

Thus the rebels idealized an isolated Korea protected from all international currents in politics and technological development. "While the grievances of the Tonghak were certainly genuine and many of their demands just, their attitude toward modernization and their hatred of foreigners placed the government in an extremely precarious position. If Korea was to escape foreign domination it was absolutely essential that she adopt Western technology, both to strengthen her armed forces and to develop a healthy economy. The rebels looked no further than their own immediate circumstances."[11]

The Tonghak revolt was eventually put down, not by the Korean government, but, ominously, by the Chinese and Japanese troops called in by the crown. With Tonghak no longer the purpose of their presence in Korea, the two powers predictably clashed with each other for the dominant influence of the Hermit Kingdom; Japan eventually won the contest. Many of the demands made by the Tonghak rebels had been seriously attended to by the government, including the dismissal and arrest of corrupt officials. A more serious consequence of that uprising, however, was that it eventually invited Japan's inroads into Korea.

Thus, Korean history up to the final defeat by Japan was an unforgiving repetition of unenlightened rulers, foreign invasions, and sociopolitical and economic chaos.

Japan began to actively interfere with Korea's domestic politics following its victory over Tonghak and Chinese contingents as the latter were driven out of the peninsula. By 1910 Korea was formally annexed by Japan as its colony, its colonial status to last until 1945 when Japan was defeated in World War II.

As the new dominant power, the Japanese colonial government attempted sweeping reforms, many of which had been tried before the formal annexation. The attempted reforms included virtually every aspect of traditional Korea:

1. Abolition of social class
2. Merit and qualification as the basis of official appointments
3. Abolition of slavery
4. Permission for the yangban to participate in business
5. Prohibition of early marriages
6. Permission for widows to remarry
7. Abolition of class privileges

Unfortunately, however, to many Koreans these reform measures, reasonable and progressive though they were, symbolized Japan's direct challenge to Korean sovereignty. As such many Koreans took pride in resisting these reforms as a demonstration of their anti-Japanese patriotism. Japan's intent was inspired by its colonial design on Korea. Without regard for the sentiments and capacities of Korean people, the colonial government viewed traditional Korea simply as an inefficient and irrational society. With brutal efficiency, the colonial government set a time limit and ordered all Koreans to abide by the alien government's decree. These reform measures, a few of them genuinely necessary, however, took little notice of how the Koreans felt. Many of them were indeed aimed at benefiting Japanese industry. The reform of dress, for instance, was designed to help the textile industry in Japan.[12]

Many yangban officials went bankrupt under Japanese rule and some entered the hitherto alien world of business. The Japanese colonial government between 1910 and 1945 did its best to keep Korea a classic colonial state, socially, politically, and economically. Koreans were allowed no participation in policy-making, and the colonial bureaucracy contained fewer than 10 percent of Koreans among its functionaries on all levels. The natives were excluded from any meaningful economic activities and the economy itself was made totally dependent upon Japan. The colonial government in Korea succeeded in creating what George McCune called ''a thirty-five-year intermission on political responsibility and administration experience.''[13]

Resistance sprang up both in Korea and abroad. The independence fighters employed both military and diplomatic means; they fought the Japanese with decisively inferior firepower and human strength, and attempted, often unsuccessfully, to call the world's attention to their plight. The Japanese retributions were methodical and terrible; many perished in prison. But some escaped. Syngman Rhee, a reform-minded young aristocrat, was one of the latter who, after a seven-year imprisonment, escaped to the United States where he established a Korean government in exile during World War II.

In the thirty-six years of relentless colonialism, Korea was transformed from a highly stratified caste society into a fairly serviceable colonial state. In both, the vast majority of Koreans suffered—first at the hands of their own masters and then at those of foreign rulers.

In August 1945, as Japan surrendered, thus ending World War II and its direct rule over Korea, Koreans suddenly found their independence. But the legacy of the thirty-six years of colonialism proved to be damning in the years to follow.

NOTES

1. A detailed analysis of the ruling yangban and other social strata is in Chapter 4.

2. The mukwan's resentment toward the munkwan often became the source of revolt and conspiracy.

3. Keun-Woo Han, *The History of Korea* (Seoul: Eul-yoo Publishing Co., 1967), p. 249.

4. Pow-key Sohn, et al., *The History of Korea* (Seoul: Korean National Commission for UNESCO, 1970), p. 150.

5. Chong-sik Lee, *The Politics of Korean Nationalism* (Berkeley, California: University of California Press, 1963), p. 11.

6. Han, *The History of Korea*, p. 250.

7. Sohn, *The History of Korea*, pp. 188-89.

8. "The most important peasant revolution in Korean history," according to Bong-youn Choy, *Korea: A History* (Rutland, Vermont: Charles E. Tuttle Co., 1971), p. 127.

9. Choy, *Korea*, p. 128.

10. Sohn, *The History of Korea*, p. 211.

11. Han, *The History of Korea*, p. 409.

12. Ibid., p. 422.

13. George McCune, *Korea Today* (Cambridge, Mass.: Harvard University Press, 1950), p. 275.

2

The First Republic,
Syngman Rhee,
and the Students

Syngman Rhee, returning from the United States a resistance hero, was elected president of the First Republic and in 1948, following a three-year tutelage under the U.S. military government on the finer points of democratic governance, formed the first modern government in Korea by Koreans. Unprepared for modern political and economic life, however, Korean society under Rhee endured an endless cycle of social chaos—accentuated by the war—in the political and economic vacuum left by the Japanese colonial experience. Rhee himself proved to be no master of politics in a chronically underdeveloped nation.

In many ways Rhee was a product of the old Korea, steeped in Chinese classics and claiming a mythical lineage to the last of the Yi royalty that had perished with Japan's advance. With this backward-looking sentiment and in his current heroic status as the "father of the nation," Rhee was actually a politician without a political ideology and a governor without a governing program. His primary political support rested on the essentially nationalistic nostalgia for a bygone era and the lore of Rhee's anti-Japanese resistance, not on political visions or economic programs.

Hence, whenever he encountered opposition to his policies he was habitually inclined to rely on physical violence and political manipulation rather than persuasion or competition on ideological grounds. "The absence of political ideology deprived his regime of any long-term goals and the country of any forward political direction. During the twelve years of Rhee's rule, no developmental program was conceived and no meaningful reform measures were enacted other than the draconian legislation in the name of national security, a euphemism for anticommunism."[1]

Lacking a political basis that could represent more than the personality of the ruler himself, the Rhee administration was from start to finish a one-man regime with enormous power concentrated in his hands alone. In addition to the absence of an ideological basis, Rhee's administration could not secure enough qualified personnel for administrative tasks that neither the colonial government nor the American tutelage had prepared them adequately. In place of long-term developmental programs Rhee implemented hand-to-mouth patchwork that served his short-term political purpose. He was notorious for his periodic cabinet shake-ups, intended and designed to maximize his political control.[2] "Periodic cabinet shake-ups deprived the administrative agencies of stability and consistency and, at the same time, engendered the temptation for the ministers to amass a fortune and pay off political debts while in office. This latter practice further undermined the stability and morale of public servants, already concerned about the wholesale turnover of low ranking administrators in conjunction with ministerial changes."[3]

Rhee's basis of personal popularity was mainly his legend as a resistance hero, which had been created during Japanese rule and carefully nurtured by his regime. Shrouded in this legacy, Rhee continued to see himself as the center of current events in Korean life. Unfortunately, Rhee possessed neither the experience nor the willingness to manage large, complex organizations. He carried on with politics surrounded by those who were personally loyal to him rather than those chosen for objective qualifications. In day-to-day government operations, the vast number of administrative tasks were handled by those who merely took illicit advantage of their positions. Elevated by his sycophants to a virtual deity, Rhee was essentially isolated from the ongoing affairs of his subordinates.[4] Charitably, "at best he was a traditional 'monarch.' "[5]

Under Rhee, Korea remained a repressive society, aided by a 300,000-man police apparatus. Corruption and incompetence characterized the regime's national bureaucracy. The police force was at the center of continuing social and political oppression. Elections during his regime continued to be scandalized with rigging, violence, and bribery—the final one of which resulted in the April 1960 student uprising that toppled his government. The press was harassed and often closed down for anti-Rhee tendencies. A few of his political opponents were assassinated or executed, or died rather inexplicably.

Economically, Rhee's Korea was an almost totally nonfunctional society. Toward the end of his regime in 1959, Korea's income per capita amounted to a mere $50. Inflation also spiraled under Rhee. Between 1945 and 1957 wholesale prices increased 1,840 times, and retail prices 1,890 times. Even taking the effects of war into consideration, few countries experienced such an extraordinary inflationary spiral. Foreign aid, chiefly from the United States, only aggravated the economic conditions further by encouraging easy consumption and haphazard spending programs. The land reform initiated by the U.S. military government and completed under Rhee's administration did little to alleviate the situation for the farmer.[6] Even a government publication admitted that "for many Koreans today, day-to-day living is not at what can be called a subsistence level—even by Asian standards."[7]

Rhee's ability to stay in power rested to some extent on his effective control of the military, whose neutrality, ironically, both helped him stay in power and, during the later student uprising, caused his fall.[8] Lacking in indigenous military tradition, the military high command was composed of factional rivals from one of three backgrounds: (1) the Japanese Imperial Army background; (2) the Chinese Army background; and (3) the Manchurian military background. Syngman Rhee controlled the military so skillfully and effectively that, despite its enormous size and the subsequent political role it would play, the military during his regime remained strangely inconsequential in Korea's political life.[9]

However, the military served Rhee well as a source of electoral votes and political funds. High-ranking officers were pressured into "delivering" their units to Rhee and his Liberal party. During elections a "persuasion" unit of political officers toured military posts to campaign on behalf of Rhee, which caused deep resentment among younger officers, some of whom eventually became the coup conspirators. As Rhee was steadily losing ground in the civilian arena, the intensity with which he sought support from the military gained momentum. He demanded and received specific financial contributions from his favored officers. Since the military was spending roughly $400 million in aid from the United States, Rhee's political machine relied heavily on the loyalty of the military to shore up his sagging political fortunes. This was at once a source of shame and embarrassment to some officers in the military establishment.[10]

Rhee was eighty-five years old in 1960—the year in which the much-rigged election caused his downfall. His chief presidential opponent, Byung-Ok Chough, died at Walter Reed while undergoing surgery, leaving Rhee with no significant opponent to speak of. Thus, the sole focus of the 1960 election shifted to the vice presidency, a position of very probable succession to Rhee, who might resign before his term expired. Ki-poong Lee, Rhee's vice presidential running mate, was primarily known more for his personal loyalty to Rhee, which went back to the days of exile government in the United States, than for demonstrable political leadership. The prospect of Lee succeeding to the presidency unnerved many Koreans. Moreover, in a previous election Lee had been defeated by John Chang for the vice presidency.[11] On its part, Rhee's Liberal party was determined not to repeat this humiliation.

In its determination to win votes at any cost, however, the Liberal party supporting Rhee and Lee apparently went overboard. Two weeks or so before the election a fantastic array of election rigging plans devised by the Liberal party was exposed by the press. The secret plans included producing ghost votes, stuffing ballot boxes, bribing voters with money and merchandise, using physical violence on opponents, openly casting ballots under supervision, and so on. The Liberal party countered by arguing that there were no such plans and the exposé was "fantastic fiction." The opposition Democratic party led by John Chang appealed to the Central Election Committee for safeguarding mechanisms. Predictably, this appeal fell on deaf ears.

The election, for both presidency and vice presidency, was won by the Liberal party, but the victory proved fatal. Reports of violence spread. At many polls Democratic ballot watchers were refused and often physically threatened and beaten by unidentified assailants. A local Democratic party official was beaten to death, and there were numerous other incidents in which the Democrats were harassed, threatened and beaten. Official electoral results were just as spectacular. In spite of his far greater preelection popularity, John Chang failed to secure one single district over Ki-poong Lee, who outgained Chang four to one; total votes for Lee, 8,337,059, and Chang, 1,843,758. Rhee, unopposed, secured 9,333,376 for the presidency.[12]

The Democratic party immediately charged that the election was "illegal, null and void." More specifically, the Democrats argued that

1. opposition ballot watchers were barred from performing their duty;
2. the election was unfair due to the many instances of "open voting," "group voting," and "voting in bundles," thus pressuring voters to vote Liberal;
3. the administration's governmental machinery, namely, the police, was involved in stuffing, stealing, and producing ghost votes;
4. government-supported organizations resorted to violence and terrorism, causing injuries and deaths.[13]

In the chaotic and tense aftermath of the election a series of small scale protests staged by students and local citizens escalated into a massive student demonstration in the capital city against the Rhee regime. By all observable accounts the 1960 election riggings by Rhee's Liberal party stood as one of the most notorious and blatant instances of force and fraud seen in any political process.

As the campaign got under way, one or two Democrats were killed; photographers wre beaten by thugs; open voting for members of the "one happy family" was practiced either by advice or by coercion; ballot boxes were "stuffed"; and corrupt police and hoodlums played their part effectively. As anticipated, there was a tremendous victory for the Liberal party candidates.

Though the aged President was shielded by his efficient bodyguards and secretaries, he knew what was happening. Big celebrations with parades and fireworks, to commemorate the victory, were cancelled, owing to the reports of growing unrest and widespread indignation against the shocking corrupt methods employed by the government party to win the elections.[14]

On April 19, emboldened by the apparently weakening authority of the once-powerful government, angry students marched to the presidential palace. The barricaded police opened fire, killing some of the students. This incident was incendiary; reports of the "massacre" spread like wildfire. The situation was now out of control while, significantly, the military stood neutral. As a measure of appeasement, Rhee announced that he would leave the Liberal party and devote himself to national tasks; this pleased no one. Soon he was forced to advise vice president elect Ki-poong Lee to resign from the posts he held both with the Liberal party and with the National Assembly where he was speaker. This Lee did.

But such gestures of atonement were too little and too late. Tasting their political power and flexing their muscles, the students refused to relent; they demanded something fairly unthinkable then: Rhee's own resignation. Under mounting pressure and seeing no way out, Rhee finally resigned from the presidency on April 27, and amid wild cheering his twelve-year reign came to an end.

As a result, for the first time university students became the center of national politics and of heroic folklore. In the Second Republic of John Chang, which succeeded the Rhee regime, however, this government-by-students proved to be the curse of the new government.

NOTES

1. Kwan-bong Kim, *The Korea-Japan Treaty Crisis and the Instability of the Korean Political System* (New York: Praeger Publishers, 1971), p. 23.

2. Kyung-cho Chung, *New Korea* (New York: Macmillan, 1962), p. 16.

3. Kim, *Korea-Japan Treaty*, p. 21.

4. Clarence Norwood Weems, *Korea: Dilemma of Underdeveloped Country* (New York: World Affairs Center, 1960), p. 25.

5. Kim, *Korea-Japan Treaty*, p. 26.

6. Choy, *Korea*, pp. 351-55; also Irving Louis Horowitz, *The Three Worlds of Development* (New York: Oxford University Press, 1966), pp. 204-5.

7. Office of Public Information (OPI), *Where Korea Stands* (Seoul: OPI, 1955), p. 39.

8. Jae-souk Sohn, "Political Dominance and Political Failure: The Role of the Military in the Republic of Korea," *The Military Intervenes*, Henry Bienen, ed. (New York: Russell Sage Foundation, 1968), p. 105.

9. Kim, *Korea-Japan Treaty*, pp. 56-57.

10. Ibid., p. 75.

11. During Rhee's administration the Korean constitution provided separate elections for the presidency and vice presidency. In 1956 the Korean electorate chose the president (Rhee) and the vice president (Chang) from two opposing parties, the Liberal party and the Democratic party respectively. The president and his vice president maintained during their tenure what at best may be described as a cordial relationship.

12. Central Elections Management Committee, *Records of Korean Elections* (Seoul: Central Elections Management Committee, 1968), pp. 814-22.

13. Chung, *New Korea*, p. 50.

14. Ibid., p. 55.

3

The Second Republic of John Chang

Following the fall of Rhee and his Liberal party, the opposition Democratic party now became the party in power. The national election administered by the interim government in July 1960 gave the Democratic party almost unlimited confidence and power. While in opposition, the party had steadily maintained its popularity, especially among intellectuals and the urban middle class, and demonstrated time and again its capacity for checks and balances, often effectively if not always successfully, against the Liberal party. Placed at the center of political power, however, the now-ruling Democratic party immediately faced two major problems: its own inner party split and the heightened national expectations. Of the two, the more devastating was its internal strife and factional feud that surfaced as soon as its ascension to power had been assured.

Factionalism within the Democratic party, mainly between the Old and New factions, had been in existence for quite some time before and during Rhee's time.[1] But the overriding task of opposing Rhee had kept them together on that common frontier. The Liberal party now ousted, and the immense power vacuum deposited in their own hands, the long-existent factional interests within the Democratic party reemerged with magnified intensity.

The first key issue to test the factions focused on who was to be appointed to the now-powerful premiership. During the Liberal party's regime, the president had wielded immense political power. Strengthened by the image of the "founding father," Rhee had enjoyed a virtually unopposed dictatorship. The new constitution, adopted after Rhee's fall, established a British-style parliamentarian system. Presidential power was transferred to the prime minister, and the president was made a figurehead.

But for the Democratic party this transition to a new political system proved to be its own undoing. A new National Assembly was formed in an election atmosphere that was not entirely free of old political scandals and wheeling-dealing. Even publicly, some Democrats aligned themselves with the badly discredited Liberals and won election. The 214-member National Assembly election resulted in a rather significant distribution.

Party	Faction	No. Elected
Democratic	New	84
	Old	83
Independent	(no party)*	42
Grand Socialist		3
Others**		

*Those who could not obtain the necessary party nomination, in addition to the old Liberals and the "pure" independents, ran as independents and occupied a significant portion in the National Assembly. Given the almost even split (84-83) of the two major factions in the Democratic party, their later ineffectiveness could already be discerned.

**A considerable number of votes were also cast for the Liberal party candidates, although none of the candidates dared hold the party banner openly.

In this election with a supposedly fresh political start, more than half of the elected assembly members were old time politicians. The most important result of the election was none other than the 84 versus 83 division between the Old and the New Democrats, no faction garnering enough members to control the assembly's majority. The internal feud among the Democrats heightened as they approached electing the prime minister, to be appointed nominally by the president pending a ratification by the assembly's majority.

Both factions managed to agree to elect the venerable Bo-sun Yun to the presidency. Since the president had the constitutional power to nominate the new prime minister, it was no secret that Yun (an Old Democrat) naturally wanted someone from the Old faction for premier rather than the one-time vice president and certainly more popular John Chang, a New Democrat. This decision by Yun to bypass Chang created a storm of controversy and a round of heated political manipulation. The independents, a sizable proportion in the assembly, held the decisive lever in the election of the country's first premier, the actual ruler. As rumored, Yun appointed Old Democrat Do-yun Kim to premiership. Both factions immediately plunged into the last phase of action, one faction to ratify and the other to reject. The New Democrats sought to solicit enough votes from the independents who realized the immense power their votes commanded to defeat Kim's ratification. Since another nomination had to be made upon Kim's defeat, the president would be forced to appoint Dr. Chang prime minister. This worked brilliantly, and Yun's first appointee suffered a hair-splitting defeat: 111 for, 112 against. The Old Democrats did not secure a majority.

The following day Chang was apppointed, apparently with reluctance, and another round of vote-getting was in full swing. Again, the key element in ratifying Chang's premiership lay in the hands of the independents who, by now, appeared determined to keep everyone in suspense and national politics in frenzy. Rumors rampaged that independent votes were sought after by both Democratic factions at a phenomenal sum of money, and given the high political stake the rumors gained credence as the voting neared. The New Democrats succeeded again by rallying 117 votes (three votes more than the necessary minimum) against 107. The Second Republic was finally inaugurated, but the two factions had already locked horns as mortal enemies.

By early 1961, as a ruling but badly crippled party, the two factions reached a point of no return in their enduring political struggle for dominance. Social, political, and economic chaos and indecisiveness characterized the short Democratic reign that was actually dominated by the New faction. In February the Old faction established its own party named the New Democratic party. Since Chang's regime received no tangible support from the rival group, the balance of power rested on the precarious and outright opportunist independents in the Assembly, who showed little concern for national political stability. Irrational politics and unproductive economy characterized the Chang regime in its short (nine-month) reign.

Among its more constructive initiatives, the government sought to normalize relations with Japan and attempted talks with North Korea, South Korea's two arch enemies. But in either case, the Chang government could not amass enough political support for the delicate and emotion-charged undertaking.

Under Rhee's government, the problem of normalizing diplomacy with Japan had been handled with extreme irrational chauvinism and high-sounding slogans. Chang's regime immediately reopened negotiation with Japan that had been more or less deadlocked before the April student uprising the year before. Even more delicate and potentially dangerous was Chang's new overture to North Korea. With all the bitter memories of the Korean War still fresh, the ideological and sometimes military conflict between the two Koreas in the following Cold War era made the approach extremely hazardous and explosive. Although most South Koreans had reservations about their emotional bitterness toward North Korea and Japan, quite a few acknowledged the need for normal relations or at least the relaxation of tension between them. Despite this positive domestic mood, however, Chang's regime was internally disorganized and powerless and seemed to have neither policy nor power solid enough to carry out the tasks.

At the crossroads of continuing social disorder and economic chaos, the country's very survival emerged as the most crucial issue of the day. During the regime's short tenure, an average of 7.3 street demonstrations occurred daily, each involving nearly 4,000 persons, totaling 1,350 separate demonstrations. Demonstrations by students alone numbered 726, and approximately 50 percent of the entire student body in the nation was involved in one protest or another. Labor unions on their part staged 675 demonstrations involving more than 200,000 employees.[2]

Although the overall situation in Korea—social, economic, and political—would hardly have ranked among the harshest of times in the past, the public's expectations were running uncontrollably high in the delirious aftermath of Rhee's fall. Any domestic and international attempt by the Democratic regime met a sharp disapproval by an ever-discontent public. The regime's dealings with Japan got bogged down in scandals while the pro-North members in South Korea openly expressed, with increasing vocality, their desire for unification as the shortcut road to the South's peace and prosperity.

What annoyed the Chang regime further was the incessant demands made by the students to whom the new regime owed its birth. Fresh from a victory in which a hated regime had been demolished, the students demanded in tirade and street demonstration a complete change in all areas of life in Korea from cultural styles to foreign policy. They often demanded and were given an audience with the prime minister, who was forced to listen to what was now called the "fourth branch of the Chang regime."[3]

The students forced their demands on the politicians by means of continuing demonstrations. After the students had shown their power so forcefully on April 19th, no politician could afford to ignore their desires. Both the interim government during the summer and the newly-elected government of John M. Chang in the fall followed the policies advocated by the college students. For six months Korea experienced "government by demonstration." As long as the students were still excited enough that they would take to the streets spontaneously to shout their demands they dominated Korean politics.[4]

"The negative effect of student demonstration on the political process"[5] during the Chang regime reached its peak when they invaded the parliament and shouted from the rostrum that action should be expedited on bills to penalize the old Liberals guilty of corruption and election-rigging. As self-righteous guardians of the nation's morals and politics the students seemed out of control, alienating many segments of the public that had generally supported their previous activities. Even among students themselves there was a desire to return to moderation.[6]

The Korean economy was mostly what had been inherited from the Rhee regime, and had deteriorated further under the Chang administration.

In less than one year the Second Republic became so corrupt and incompetent that economic deterioration, social unrest, and political instability were rampant. In April, 1961 more than four million city dwellers representing 28 percent of the total working labor force were unemployed. Business and industry stagnated because of shortages of capital and electric power; industrial production declined by 75 percent, and many small and middle-sized business establishments went bankrupt. Meanwhile, living costs went up; the price index had risen 30 percent since the student revolution the year before. In the rural areas, more than five million farmers were desperate—caught between crop failures and payment of exorbitant interest on loans (in some cases as high as 80 percent per year). Large numbers of the rural population were on the brink of starvation.[7]

During the short period of Chang's government, inflation soared. Pressured by the high hopes created after the fall of Rhee, and particularly harassed by the ever-demanding student activists, Chang's administration was characterized by short-term patchwork, chaos, and a sense of impending crises. "Lacking political organization and ideology, the Chang government was unable to offer either short-term relief or long-term hope to the populace. In fact, as a result of Chang's weakness, socioeconomic conditions deteriorated from bad to worse."[8] Particularly in the economic sphere, what Chang had inherited from Rhee was already bad enough, critically hurt by the Korean War, for Rhee himself had no long-range economic plans drawn or implemented. With the past consequences and the present conditions combined and compounded, the Korean economy was on the verge of collapse.

Over the previous five years, the ratio of capital goods to raw materials administered through the International Cooperation Administration widened from 47:53 in 1955 to 22:78 by 1960, upon which an observer later remarked: "Extreme luxury and vanity encouraged the infiltration of various foreign commodities. Shortly before the [military] revolution the Republic of Korea was an unchallenged market for a third world nation."[9] The heavy emphasis on raw materials encouraged consumption and discouraged long-term capital investment in production and industry. Furthermore, rather small portions of capital goods had anything to do with a productive economy. Most state-owned enterprises were also operating in the red. By 1960, twelve major state enterprises sustained a deficit of $63 million. In most cases liabilities cancelled out all assets, leaving them in a state of bankruptcy. The 34 leading industrial firms were in debt to the state, owing an average of $1,530,000 in principal and $330,000 in interest. The loans "to the privileged stratum of society" could not be repaid in most cases without auction-ing. U.S. aid gradually decreased, and the shaky Korean economy sustained an average annual trade deficit of almost $300 million.

The agricultural sector, which was comprised of about 70 percent of the Korean population, suffered no less. At the end of World War II, the terminating point of Japanese colonialism in Korea, about 68 percent of rural families owned less than one "chungbo"; this increased to 80 percent by 1959, "indicating the pauperization of the landowning rela-tionship in the composition of South Korea's land ownership."[10] Despite the high proportion of rural population, agricultural production fell far below self-sufficiency. Ironically, on the Chang regime's last day in power a newspaper ran a headline about a tenant farmer with a family of six who was unable to meet the landlord's final notice on unpaid rent, and killed himself.[11] The "Spring Poverty," as it had been called traditionally, was exceptionally hard in that year. Tenant farmers peren-nially suffered between the end of the previous year's crops and what little cash was left, and the coming of the barley harvest in the early summer. Every year the Spring Poverty invariably reappeared, and any effort to stamp it out was either a policy failure or the government's lip service paid to farmers.

The Korea of early 1961 was highly charged with political passions accentuated by raised expectations and the repeated frustration of those expectations. Largely preoccupied with the urgent needs of political consolidation after the party's split, the Chang administration was unable to do much in the economic sphere.

The government of less than a year was toppled by a military coup on May 16, 1961.

NOTES

1. See Chapter 4 for the origins of factionalism within the Democratic party.

2. The Supreme Council for National Reconstruction (SCNR), *History of the Korean Military Revolution* (Seoul: Publications Committee, 1961), p. 15.

3. John Oh, *Democracy on Trial* (Ithaca, New York: Cornell University Press, 1968), p. 90.

4. William A. Douglas, "Korean Students and Politics." *Asian Survey*, Vol. 3, No. 12, 1963, p. 586.

5. Kim, *The Korea-Japan Treaty*, p. 30.

6. In the fall of 1961 the students were asked how much political activism was considered desirable; 44 percent preferred "moderate," 28 percent "passive," and 8 percent "very positive." (Reported in Robert A. Scalapino, "Which Route for Korea?" *Asian Survey*, September 1962, Vol. 11, No. 7, p. 10.) However, the fall of 1961, when this survey was taken, represented the peak of the new mili-tary government's crackdown on student militancy, which may have discour-aged their political activism.

7. Douglas, "Korean Students," p. 589.

8. Kim, *The Korea-Japan Treaty*, p. 28.

9. Park Chung Hee, *The Country, the Revolution, and I* (Seoul: Hollym Corp., 1970), pp. 31-32.

10. Dong-Pil Cho, "Agricultural Problems in Korea." *Koreana Quarterly,* Vol. 1, Winter 1959, p. 118.

11. *Dong-A Daily*, May 15, 1961.

4

Social Forces and Social Change

We shall conclude the discussion on the precoup social conditions in Korea by considering the following three aspects in this chapter: (1) the specific consequences of Japanese rule in sociopolitical and economic spheres, especialy its impact on the various social strata that had constituted the Korean caste system; (2) an analytical look at why the Rhee and Chang regimes failed, and the historical and ideological reasons for their failure; and (3) a discussion on other social forces and institutions in Korea, for example, labor unions and students, and why these forces could not have brought about meaningful social change toward a more functional society.

SOCIAL STRATIFICATION AND MASS SOCIETY

During much of the Yi dynasty, the last of the Korean kingdoms, social restrictions had discouraged activities that were generally regarded as "economic" in nature. Most learned Koreans took a fairly cavalier attitude toward economic activities as ungentlemanly and vulgar even when their circumstances warranted a more active interest. Influenced by the Confucian teachings, the yangban class was legally forbidden to engage in trade, and the merchants (a great many of them peddlers) were socially frowned upon. Those belonging to the merchant class, constituting about 6 percent of the total population, received encouragement from neither the national policy nor the normative social system. International trade toward the end of the nineteenth century was both scarce and weak; Pusan was the only port open to trade with Japan.

Although Kaesong functioned as the center of foreign commerce, its scale was nothing like China's Canton or Japan's Osaka by comparison.

Unlike either Japan or China, Korea had never been favorably disposed to robust business acumen. The general social attitude toward commerce was perhaps more important than any specific government policy to discourage entrepreneurial activities. While skill in small trade—the way farmers demonstrated their competence in bargaining for bulls, for example—was always admired by the villagers, the "trader-specialist" himself was never very high on the scale of social respect. He was despised as an exploiter during much of the Yi dynasty and was barred from owning land. It was the farmer-trader, not the trader-specialist, who owned and dominated the network of small markets. Discouraged both by the negative social attitude toward commerce and by stifling government control, entrepreneurship and capital formation remained totally dormant in Korea until the coming of the Japanese merchant in the late nineteenth century. Shops were few and small, and merchants above the peddler level were also few and had negligible social influence.[1]

Industrialization began under the Japanese occupation, especially toward the beginning of World War II, primarily designed as part of the Japanese war efforts in supply and transportation. The acceleration of military industrialization was such that industrial productivity almost matched that of agriculture. Yet, "most of the industry and the better farmland were owned and managed by the Japanese, with Koreans serving as laborers and lower-level supervisors."[2]

The really significant Japanese settlement did not occur until the 1880s when many impoverished Kyushu families emigrated to Korea under the government's protection and subsidy. By the early twentieth century, the Japanese small shops and trading posts covered the entire peninsula "like a network." With the expanded political role of Japan over Korea, the number of Japanese migrants increased phenomenally: 3,622 in 1882, 42,460 in 1905, 171,543 in 1910, 336,812 in 1918, and finally 708,448 in 1940, or about 3.2 percent of the population. "As a ruling class, the Japanese outnumbered even the yangban whom they displaced." Many of them were in agriculture and commerce, but the largest group was in government service, 41.4 percent as opposed to 2.9 percent of Koreans in offices of small significance.[3]

Other indicators of contrast between the Japanese settlers and Korean natives were equally sharp. About 97 percent of all gainfully employed Koreans (men and women) were laborers, while a matching percentage of Japanese were in top or middle level ownership or management, both in and out of government. About 71 percent of the Japanese population was urbanized as opposed to 11.5 percent of Korean natives. With increasing war efforts, the gap steadily widened. Toward the end of colonial rule, the Japanese constituted the absolute ruling elite in politics and economics.[4] Industrial activities, picking up tempo, increased fifteen times between 1932 and 1945. Household industry dropped from 40 percent of the total composition of industry in 1933 to 24.7 in 1938, while heavy industry, mostly war related, rose from 38 percent in 1930 to 73 percent by 1942. On the surface, Japanese industrialization in Korea brought with it all the potential factors for modernization, such as increased skill levels, urbanization, specialization, and a progressive, orderly society, presenting an alternative to the traditional, backward social system.

But beneath this surface was a process that fulfilled little of this assumption. The tempo of growth was without rational control. Strange towns emerged overnight with no local ties, and laborers were recruited haphazardly from the south to the industrial north. There was no control over the overuse of facilities and resources. Much overtime work and prohibition of union activity made the formation of new ties impossible.[5]

The colonial administration carefully controlled capital investment in Korea, through the Zaibatsu and Japanese Overseas Department,[6] aimed at creating the Korean economy's total dependency on Japan. "The Japanese owned 90 percent of the total paid-up capital of all corporations in Korea in 1938 and 85 percent of all manufacturing and industrial facilities in 1944 as well as controlling all major banking, insurance, and so on." It is believed that the Korean share of overall industrial capital investments was less than 6 percent, and about 90 percent of capital for even Korean-operated industry originated from Japan.[7] Such heavy concentration of Japanese ownership and skills in the Korean economic system became an obvious factor for the chaos and stagnation that surfaced when the Japanese abruptly withdrew from Korea with the ending of World War II. "Administration virtually collapsed. With the uprooting of all Japanese, routine vanished. No one knew to whom to apply for daily needs, let alone for mountainous exigencies. The economy, instead of expanding to absorb this enormous increase, declined, the industrial sector foundering. . . . The departure of 700,000 Japanese civilians removed almost all the country's technical and managerial skills and its industrial capital resources."[8] "Without the Japanese managers and technicians, such key industries as transportation, communication, electricity, and the manufacture of fertilizers could not be operated."[9]

Korean social strata, rigidly defined in form only, went through a fundamental change during Japanese rule. The traditional Korean aristocracy in the Yi dynasty had been quite different as a social class from those classic aristocracies of other societies. As a class they maintained virtually no cohesive class interests, collectively defined and defended. Even the status definition had never been very clear. Only a small group of yangban officials mostly residing in the capital could properly be so defined. But their propensity for court manipulation aimed at achieving petty personal gains created more rivalry than cohesion.[10] Although there were some yangban who, in and out of government, jockeyed for political influence, they were extremely small in number. The nation's entire yangban class, or those who so claimed, however, far outnumbered both the above groups of yangban. Record keeping of the yangban status in Korea was notoriously inaccurate, and it was commonplace for the wealthy and enterprising non-yangban to purchase yangban status.

The Korean folklore is full of the legacies of yangban who fell from, and those who rose to, the status through luck and ingenuity. Often "heavy debt brought sale or exchange of status. To thousands, a yangban status past became a dusty record in the family register and a horse laugh in village gossip." Some families attempted to retain their yangban status through political connections. However, their capital connections wore thin and their influence on the local government accordingly waned. It became increasingly difficult to maintain the paraphernalia of being yangban: strict marriage customs, contempt for work and money, and the expenses of Confucian ceremony between birth and death were enormous. Marriage with lesser local families, even slave families, eventually resulted.

The principal factor for the looseness of yangban status and the ease with which the status changed hands was the enormous number of those who claimed, from one source or another, to belong to the class. No exact number of yangban is available for the last century of its existence. Including the "hyangban" and "toban" (local yangban varieties), a 1910 contemporary observer from Japan, according to Henderson, estimated the number of yangban as something between 1,500,000 and 2,000,000.[11]

The jungin, the "middle" functionary class, often took advantage of yangban aloofness from practical matters and climbed to the yangban class, or took actual command of situations in daily matters. For their functional and practical disposition, the jungin were potentially the most modernized of all social classes in Korea. When the opportunity for their service arose, such as during the Japanese invasion or the installation of the U.S. military government in 1945, their administrative skills at least on the clerical level were greatly utilized.

The ineffectiveness of the yangban class as an elite in Korean society was further aggravated by the remaining two social strata—the sangin and chunin, commoners and slaves respectively. One statistic indicates the extent to which the line of social caste had deteriorated: about 48 percent of the local yangban became farmers, even slaves, when taxation and military obligation became too severe for them to bear. By the end of the Yi dynasty, "the farming occupation no longer corresponded clearly with what had been the farming class, and farmers whose families had never known any other social status than that of farmer may well have become a minority of the farming population."[12]

Although the chunin class had elements (for example, butchers) that were clearly defined and degraded, the actual operation of the lowest social stratum was considerably ill-defined and broadly constituted. Private slaves, for example, were generally recruited from sangin, but often they were also from the yangban class, pressed by "debts, taxes, funeral expenses, and the like." They either sold themselves or sought protection from powerful families, the pattern of which significantly altered the society's general and considerably lax attitude toward class distinctions. The slaves could become yangban almost as easily as the yangban became slaves. Henderson observed that "only in such a way can one explain how, when slavery was 'abolished,' the slave population tended to vanish so quickly that, miraculously, though it married and reproduced, almost no one claims to be or is even accused of being its descendant among present-day Koreans."[13]

One village study, included in the statistics above, shows the true nature of Korean caste as it existed before its final formal collapse. The study period, 1690-1858, revealed no significant "natural" growth in the yangban class. Nevertheless, toward the end of the period yangban rose from about 7.4 percent of the numerical population in the beginning to 70.3 percent of the number of households, while sangin households decreased from 49.5 percent to 20.1 percent in the same period. The slaves decreased from 43.1 percent of the population to 15.9 percent in the 1783-1789 period, and rose again to 31.3 percent by 1858.[14] The conclusion invariably leads to the kind of status fluidity that demonstrates the peculiar inner workings characteristic of the seemingly rigid class system, which did much to define the Korean psyche in "homogeneity" and "fluidity" in its crucial stage of modernization later.[15]

What was left of the yangban class received its final blow from the wholesale acquisition of land by the Japanese. Without land and never having been engaged in commerce, the Korean aristoctracy completely lost its hold in society. When the Japanese came to Korea to rule, some yangban gladly collaborated. When the 84 most prominent yangban were offered a $10,000 per annum retirement stipend, as part of a yangban liquidation campaign, only eight refused. Top Korean officials, 3,645 in all, were pensioned off, marking the final elimination of yangban as a nominally ruling elite. "At least from 1919 on, Korea may be said to have become a country without a leadership class."[16] The disappearance of aristocratic patterns in culture and behavior was astonishing indeed. After more than five hundred years of continuous existence, Korean aristocracy vanished more completely than that of

Europe, Japan, India, or South America. No remnants of a class society—the class personality type, the behavioral traits, and the distinguish-
ing class accents—remained in Korean society once the aristocracy was
dismantled. No significant social custom, with origins in the aristocracy,
remained a permanent part of contemporary Korean society.[17]

WHY THE FIRST TWO REPUBLICS FAILED

Although Rhee's fall stemmed directly from the 1960 election rigging
and the subsequent killing of students by the police, the historical and
structural origin of his leadership, which led to his eventual fall, goes
back to the beginning of the current century. The general composition of
the power elite under the Rhee regime heavily reflected the archaic
ideology of the national liberation and independence movement in
which Rhee's own worldview was shaped. Those who served under
Rhee, largely "docile agents" of the power holders and leaders of the
outdated independence movement, lacked the functionally disposed
modern organizational skills.

The nation-building leaders did command brief but considerable en-
thusiasm and respect from the grateful postcolonial population after the
Japanese withdrawal. But as soon as their managerial shortcomings
became evident as problems mounted, they were replaced by career bureaucrats who had acquired low-level administrative experience during
the colonial government. Both groups under Rhee did little to exert
more powerful and functional influence on Korea's developmental administration. On one hand, the nation-building leaders led by Rhee
were technically ill-equipped to handle the pressing affairs of practical
government for which the charisma and rhetoric of the nationalist past
remained fairly useless. On the other hand, the top-level bureaucrats
under Rhee, many of whom had entered the administrative ladder
through a legalistic public examination during colonialism, were neither
innovative nor efficient in managing public affairs. Their limited functional capacity saw its best moment during the brief postwar period.[18]

As a charismatic and legendary hero of Korean resistance against
Japan, Rhee's initial leadership position was both broad and solid. But
by extending his leadership beyond the largely symbolic nation-building
phase into a developmental phase of national government, he outlasted
his own usefulness and capacity to lead.

Unfortunately for Rhee and his country, the world of his youthful
reformist zeal and his actual assumption of power were separated by
over half a century. In this passage of time he lost much of his earlier
commitment to reform. The country he was now chosen to lead was not
the same country in which he had earlier formed his self-image and
worldview. A close relative of Rhee wrote to a reporter after Rhee's

death: "When at last he arrived at his life's goal, he was already an old man." As an old man, the political and psychological makeup that defined him and his ideology were similar to those of the old order that he had despised as a young man.[19]

Since Rhee possessed neither the inclination nor the competence to manage the national government effectively and purposefully, he expressed strong aversion to anything that resembled planning or rationalizing the bureaucracy and national affairs. The Nathan Plan, the first of a series of abortive economic plans conceived before the military coup of 1961, was intended as an overall program for developing the economy; the Rhee regime, preferring "negotiations with aid donors (principally the United States) by proceeding on an ad hoc basis and avoiding the overall commitments and constraints of a plan," refused to adopt it.[20] The basis of Rhee's economic policy, where such was the case, consisted of obtaining as much foreign aid as possible and, from this viewpoint, committing the nation to a rigidly set plan was considered a significant political risk.

This short-run tendency in the general direction of national government invariably created an atmosphere of temporary "consumption mentality." Between 1955 and 1960, for example, government consumption as a percentage of the nation's total available resources rose gradually from 9.2 in 1955 to 9.4 in 1956, 11.2 in 1957, 13.1 in 1958, 14.6 in 1959 and 14.9 in 1960. But this increasing input, the governmental expenditure, had the negative effect of reducing private investment in the same period, which declined from 9.1 to 6.2 percent.[21]

In foreign policy, Rhee also lacked the pragmatic and practical bent of internationalism, holding on to his rigid nationalism in a rapidly changing world. His main diplomatic ties were almost exclusively with the United States, rejecting any nation neutral to or tolerant of communism. Under Rhee, communism became the single most important basis of national direction and daily mindset to the extent of obsessive rigidity and irrational judgment; this obsession intensified after the Korean War. "Under the formula of anti-communism few distinctions existed between political opposition and political enemy, between progressive parties and the communist organizations, and between Rhee's enemy and the national enemy. Rhee and his elite publics (power elite) seemed to confuse themselves with the state. They often charged those who disagreed with them as enemies of the state rather than as their political opponents."[22]

Lacking both the willingness and capacity to rationalize the governing process through functional reform in government, Rhee predominantly relied on personal loyalty and intrigue rather than on open, merit-based systems of management. Competing for his personal confidence became the mode of political ascent. Different organizations, headed by those

with Rhee's implicit recognition, formed competing factions to monopo-
lize this attention. In this atmosphere, rivalry encouraged political con-
spiracies and even assassinations.[23]

During Rhee's tenure the entire arena of political and economic
activity centered around Rhee's singular persona, and in the charged
atmosphere of intrigue and counterintrigue, there was little desire or
capacity to establish a future-oriented national direction through positive action.

If the Rhee regime suffered from such internal inadequacy, the succeeding Chang administration suffered from both external and internal
handicaps. For the most part, the Chang regime was created by external
factors over which it had little control, and was subsequently paralyzed
by the internal factors dating back to the earlier nationalist movement.
The Democratic party of John Chang that eventually split up into two
parties, as seen in the preceding chapter, had always been a shaky
political alliance against the common enemy, Rhee and his Liberal party.
The Democratic party was organized out of the sheer urgency of opposing Rhee by the convergence of the independents from the Parliamentary Liberal party and the Democratic Nationalist party.

The leadership element of the former was made up largely of civil servants from the colonial government, somewhat favorably disposed to
functional management and liberal politics. John Chang was the leader
of this faction, later identified as the New faction. The Democratic Nationalist party, on the other hand, was composed of political leaders
with the conservative background of former landlords and rural elders,
although the party possessed some commanding figures who ran later
against Rhee in presidential elections.

When they were finally brought to power after the fall of Rhee, the
Democratic party, now without a common target for alliance, reverted to
its traditional factionalism. Although Chang was nominally the prime
minister, he was badly crippled by the Old faction's defection from the
coalition—thus losing effectiveness in the governing process. "By
patience, persuasion, the use of power, and financial lures," Chang for
a time managed to maintain enough support for the Democratic party
(now solely made up of the New faction) augmented partly with defec-
tors from the Old faction, which eventually established itself as a new
party. Chang's position was thus made extremely vulnerable and his
leadership tenuous by implication. His political foes, separated from
him with no ideological or programmatic differences, continually
harassed his administration. With the unity, stability, and viability considerably damaged, Chang's regime was at the center of the age-old
cynicism about the political process in Korean society.[24]

In addition to the internal handicap that severely paralyzed governmental effectiveness, the structural rearrangement in the political

system considerably reduced administrative effectiveness and function-ality, a parliamentary system was established in place of the presidential system with centralized authority. Partly as a reaction to the negative memories of an autocratic president and partly from a national mood for change, the parliamentary-cabinet and the two-chamber National Assem-bly were enacted. However, "a good case might have been made in favor of the existing [presidential] system given the state of general turmoil and unrest" with the student uprising.[25]

Much the same pattern practiced under Rhee reappeared to character-ize the Chang government: for example, using the military as the source of political funds and votes. Yet Chang was unable to protect the military from the political harassment of the now all-powerful National Assembly. The Chang regime also faced the dilemma of having to choose as a major national task between the urgent need for political consolidation and the equally urgent need for economic development. The public euphoria after Rhee's fall, raised to the level of impatient de-manding of immediate results, allowed little time for the Chang admin-istration to plan and act. A three-year economic development plan, a modified form of the Nathan Plan, was worked out by a group of eco-nomic planners. But the political leadership, preoccupied with its own political problems, paid scant attention.

Another more fundamental defect in the functioning of the govern-ment was an outgrowth of the internal factional strife: the Democratic party had been in opposition so long that they never thought of taking actual power as a possibility; they had become a permanent opposition party. After the years of struggle against the Rhee government, when their turn suddenly came they found themselves without a coherent governing plan. A small element, mostly the New faction members who for years had planned a broad chart for national and international policy, remained unsupported. "[O]wing to the inherent lack of cohe-sion and the dissipation of energy in opposition struggle, the policy thinking of these individuals, though expressed in public announce-ment, was not widely shared by other leaders of the party."[26] Those who possessed political power had no developmental disposition, while the functionally oriented elements in the government had no power to implement their plans.

With these internal difficulties came the external handicaps. The pro-gressive political leaders having faded away as procommunist during the Rhee era, the Chang government was little different in its broad out-look on politics and personality from the regime it replaced. The political leaders within the Democratic party did struggle against Rhee, but "were not and could not be revolutionary in character because their power was not acquired by their own revolutionary effort but was 'given' by the students" after the April uprising.[27] "The implication of such a handicap was that the party was subject to a whole array of demands from the various new social forces that were unleashed by the upheaval and that the ultimate survival of the regime was dependent upon the extent to which the party succeeded in absorbing such new forces."[28] The most tangible manifestation of the implication was the general disorder of society. Between April 1960 and May 1961, street demonstrations had become a Korean way of life and politics as the following numbers indicate:[29]

Organizations	Number of Demonstrations	Number of Persons Involved
Political organizations	57	76,280
Students	747	527,819
Labor	675	219,303
Religious, cultural groups	35	40,713
Others	486	310,678
Total	2,000	1,174,802

Pent-up grievances, legitimate or otherwise, poured out in daily street protests. Wavering between the need for law and order and the commitment to liberal democratic ideology for which the Democratic party had struggled so long under Rhee, Chang chose the latter. He refused to suppress the street demonstrators despite the increasing social unrest and disorder. As the parliamentary-cabinet system partially paralyzed the governing process, the overcommitment to free popular expression, also as an emotive reaction to what Rhee had represented, greatly immobilized the Chang administration.[30] The press and intellectuals had no thoughtful regard or sympathy for the problems the Chang regime was struggling to solve within a democratic framework with tolerance. Habitually at odds with the government since the Rhee era, the intellectuals and students had become a highly vocal and critical group, which, without offering concrete plans or policies, continued to criticize the Democratic party especially after its split.

A combination of such internal and external circumstances made the Chang administration, for its brief tenure, appear a highly ineffective and incompetent national government.

THE ROLE OF SOCIAL FORCES

Many social observers have often noted that Korea is a society of no significant pressure groups. When numerous organizations appeared overnight during the Rhee regime as a strong demonstration that was deemed necessary against the Japanese intention to expatriate Koreans in Japan to North Korea, one observed that "from the outset, they are organized as a subsidiary to the government party. They are agents of the government or a political party, and the leadership within a group is decided not on the basis of the majority support of its members, but on the amount of support that one receives from the parent organization."[31]

The weakness of social organizations concerned with fairly narrowly defined interests and aims was characteristic of social forces in Korea—students, labor unions, radical political parties, or sociocultural interest groups. Generally they lacked firm articulations of purpose and ideology and ordinarily were organized top-down for a particular objective the parent organization deemed useful at the moment.

A strong personality as the center of the organizational activities, not the policy or the structure itself, was another common feature of Korean pressure groups. A contemporary observer remarked that "if a pressure group is a pressure organization to the extent that it is capable of exercising pressure on 'politics,' or more specifically, on the functioning of political power . . . Korean pressure groups which are merely useful agents of the government can hardly fit themselves into the definition."[32] Still another observed similarly that "political parties, labor unions, student groups and businesses are often merely factions composed of one leader and his personal followers. This makes it difficult in Korea to build any organization larger than the number of persons one man can personally gather around him. Larger organizations can be built only putting various factions together, and therefore they suffer from disunity. Koreans often seem to have no clear concept of an organization as entity in itself."[33]

The students, however, enjoyed more effective political influence than any other group in Korea; they toppled one government and thoroughly dominated another. In April 1960, outraged by Rhee's election rigging, they marched to the capitol building and dismantled the Liberal government. "It was completely the student's show, for the adults merely stood on the sidewalks and applauded."[34] Spontaneity and unstructuredness, however, characterized their activities. "Indeed the lack of any organized leadership was a significant characteristic of the April" uprising.[35]

For Korean students there were several factors that hampered the development of an effective, national organization of lasting significance:

1. In common with other social organizations in Korea, factionalism among leaders and groups made any coordinated effort toward national unity among students virtually impossible; leaders exaggerated claims of strength by inflating the number of followers, and ideology or principle was fairly ignored in their activities.

2. Corruption was another common feature of student activities rivaling those of the real political world. In student body elections, from which leaders generally emerged, student votes were purchased, bribery was openly practiced, and opponents were often harassed and beaten; and scandals involving student leaders, faculty, and politicians in collusion frequently appeared in the media.

3. Students were too preoccupied with their own career pursuits by making connections with the established order, which seriously weakened their commitment to social causes. The landing of a bureaucratic job in the establishment was considered so imperative that different factions often emerged as rival groups vying for right connections and support in the government.[36]

If leaderlessness was the general feature of their organizations, the absence of a firm ideological commitment and a clear programmatic articulation characterized their specific political activities, especially between 1960 and 1961. A survey after the April uprising on the students' reasons for having participated in the anti-Rhee movement revealed the following rather wide-ranging results:

1. Dissatisfaction with the lawless and corrupt Rhee regime (72%)
2. Anger at police atrocities (65%)
3. Anger at the society ruled by violence (65%)
4. Dissatisfaction with social corruption (64%)
5. Dissatisfaction with arrogance of the privileged class (64%)
6. Attempt at supporting organizations defending democracy (53%)
7. Realization that only students can stand up for the nation (48%)
8. Influence of newspaper agitation (45%)
9. Anger at distorted reporting by the ruling groups (44%)
10. Anger with the hoodlums who assaulted students (35%)
11. Anger at the corruption in educational institutions (37%)
12. Inability to sit idly by while students were involved in protest (17%)
13. Conviction of the certainty of success with student protests (14%)
14. Influence of the appeals of professors to get involved (13%)[37]

(The choice of reasons in this survey was preestablished. The fourteen most likely reasons were selected by the researcher and then presented to the subjects. Given the range of choice, the respondents were not allowed to present their own reasons in this survey.)

When asked about the factors that contributed to their success in the uprising, the students gave "courage shown by students," "influence of education," "neutrality of the military," "influence of newspapers," "professors' demonstration," and "leadership shown by the opposition party," as listed in order of preference. The students offered virtually no ideological reference in this survey as reasons for their political success.[38] Asked about their reasons for participating in the movement when the choice was open, the students still gave similar responses, such as "election rigging," "corrupt Rhee regime," "police brutality," and so forth.[39]

Regarding student ideology, another survey revealed the fairly startling extent of disillusionment concerning democratic ideals and their usefulness in actual practice in Korean society. Over 40 percent showed a negative reaction, saying that Western style liberal democracy was not appropriate for Korea, 71 percent opposing a two-party system as inefficient, and 40 percent equating the political system appropriate for Korea with "good employment conditions and improved material standards."[40]

During the 1960 uprising the protesting students and professors routinely demanded "justice, truth, liberty, and democracy, but they failed to spell them out in exact terms; nor did they advocate new political and economic reform programs. Consequently, no new political forces or parties that could challenge the supremacy of the old political forces emerged from the student movement."[41]

Nor were the students able to shake off the lingering tradition of personal loyalty to the leaders of the anti-Japanese nationalist legacy, of which Rhee was the most dominant figure, even as they were violently denouncing his very regime. Eighty-five percent of the students surveyed identified the Rhee regime as the target of their opposition while only 13 percent held Rhee personally responsible, generally stating that "he was too old" or "he did not know what went on below him."[41]

Lacking a clear ideological direction in their political movement, since they were the only political group in the absence of other strong social forces (labor unions were nonexistent and the military stood neutral, for example), the student movement turned into a semimoralist demand.[43] "Recognizing the difficulty of pursuing vague principles, some student groups turned to more pragmatic goals (after April). . . . They stopped official cars on the streets to see if they were being used for private purposes. They stopped pedestrians to search them for illegal foreign goods. Some of the more ambitious students ran for National Assembly election in their home districts."[44]

A strain of chauvinistic nationalism was inevitable in the absence of a more progressive political ideology. They not only denounced foreign goods consumed in Korea but also opposed any superpower (including the United States) intervening in the domestic affairs of Korea. Having neither a clear political consciousness nor articulate plans for Korea's future, the movement degenerated into an aimless students-for-all mentality. The students at will demanded audiences with the prime minister and occupied the National Assembly floor with endless complaints and tirades. The more radically inclined groups demanded a hand in foreign and domestic policies and proposed a direct North-South student conference that was received enthusiastically by North Korea. Only three days before the military coup, the radicals supported a rally of the People's Self-Reliance party (which had been directly inspired by North Korean President Kim Ilsung's "juche" concept).

This frenzy of student activity came to an abrupt halt in May 1961 when the military took over. The hitherto tolerant if not always friendly relationship between students and government altered dramatically in the subsequent years of the junta government. The military junta, as a reaction, would accept none of the student powers displayed during Chang's government. Yet it co-opted the willing and able graduates into the mainstream of administrative resource.[45]

Labor unions have never been effective in Korea either as political organizations or as trade pressure groups. A contemporary observer of the Korean labor scene declared that "there is no labor movement in South Korea. . . . Many union leaders are closely related to the government party."[46] At the time of this observation the organized laborers barely exceeded 10 percent of the total labor force. "The labor movement during the Japanese rule gained virtually no foothold for its development. After Korea's liberation from Japanese rule, the present national labor organization started as a front organization of right-wing politicians to destroy the powerful Communist infiltration in the ranks of labor. Under Rhee, it became a subservient instrument of the Liberal Party, as well as the object of political spoils of the 'labor aristocrats.' "[47]

What little labor organization existed mostly served as an extended arm of the government as its front organization. To most Koreans labor unions frequently conjured up the images of "lowness, meanness, gangsterism, and covert collaboration with the government to destroy private interest and, when it appeared, liberalism."[48] Although the labor unions were increasingly vocal in subsequent years,[49] they still remained largely without influence primarily because of (1) the government's active interest in controlling labor, and (2) the general social resistance to class consciousness, especially relating to the urban working class.[50] Ironically, one of the chief reasons cited for the remarkable economic development in the decade 1961-1971 was the absence of "powerful trade unions."[51]

Under the Rhee regime, labor unions functioned as political organizations heavily subsidized by the Liberal party. But under Chang, the general composition of labor membership and political contour took a sharp turn. "New labor organizations sprang up, especially among white collar workers such as bank employees and school teachers, and a new movement was initiated to coordinate or amalgamate scattered labor organizations. Labor organizations increased in number and membership during the few months following the April uprising. In less than six months, the number of labor unions increased by almost one-third (from 621 to 821), and membership increased by more than 25,000."[52] It was in this period of general social upheaval under the more liberal Chang administration, and the increasing vocality and membership of labor unions, that most of the labor demonstrations, 675 in all, took place.

The most vocal and radical of the mushrooming unions was the National School Teachers' Labor Union, which had been suppressed by Rhee. Many radical elementary and secondary school teachers sought to attain the union's autonomy from governmental interference and to protect the interests of low-ranking members in wage increase and job security. As the most effective labor movement under Chang, the protest spread nationwide; nevertheless, only a fraction of the claimed 20,000 members actually engaged in activities supporting the ideologically radical orientation of the leadership.[53] Moreover, a procommunist strain, real or imagined, was imputed to the movement and a severe crackdown followed, ending the only viable labor activity in modern Korea.

The least effective of all as a social force, much less as an institution, in Korea was the leftist-leaning organization, be it "communist," "socialist," "progressive," or even "reformist." The various ideological banners were all lumped together as antistate organizations, and to varying degrees both regimes suppressed, harassed, and persecuted the ideological dissent.

Communism was outlawed after the 1945 liberation, and the remnants of leftist structure in South Korea were thoroughly purged through the subsequent anticommunist campaign under the U.S. military government and the 1947 Communist-led military rebellion. Following the 1950-1953 Korean War against the Communists, the Rhee regime established "the official doctrine of anticommunism" and also succeeded in "generating a popular revulsion against the communist in the wake of the cruel destructiveness of North Korean forces."[54]

Emerging as legal political organizations during the more liberal Chang regime, the reformist parties, nevertheless, suffered a political defeat at the ballot box. Lack of political funds, the disunity among the parties, and the hostile relationship between the two Koreas contributed to their defeat. A campaign for open discussions on fundamental political and economic issues could not be waged under the restraining ideological structure in the South perpetually engaged in a cold war with the North. Having elected only a marginal proportion to the National Assembly, a total of seven in the two-chamber assembly, moreover, "they were not inclined to rely on the regular political process to affect government policies; instead they became generally conspiratorial and resorted to anomic forms of political action. Hence, to many people

in South Korea, the reformist parties appeared to be basically uncon-
structive, untrustworthy and insubstantial."[55] Their activity in and out
of government managed to attract some radical students and intellectuals toward the end of the Chang administration. The government eventually launched its own antileftist campaign, and this was effectively
and thoroughly accomplished by the military government upon its
ascension to power.

As for the peasants in Korea, the Tonghak rebellion marked the last
effective peasant movement in Korean society, although they played
another significant role in the 1919 movement against the Japanese
colonial government. For centuries, peasants had been the least active
and most paternalized group, showing little interest in politics, and by
and large common rural action remained difficult to achieve.[56] It was not
until the junta government's sweeping rural program called "The New
Village Movement," some years later, that the farmers in Korea gained
an equal footing with their fellow citizens.

It was in this power vacuum of Korean politics, with virtually no
coherent social force to compete for political dominance when the
regime faltered, that the military emerged as the most organizationally
capable social force in Korea.

SOME QUESTIONS RAISED AND ANSWERED

In concluding this chapter, some questions that are an integral part of
our current analysis still must be raised and answered. Let us raise the
few pertinent ones below:

I. Why did anticommunism so strongly prevail in Korea under Rhee?

The role of communism in Korea (both South and North)[57] is historically explained first by World War II, upon whose conclusion the
United States and the Soviet Union divided Korea along the 38th parallel. The North was occupied by the USSR and the south by the United
States, a temporary and administrative division that eventually froze
into permanence through the irreconcilable political differences between
the two superpowers. Second, in the Korean War the Communist North
(backed by the USSR) and the capitalist South (backed by the United
States) clashed, and as a result anticommunism under Rhee became an
ideological and political weapon of control as well as an emotive reaction
to the war enemy. Third, in the ensuing Cold War the drift between the
two world blocs further widened, affecting the two Koreas. For Rhee
and his Liberal government, communism and the Communists posed an
actual mortal threat: not only was the South's sovereignty perceived to
be physically endangered by the Communist counterpart in the North,

but also the entire national psychic makeup was eventually molded into this perception of clear and imminent danger about communism. The psychological and physical causes of anticommunism for Rhee and his regime and his Korea are not difficult to comprehend. Nor is there any hidden explanation of why anticommunism heavily swayed the mood and structure of Korean society in Rhee's days. This ideological conflict was intimately and immediately interlocked with the mindset of those in power and with the superpowers that supported their respective regimes.[58]

II. Is there a structural, class-based explanation for the rise and fall of the Rhee and Chang regimes? How was it possible for Rhee to stay in power for over twelve years?

The answer lies in some of the more widely available historical explanations that were structural components of Korea under Rhee and Chang:

First, Rhee's regime (and to a great extent Chang's) was primarily based on the precolonial social structure and sentiments, notably the Yi dynasty's. Rhee put his mythical genealogy, believed to be traceable to the Yi (Rhee) royal family, to good political effect; the farmers, the numerical majority under universal franchise instituted after World War II, became his power basis that had remained traditional, conservative, and at times reactionary. While the political lid was being kept on the disgruntled intellectuals and urban population in the hectic aftermath of national liberation, the Korean War, and the postwar nation-building, the farmers continued to give him the political support he needed. However, in the postwar period dissatisfaction and grievances mounted among the intellectuals and urban population, which, as we have seen exploded with the student protests over election riggings. The inherent structural weakness of Rhee's political basis became apparent in the days of political crisis when he found that he had no reliable constituency for support. The farmers did give votes even though they were not articulate or active supporters of Rhee and his regime; their precolonial sentiments and gratitude toward Rhee for resistance activities were growing thin in the period prior to the 1960 crisis. With the military standing neutral, Rhee found himself powerless against the violent students. The brief tenure of Chang's regime in this sense needs no further elaboration with the exception that from the standpoint of farmers, Chang essentially represented the same class of old society.

Second, the Korean social structure under Rhee, despite the war and the political conflict between the two Koreas, was an exceptionally stagnant one from the contemporary perspective of functional development and rationally planned action. The bureaucracy had degenerated into ritualism with corruption becoming an end in itself;[59] government spending was haphazard and increasing, with capital-intensive investment considered "evidence of progressiveness."[60] There was no long-term plan conceived with national development in view. Through one crisis after another, both political and economic, the Rhee regime was able to sustain itself against its Democratic opposition with its intellectual and urban basis, but Korea in general remained primarily a dormant society. An instrumental government or an active administrative role was neither perceived as desirable nor pursued as possible. It was as if the shadow of the old Hermit Kingdom had returned. All in all, in the absence of a dynamic political participation and leadership in national development, the Korea of this period was characterized chiefly by political repression and economic stagnation.

Third, the political and psychological influence of Rhee as the sole leader of Korea cannot be underestimated. As such, his administration continued to be a traditional bureaucracy[61] thoroughly dominated by those personally loyal to Rhee and with no clear direction for social development. Rhee's charisma, built upon old Korea, his anti-Japanese movement, and exigencies of the Korean War contributed to the concentration of enormous power within the man and his close subordinates. While the appearance of electoral modernity was maintained, Korea under Rhee was still a traditional society in substance. This traditionality, coupled with the passive and tamed constituency that had made the ruling elite complacent, left Rhee and his regime shell-shocked and paralyzed with no ideological or programmatic defense when the urban citizens and students rose in protest.

Last but not least important is the frustration the educated segment of the population felt during the Rhee regime. Korean society had few international outlets, severely bound by its own self-imposed anti-Japanese and anticommunist restrictions. Korea, as many intellectuals felt, was a hermit kingdom again, isolated from the dynamics of contemporary world events. Predominantly nationalist and emotive themes were played up by Rhee and his regime to justify their own reactionary international politics. The political and economic stagnation was undoubtedly the basic Korean structure. This psychological alienation (deeply felt amng the urban and educated population and fostered in part by that very sociopolitical structure) became intolerable. In retrospect, the election rigging of March 1960 was merely the last straw that broke the camel's back. Structural weaknesses of Rhee's political basis; the traditional outlook that looked away from, if not outright rejected, political rationalization and economic development; and the emotive styles of Korean politics under Rhee that effectively shut the society off from the outside world—these constituted the broad outline against which the Rhee regime ruled Korea.

III. Why was there no sizable radical force in Korean politics at the time of Rhee's fall? Why were students and labor unions unable to exercise power more effectively on the national level?

Radical theories on social change with intellectuals, workers, and peasants as its spearheading force necessarily assume certain ideological conditions within the given society. The ideological conditions that may lead to a "class consciousness," using the Marxist concept, for example, must be created by the structural conditions representative of the objective social system. The structural conditions and subjective (ideological) conditions must coincide in order to bring about the desired social change.

The Korean social conditions, as they were, did constitute the objective social structure: there were workers, peasants, and intellectuals; and there was the class system in which one class ruled and the other obeyed. Yet, the subjective recognition of social revolution by the working class did not exist at the time of the power vacuum following Rhee's fall. Neither the workers, nor the students, nor the peasants, utterly ignorant of political ideology, had any idea of what to do to take power actively or step into a power vacuum when it materialized. Students revolted and workers demonstrated, but because of their lack of political experience in the previous eras they found themselves unable to formulate political alternatives. The student agitations, continuing after their triumph over the Rhee regime, never crystallized into a concrete political form; the workers tasted power in numbers but their objectives were small and immediate—higher wages, better working conditions—nothing that could properly be called a workers' movement. The political and ideological repression under Rhee in particular had left little room for system alternatives.[62] Radical social systems, such as socialism or communism, had been thoroughly eliminated between 1947 and 1960, and it is no wonder that there was no major voice with a different ideological articulation when suddenly a power vacuum appeared in Korean politics.

IV. What types of system change occurred before and after World War II, and what was the dominant feature of status groups that arose?

The Japanese colonial government in its thirty-six-year reign had effectively dismantled the old ruling class, yangban, and as a result, when Japan withdrew there was total chaos in the Korean social and political scenes. Economic production had been geared mainly to Japan's war efforts during World War II and government positions were staffed by the Japanese at the top and in the middle, which almost paralyzed the administrative processes when the war ended.

With these backdrops in Korea's social structure, there arose two status groups after the war to become the dominant ruling class: the resistance leaders and the nouveaux riches. The anti-Japanese resistance leaders, based mainly in the United States and China, returned and immediately became the predominant political figures.[63] Some of these resistance leaders were self-made men, but many had been members of the dismantled aristocracy of the Yi dynasty. The nouveaux riches often comically seized the opportunity of a hasty Japanese withdrawal and grabbed their land and property either by force or in exchange for token payment. Under the circumstances the Japanese had no chance of properly disposing of their assets. These new entrepreneurs had been in employment (but rarely in partnership) with their Japanese superiors, but overnight they became the owners of some sizable heavy machinery, large factories, and farmlands in the chaotic post–World War II period. These nouveaux riches, under the strangest of circumstances, were to act as the new capitalist class of Korea in the coming years under Rhee and Chang and Park's military government. In addition to these new status groups, there also reemerged a handful of old aristocrats who survived the colonial government. These three gorups, two of which emerged practically overnight, established themselves as the new ruling forces in Korean society.[64]

We here reiterate our previous observation on the dismantling of the Korean social system through the colonial period and World War II. Korean society, as Henderson has elaborated, was a mass society uncertain in structure and fluid in status mobility. This traditional ambiguity was suddenly lifted, however, when yet another and entirely new ruling class suddenly emerged: the military establishment that came to power to forever alter Korea's political and economic landscape. This is the main theme of the subsequent chapters in this book.

NOTES

1. Gregory Henderson, *Korea: The Politics of the Vortex* (Cambridge, Mass.: Harvard University Press, 1968), p. 51.

2. David Cole and Princeton Lyman, *Korean Development: The Interplay of Politics and Economics* (Cambridge, Mass.: Harvard University Press, 1971), p. 122.

3. Henderson, *Korea*, p. 75.

4. Ibid.

5. Ibid., pp. 94-95.

6. Harold Sunoo and Se-jin Kim, "Historical Perspectives on Korean Politics," *Government and Politics of Korea*, Se-jin Kim and Chang-hyun Cho, eds. (Silver Spring, Maryland: The Research Institute of Korean Affairs, 1972), p. 19.

7. Henderson, *Korea*, p. 75.

8. Ibid., p. 137.

9. Sunoo and Kim, "Historical Perspectives," p. 10.

10. Gregory Henderson's analysis of the yangban is the most extensive and original piece of literature on the topic. I have borrowed heavily from his *Korea: The Politics of the Vortex* for this section. Henderson's thesis is that the past failure of Korean society lies in the directionless homogeneity of social structure characterized by the centralized influence, in place of many competing occupational or ideological strata.

11. Henderson, *Korea*, p. 43.

12. Ibid., p. 50.

13. Ibid., pp. 54-55.

14. Ibid., pp. 41-42.

15. Cole and Lyman, *Korean Development*, p. 17.

16. Henderson, *Korea*, p. 77.

17. Ibid., p. 44. Cole and Lyman observed, "It is interesting that, throughout the postwar period, the redistribution of income or wealth has not been a major concern of economic policy. This presumably reflects the equalizing effects of a colonial status during which the Japanese had held most positions of economic power and the Korean aristocracy had been largely destroyed; of the land reform carried out in 1945-50; and of wartime destruction, which eliminated any large elements of extreme wealth in the country. There has been concern about poverty and underemployment, but little evidence of a conviction or expectation that the government should or could do much of a direct nature about these problems in the short run." Cole and Lyman, *Korean Development*, p. 167.

18. Hahn-been Lee, *Korea: Time, Change, and Administration* (Hawaii: The East-West Center Press, 1968), pp. 97-99. Extensive comparisons of the three regimes' administrative styles will be made in Part Three.

19. Ibid., p. 79.

20. Cole and Lyman, *Korean Development*, p. 217.

21. Lee, *Korea*, pp. 99-100.

22. Sung-chul Yang, "Political Ideology in Korean Politics: Its Elements and Roles," *Government and Politics of Korea*, p. 30.

23. Henderson, *Korea*, p. 350.

24. Ibid., p. 178.

25. Lee, *Korea*, p. 127.

26. Ibid., p. 135.

27. Yang, "Political Ideology," p. 31.

28. Lee, *Korea*, p. 126.

29. Kim, *Korea-Japan Treaty*, p. 126.

30. There were sympathetic voices in defense of John Chang to be sure: "Conscientious, hard-working and intelligent." Henderson, *Korea*, p. 431; ". . . demonstrated and practiced faith in popular government and liberal politics." Kim, *Korea-Japan Treaty*, p. 126.

31. Sang-cho Sin, "Interest Articulation: Pressure Group," *A Pattern of Political Development: Korea*, Eugene Kim, ed. (Detroit: The Korean Research and Publications, Inc., 1964), p. 43.

32. Ibid.

33. William A. Douglas, "The Current Status of Korean Society." *Koreana Quarterly*, Vol. 1, No. 4, 1962, p. 395.

34. Ibid., p. 385.

35. Oh, *Korea: Democracy on Trial* (Ithaca, N.Y.: Cornell University Press, 1968), p. 69.

36. Douglas, "Korean Students," pp. 587-89.

37. Oh, *Korea*, p. 69.

38. Eugene Kim and De-soo Kim, "The April 1960 Student Movement," *A Pattern of Political Development*, p. 56, 69. "Ideological" here refers to politically established systems of ideas. The predominance of liberal capitalism (at least in form) and anticommunism in the forties and fifties had its impact on student thinking in the early sixties. Continually denied articulate ideological voices, students were unable to present an alternate political system other than the demand for a "moral" and "clean" government.

39. Kim and Kim, "April 1960," p. 55.

40. Woun-sui Lee, "Student Power and Politics in Korea," *Theses Collections*, Vol. 4 (Taegu, Korea: Yeung Nam University Press, 1970), pp. 147-48.

41. Choy, *Korea*, p. 314.

42. Kim and Kim, "April 1960," p. 56, 59.

43. Kwang-man Kauh, "Problems Concerning Student Participation in Korean Society." *Koreana Quarterly*, Vol. 10, No. 3, 1968, p. 260.

44. Byung-hun Oh, "University Students and Politics in Korea." *Koreana Quarterly*, Vol. 9, No. 4, 1967, p. 14.

45. Y. C. Han, "Political Parties and Elections in South Korea," *Government and Politics of Korea*, pp. 64-65.

46. Gerhard Breidenstein, "Capitalism in Korea." *Korea Focus*, Vol. 2, No. 1, 1973, p. 15.

47. Kim, *Korea-Japan Treaty*, p. 265.

48. Henderson, *Korea*, pp. 52-53.

49. Chae-jin Lee, "South Korea: Political Competition and Government Adaptation." *Asian Survey*, Vol. 12, No. 1, 1972, p. 42.

50. Cole and Lyman, *Korean Development*, p. 247.

51. In-sang Song, "A Case Study in Export Promotion: Korea." *Korean Observer*, Vol. 2, Nos. 2-3, 1970, pp. 87-88.

52. Han, "Political Parties," p. 61.

53. Ibid., p. 62.

54. Cole and Lyman, *Korean Development*, p. 27.

55. Han, "Political Parties," p. 57.

56. Henderson, *Korea*, p. 51; also see Clarence Norwood Weems, *Reform, Rebellion, and the Heavenly Way* (Tucson, Arizona: University of Arizona Press, 1964).

57. For the origins and activities of the Communists before 1945, see Dae-sook Suh, *Documents of Korean Communism* (Princeton, New Jersey: Princeton University Press, 1970); Robert Scalapino and Chong-sik Lee, *Communism in Korea* (Berkeley, California: University of California Press, 1973); and the same authors' shorter version, *The Origin of the Korean Communist Movement* (Seoul: The Korean Research Center, 1961).

58. For the best and most concise account of the role of Communists in Korean politics, see Henderson, *Korea*, pp. 113-36, 312-33.

59. Corruption in the military regime under Park will be discussed in Part Four.

60. Peter Bauer and Basil S. Yamey, *The Economics of Under-Developed Countries* (Chicago: University of Chicago Press, 1966), p. 204.

61. Discussion on traditional and rational bureaucracies will be taken up again in Part Three.

62. A purely Marxist analysis, as an alternate mode of analysis, has been suggested by Professor Sam Friedman in the following scenario: (1) Students as the only able and willing force topple Rhee; (2) unable to articulate themselves, the student movement fails to be the major force; (3) in the meantime, repression is reduced, and labor is able to exert itself, thus threatening the existing ruling class; (4) then the military, backed by U.S. imperialism, steps in and stamps out the chance for a social revolution by the workers.

63. It was this homogeneity of background and experience that made both the Liberal party and Democratic party, created by their earlier groupings and regroupings, so much alike, thus reducing any chance for genuine social change when the latter replaced the former after the Spring 1960 student uprising.

64. As it was, both capitalism as a mode of production and the capitalists as a class were in the infantile stage, virtually undeveloped during the colonial period. No so-called capitalist had any established position in the economic sphere at the time of liberation in 1945. The overnight fortune hunters for the Japanese assets abandoned in Korea (which became a thorny issue in the Korea-Japan Treaty in 1965) were hardly in a position to dominate the Korean economy with any certainty in the years following the liberation. More nouveaux riches were created through the postwar reconstruction and the extensive U.S. aid that followed. Coupled with the extensive ideological struggle in anticommunism, this economic situation allowed little room for the formation of a class consciousness in Korea. Both ideologically and structurally, Korea was an anomic society in 1945-1960, virtually everyone scrambling for himself.

It is for this reason that the persona of Syngman Rhee as a traditional and charismatic leader loomed large in the Korean political scene. With the fluid and uncertain sociopolitical structure, yet static economics in the background, his persona became the dominant feature of Koran life; his emotive and nationalist whims dictated the terms of politics; his favoritism determined the fortunes and misfortunes in the economy; and those around him rose and fell as their grace flowed and ebbed. Political parties were virtually one-man organizations, like Rhee's Liberal party, without mass constituents. This composite picture of Korean society makes class analysis an unprofitable application. It is perhaps for this reason that there is scant literature on class in Korean social science.

Part II

THE MILITARY TAKEOVER

5

The Military Establishment, 1945–1961

At the time of Japanese takeover in 1910 there existed only a handful of palace bodyguards that could properly be called a standing military organization in Korea. During the thirty-six years of Japanese occupation through World War II, no military unit native to Korea was ever organized. Korea was administered by the colonial bureaucracy overwhelmingly staffed by the Japanese. Law and order were maintained by the Japanese military police dispatched from Japan for the purpose. A handful of natives served as underground informers and assistant constables in it. Thus, the later Korean military establishment was formed "without the benefit of any established tradition of military experiences,"[1] for the withdrawal of Japanese colonial rule from Korea left behind "no self-contained native army."[2]

In September 1945, the U.S. military government established the National Defense Command (NDC), charged with the task of forming a defense force in Korea. In the same year the NDC organized the Military English Language School (MELS) with the objective of training an officer corps for the development of a future army in Korea. The most common candidates for the MELS were those with previous military experience in either the Japanese or the Chinese army before and during World War II, who had returned to Korea after the war. Early 1945 saw the establishment of the South Korean National Constabulary, which in 1946 replaced the MELS as the South Korean Constabulary Officers Candidate School (OCS). The OCS in 1948 became the Republic of Korea Army Officers Candidate School with the formal establishment of the Republic of Korea Army (ROKA). The regular Korean Military Academy, patterned after West Point, grew out of the OCS in 1950. At the time of the Korean War the total force of the ROKA stood at 100,000, which soon expanded to 1,000,000 in the peak of the conflict and was eventually reduced to the current size of 600,000.[3]

The sudden expansion of the military without a previously established military tradition had significant implications in the later development within the military establishment. The top-ranking officers in the early days of military development were conspicuous for their lack of proper military training as well as for their equally poor civilian education. Any Korean male over 21 years of age with an eleventh grade education, having established no criminal record, was eligible to join the original OCS. The training generally lasted anywhere from six weeks to three months. Those who entered the OCS btween 1946 and 1947 with that training, however, attained ranks from full colonel to general as of 1960. By 1960 the burgeoning military boasted 7,000 from major to full colonel and 170 generals, all within only 12 years of the establishment of the ROKA. Among them, only three field officers, one major and two lieutenant colonels, were those who joined during the war.[4] The military budget rose from 24 million won in 1949 to 16,599 million won by 1961. The speed with which the miltary establishment grew into a colossal force within less than a decade can clearly be seen in the key commanders of army field units in 1956. The Army Chief of Staff, Il-kwon Chung, full general, was only 37 years of age, and three of the main corps commanders were 34. The oldest general to command a combat corps in this period, Lt. General Tuk-shin Choi, was only 42.[5] This phenomenal growth, coupled with lack of a firm modern military tradition and numerous underqualified high-ranking officers, naturally caused problems especially within the upper echelon. In retrospect, it was obvious that the army had grown too big much too fast, and its generals had been promoted much too soon and too young.

During the fifties the military's demand for high-ranking officers was voracious. The newly created positions had to be filled, and they were filled by the inexperienced and underqualified officers who had suddenly found themselves promoted to the ranks of colonel and general in no time at all. As brigade and division commanders, these officers were thrust into positions of considerable authority as well as material abundance that such positions conferred upon them. Inevitably, these senior officers succumbed to silly overindulgence and other deviant behavior highly unbecoming to their lofty military ranks. Embarrassed by their lowly social origins, they began to display the typical zeal of the nouveaux riches. Some of them proceeded to divorcing their humble wives in preference for more sophisticated urban women; others conspicuously patronized stylish nightclubs to demonstrate their new affluence. Many of them used enlisted men as their cooks, errand boys,

and tutors in English, in ballroom dance, and in other modern requirements of elitism.[6]

With no indigenous military tradition upon which the later military
buildup could be based, the military vacuum left by Japanese rule was
filled by three major competing factions according to their previous
backgrounds: Japanese, Chinese, and Manchurian. Under Rhee's skill-
ful manipulation each faction, including the latecomer North Korean
faction, rose and fell from grace as his political needs shifted. Thus the
original OCS was composed of divergent officers who had served under
the Japanese, Chinese, or Manchurian army, and these heterogeneous
groups soon developed a fierce factional rivalry.[7]

The Chinese background officers dominated the ROKA in the early
phase of the Korean military. Their prominence had to do to a large
degree with the nation's acknowledgement of their armed struggle
against the colonial ruler in spite of their meager formal training and
education. Lack of these essential ingredients among the Chinese background officers soon became apparent when they began to compete
with the better trained and more prestigiously prepared Japanese background officers. Toward the end of World War II, many Koreans had
been drafted into the Japanese army and quite a few had risen to the
officer ranks. The 1949 assassination of Koo Kim, Rhee's respected rival,
further damaged the already weakened Chinese faction when the assas-
sin confessed an association with the faction. Ostensibly, Rhee installed
the Japanese faction in high command posts to fully utilize its military
experience for the then-growing Korean army; the real purpose for
Rhee, however, was to "dislodge some of the members of the well-
entrenched Chinese faction at the highest levels of the army."[8]

The Japanese faction officers in high command shouldered the ROKA
during the Korean War. However, they soon fell from Rhee's confidence
after an incident when one of their generals refused to remove a division
to solidify Rhee's beleaguered political position. Other officers of the
same background proved to be equally independent and unpliable for
Rhee's political designs. Rhee appointed and kept in high military posts
only those whom he could handle with relative ease, which meant that
"those highly respected military professionals from Japan—the ones
from China were already in eclipse—were to be eased out of key positions and subsequently from the military service itself."[9] The Manchurian faction, consisting of the Korean officers who served in the puppet
Kwantung Army, soon became Rhee's favorites. Right behind them the
upstart right-wing North Korean background officers were rising rapidly
under Rhee's tutelage. The Manchurian faction dominated the ROKA
during much of the 1950s. The highest commanding post, commander of
the Constabulary and later of the Republic of Korea Army, was held suc-

cessively by groups who were alternately in Rhee's confidence at the time. The following chart reveals the succession pattern:[10]

Year	Commander	Background
1946	Dong-yol Ryu	Chinese
1946	O-song Song	Chinese
1948	Ung-jun Lee	Japanese
1948	Pyung-duk Chae	Japanese
1949	Tae-yung Shin	Japanese
1950	Pyung-duk Chae	Japanese
1951–52	Chong-chan Lee	Japanese
1953	Sun-yup Paik	Manchurian
1954–55	Il-kwon Chung	Manchurian
1956	Hyung-gun Lee	Japanese
1957–58	Sun-yup Paik	Manchurian

While these groups competed for dominance in the ROKA, matters relating to assignment and promotion were regularly overshadowed by factional disputes and interests so that incompetent personnel management was commonplace, and discipline in the officer corps was weakened accordingly.[11] Up to the very eve of the coup d'état in 1961, the factional rivalry had continued in the military. A newly added rivalry was that between the northeastern and northwestern cliques within the North Korean background officers. The latter scored a major victory when General Do-yung Chang, later to become the junta's figurehead leader, was appointed army chief of staff.

Corruption in many varieties was characteristic of the Korean military prior to the May coup d'état. As Rhee used the military as a source of political funds and votes, the generals who refused to cooperate fell from his grace and out of their careers. General Kyung-rok Choi, a respected army officer later replaced by Do-yung Chang, for instance, had refused John Chang's request to raise $2.5 million in political funds, and the refusal subsequently cost him his job.

Corruption rampaged especially with the Manchurian faction in control. Luxurious life-styles among generals were common while "the great majority of field-and-company-rank officers and enlisted men of the military forces led a life at the subsistence level."[12] The military reform movement, which had started as a reaction to such corruption at the end of the Rhee administration, became more vocal and widespread under John Chang. The movement was initiated by a group of colonels later known as the "sixteen hakuksang officers" (hakuksang meaning insubordination) who later spearheaded the coup conspiracy. Corruption among the high-ranking military officers in the Rhee and Chang regimes was so pervasive that many indignant field-rank officers were determined to clean up the high echelon of the military.

The effect of repeated and openly practiced election irregularities under the auspices of Rhee's Liberal party was particularly significant on the Korean military. The illegal delivery of votes, often in hundreds of thousands by the top-ranking generals, deeply eroded the morale of the command structure. Many of these generals no longer enjoyed the necessary respect of their officers and men, but held on to their high posts through the political patronage system. Rhee, Ki-poong Lee (second in line within the Liberal party), and even some lowly assistants manipulated the generals at will by using the lures of promotions, assignments, and retirement benefits.

The field-rank officers, mostly colonels and lieutenant colonels, were now publicly insistent upon ridding the army of the "corrupt elements," meaning the generals in high command who partook of election rigging and political patronage. The young "mutinous" officers called for

1. punishing the high-ranking generals who participated in 1960 election rigging;
2. punishing those officers who amassed a fortune through illegal means;
3. eliminating incompetent officers from key command posts;
4. maintaining military neutrality from politics; and
5. improving the status of military personnel.[13]

Pressured by Rhee's relentless demand for money, many senior officers had resorted to the outright sale of military hardware given to the ROKA as aid from the United States. The generals then replaced the materials with lower quality substitutes, thereby compromising the very essence of the 600,000-member armed forces. This method always yielded easy and considerable funds. John Chang's inability to protect the military from the then all-powerful National Assembly's harassment, which had accelerated with the criticism of General Do-yung Chang's appointment, further aggravated the grievances. It seemed that the eruption of a reform spirit within the military, though unprecedented in its scale, was almost inevitable.

General Yo-chan Song, martial law commander and army chief of staff under Rhee, resigned under pressure from the reform agitation staged by the hakuksang officers. General Sun-yup Paik, chairman of the joint chiefs of staff, followed suit under pressure. (As was the unwritten tradition, both generals were immediately sent abroad.) The reform movement, now a popular public spectacle, was also active in other branches of the military, the marine corps, and the navy. Similar agitations and consequent command shake-ups also followed in these branches.

Emboldened by the initial success of their movement, the reform officers not only continued their agitation but also expanded their demands, making anything short of a complete housecleaning unacceptable. The Chang regime, bowing to the pressure, replaced a few cabinet members and high military commanders implicated in election rigging and financial corruption. At the same time the hakuksang colonels were placed under military custody for court-martial regarding their insubordination. (The much-publicized court-martial, however, turned out to be a farce. The colonels put the judicial officers on the defensive by insisting that the latters' proven collusion with the established hierarchy had disqualified them from sitting in judgment. The ringleader, most senior of them, received a token prison sentence and the rest were acquitted.) As a result of this trial, Jong-pil Kim, the real leader, and three others were forced to resign from service. Kim was to become the key figure who masterminded the full-scale military coup. Colonel Kim's free status and previous experience as an intelligence officer were of significant value in carrying on with the coup conspiracy.

The colonels' open challenge against the high-ranking generals was fatal in view of the fact that the alleged corruption in the armed forces was an undeniable reality. Few generals could claim to have been un-involved and untarnished. Although one general after another was either replaced or forced to retire, the Young Turks were far from satisfied. It is uncertain at exactly what point this reform movement, first an attempt at simple housecleaning, was transformed into a military coup d'état to topple the legitimate government. Reportedly, however, the colonels had their decisive moment in August 1960 when they requested to see the defense minister but were rejected and then severely repri-manded for their behavior by the provost marshal. "It was in the evening of the very same day," one observer reported, "that nine indig-nant colonels met with Major General Park Chung Hee at a Seoul res-taurant and unanimously resolved to execute a coup. Every one of them readily agreed on the futility of reform efforts through peaceful recom-mendations. They agreed that drastic reforms were urgently needed in the entire political and governmental establishment."[14]

From the standpoint of the young reform colonels, corruption in the armed forces had more immediate repercussions in their personal lives. These "corrupt" generals, who were admittedly inferior in training and education, were occupying all the general ranks at the time, thereby blocking future advancement for the junior officers. The graduates of the Military English Language School, now mostly senior generals, had received slipshod training—in 1946, for example, it lasted only one month. Their military experience in the Japanese or Chinese army was at best a dubious claim. Nearly 80 percent of the MELS graduates (72 out of 91) had reached the general ranks within five and half years of their commission, although the Korean War helped speed up their promotions. On the other hand, the better trained and educated eighth class of the improved Officers Candidate School took nearly 12 years to become colonels. General ranks were saturated with graduates of the MELS and the Constabulary, and none of the eighth OCS class had made general. The major component of the hakuksang group consisted of these eighth class colonels and lieutenant colonels who had apparently reached the plateau of their professional careers in the military.

The discrepancy in promotion between the two typical groups of officers in the ROKA—the old, tainted generals and the better qualified and idealistic colonels, in many ways a classic confrontation—was as obvious as it was critical. It took longer for the latter to be colonels than for the former to become four-star generals.

These officers were sandwiched between the generals who enjoyed numerous and substantial privileges, and company-rank officers, the workhorses of the officer corps, who had to be largely preoccupied with their daily chores. The colonels occupied important positions in the chain of command of the army, as battalion commanders or general staff members of various units, from army headquarters down to combat units. In their positions, they had direct control over field-rank officers and frequent contact with many generals who were targets of their daily criticism. They had long felt a sense of uncertainty about their future.[15]

Thus, a combination of circumstances led to the military takeover of May 1961. The military, without any previous indigenous tradition, had grown from a handful to world-ranking size in just a few years. In common with the long-standing history of political factionalism in Korea, this lack of military tradition led to factionalism skillfully but unwisely manipulated by Rhee and further demoralization under the ineffective Chang regime. The general tide of radical movement sparked by the student uprising of April 1960, and aggravated by Rhee's unchecked corruption and by Chang's abortive laissez-faire policy, substantiated the vaguely defined reform efforts in the armed forces.

Finally, but perhaps more importantly, the revolutionary impetus received its green light from the more immediate and personal frustration of the younger officers. Their careers were made virtually hopeless by the low caliber generals whose corruption and cowardice, inferior military training and education, seemed beyond doubt.

The hakuksang officers coordinated by Colonel Jong-pil Kim (retired) and led by Major General Park Chung Hee (the two military men who would largely shape the future of Korea) proceeded to plan an overthrow of the Chang government. The clandestine group sought out potential coup supporters and persuaded the unit commanders sympathetic to their cause whose troops could be mobilized.

On May 16, 1961, one of the most critically significant dates in Korean history, the military men, pledging their lives and fortunes, struck the peaceful, sleepy capital in a lightning maneuver.

NOTES

1. Se-jin Kim, *The Politics of Military Revolution in Korea* (Chapel Hill, North Carolina: University of North Carolina Press, 1970), p. 37.

2. Jae-souk Sohn, "Political Dominance and Political Failure: The Role of the Military in the Republic of Korea," *The Military Intervenes*, Henry Bienen, ed. (New York: Russell Sage Foundation, 1968), p. 104.

3. Kim, ed. *Military Revolution*, pp. 39-40. See also *History of the Republic of Korea Army (ROKA)*, Vol. I (Seoul: Ministry of Defense, Republic of Korea, 1968).

4. Kim, *Military Revolution*, pp. 40-42.

5. Ibid., p. 62.

6. Ibid., p. 66.

7. Sohn, "Political Dominance," p. 104.

8. Kim, *Military Revolution*, p. 48.

9. Ibid., p. 52.

10. Ibid., p. 46.

11. Sohn, "Political Dominance," p. 107.

12. Oh, *Korea*, p. 99.

13. Kim, pp. 77-78.

14. Oh, *Korea*, p. 103.

15. Ibid.

6

The Military Junta and Rational Orientation

The political leaders under Rhee and Chang were primarily the men of old Korea, descendants of the aristocracy that once ruled Korea, educated in the mold of Chinese classics. Although some did graduate studies in the United States and elsewhere, they nevertheless represented the old Korea in ideology and general worldview. Included in their habits of mind was the easy acquiescence to political pressure for corruption and factionalism that had been the hallmark of Korean life. Predominantly in pursuit of self-interest, their style of life and ideology could not be populist or progressive. Hence, "none of them had popular support as national leaders because they did not fight for the interest of the people, but for their own."[1]

By contrast, the new military leaders of the sixties belonged to an entirely different generation. They emphasized economic progress to overcome Korea's chronic underdevelopment and, as such, they recognized the instrumental powers of an active national government. They were "recruited from middle and lower classes and from rural areas," and most were seeking upward social mobility from rather "humble families."[2] The officers of the Korean Military Academy graduating between 1955 and 1962, for instance, were mostly from the lower middle stratum: 31 percent of these officers' fathers were tenant farmers; 29 percent small businessmen; and 20 percent white-collar workers.[3] In the initial stages of the Korean military establishment, the officer corps was made up largely of those who came from rural and indigent families.[4] "The majority of the revolutionary activists were recruited from a group of outcasts—the malcontent and rural oriented officers from the eighth and the second classes of OCS. Personal dissatisfactions, however, were only partly responsible. These officers were also deeply aware of social injustice and seized power in the name of, and for the sake of, the masses.''[5]

One contemporary observer of the postcoup government character-ized the leadership as those ''who came from rural backgrounds and who, in many cases, have known poverty at close range,'' and it was ''natural for these men to have a rural orientation—to feel an empathy with the farmer. They associate urbanism with corruption, immorality and selfishness.''[6] Although these new leaders displayed staunch na-tionalism and patriotism, their military background and relative youth equally encouraged a tendency toward rational solution and functional organization. Their age was one of the more pronounced characteristics that set them apart from the older leaders. The junta leaders by virtue of their singular military status were younger than their counterparts in the previous administrations by more than a decade. Nearly 95 percent of the revolutionary leaders were under 50 years of age, nearly 40 percent under 40 as the table shows.

Age Distribution of Korea's Political Leaders Compared

Age	Liberal (%)	Democratic (%)	Junta (%)
30–39	2.0	3.5	39.6
40–49	24.3	32.5	55.2
50–59	38.5	36.1	3.5
60–69	29.1	27.9	1.7
70–79	4.7	0.0	0.0
Over 80	1.4	0.0	0.0
Total	100.0	100.0	100.0
(Mean Age)	(53.4)	(51.8)	(41.7)[7]

The following table compares the age distribution in a more simplified manner.[8]

Average Age of Governmental Executives Compared

	Pre-Junta (years)	Junta (years)
Ministers	51	43
Vice Ministers	49	40
Directors	42	40

The predominantly youthful composition of the ruling elite was indeed an important development. The new military regime was charac-terized by the inroads of fresh energy made by the young elite, radically different from the Rhee and Chang regimes of old. Many positions of power were in the hands of a new generation.

Unlike the first two republics, an absolute majority of the junta government's leaders, with lower social origins, had attained their ranks
through a military education. Composing nearly 84 percent of the new
leadership, they were alien to the usual political ladder and patronage
system, and none (compared with 17 and 22 percent respectively for the
first two regimes) owed their career to party politics. Their respective
career distributions are as follows:[9]

Principal Life Careers of the Leaders Compared

Life Career	Liberal (%)	Democratic (%)	Junta (%)
Civil Servant	25.7	18.5	8.3
Education	17.1	18.5	8.3
Professions	17.1	3.7	0.0
Business	11.4	11.1	0.0
Bank Clerk	2.9	0.0	0.0
Political Party	17.1	22.2	0.0
Journalist	0.0	3.7	0.0
Military	0.0	0.0	83.4
Police	3.0	18.6	0.0
Prosecutor	5.7	3.7	0.0
Total	100.0	100.0	100.0
(Number)	(35)	(27)	(12)

A comparative study of the administrative elites demonstrates the
dramatic changes that occurred in the leadership. Of the old elite, 80
percent had only Japanese as their foreign language; the percentage
declined to 40 percent among the new elite. Western educational background increased from 14 to 23 percent while Japanese background
declined from 34 to 11 percent. As for class origin, 43 percent of the new
leaders came from the middle class compared with 20 percent for the old
ruling elite, and the sons of landlords declined sharply from 50 to 24
percent. A significant shift was also evident in their birthplaces. Those
born in the rural areas increased from 27 to 52 percent and at the same
time those born in Seoul declined from 25 to 16 percent, thus moving
away from the tradition of Seoul-born dominance in the elite.[10]

As in any significant social change, the social, political, and economic
atmosphere of a society is directly and intimately affected by its leaders.
In the case of Korea, the origin and composition of the revolutionary
leadership decisively influenced the new direction of Korean society,
and no one epitomized this shift more dramatically and forcefully than
Park Chung Hee himself.

Rhee and Chang shared many similarities; both were Christians, born
in the nineteenth century, both at least theoretically committed to a
libertarian form of representative government. Both were "urban, civil,

and cultured . . . and were Western-educated heirs to the aristocratic or landed class of traditional Korea.''[11]

Park Chung Hee was rather different from either of the earlier leaders in temperament, ideology, class background, education, and career. He was born in a small, mud-walled, thatched-roof house—where his oldest brother still lived for many years even after his more famous brother's ascension to power. His birthplace was a small farming village in Kyung-sang province, inhabited by mostly poverty-stricken tenant farmers, one of whom was his father Sung-bin. Young Park excelled in his schoolwork and, upon completing grammar school, was given the opportunity to attend a teachers' high school in Taegu, the provincial capital of Kyung-sang. Graduating in 1937 with a teaching credential, he spent the next two years in a small town as a schoolteacher. In 1940, Park entered the Military Academy of Manchukuo, Japan's puppet regime in Manchuria. He then was sent to the Japanese Military Academy where he graduated in 1944 as a second lieutenant and was assigned to an army unit in Manchuria. When World War II was over, Park returned to Korea and in 1946 entered the Officers Candidate School, from which he graduated as a captain. In the following seventeen years of military career[12] in the ROKA, ''Park remained outside of the main political traffic in the army.'' When political patronage was both a necessary and accepted form of military careerism, ''he was never aligned'' with any of the powerful generals who were then in high command.[13]

General Park by and large presented an enigma in sharp contrast with his predecessors Rhee and Chang. A professional soldier of humble rural background, he was at once Korean and western, revolutionary and managerial, a follower of Confucianism and a true believer of modern science. ''He was not a party man during the Rhee administration, and he seldom attended the popular American cocktail gatherings; he was considered one of the few Korean military officers who did not take part in corrupt practices.''[14] As Park emerged as the principal figure following the coup d'état, some American observers marvelled that Park was a general who never played golf, a sport that conferred prestige and culture on the often insecure Korean high officers. Even during the mudslinging election campaigns in later years, ''Park himself remained exempt from any suspicion or charges of corruption,'' and the failure of Dae-jung Kim, Park's opponent in 1971, was attributed to Kim's ''inability to include Park himself in attacks of government corruption.''[15]

Throughout his military career, he had been known for almost total absence from the gay social functions attended by most highranking government and military advisors. While many young, dashing Korean army generals conspicuously enjoyed their newly won social positions since the Korean War, General Park was an exception. He was never a great mixer, social functions being too rich for his blood; and he did not particularly enjoy petty salon politics.[16]

It is well known that Park disliked "political" chores that politicians must bear as part of their public duties, and preferred to go about the business of modernizing his country.

With his profound affection for things oriental and Korean, Park himself was a typically Asiatic leader. Yet, at the same time, he was more rationally disposed toward political modernization and economic development than his seemingly more western-styled predecessors. The theme of modernizing Korea through technology and efficient management permeated his words, attitudes, and policies.

This function-oriented shift in the leadership element is most dramatically revealed in a study comparing the speeches made by Syngman Rhee and Park as the traditional and new leaders respectively. The study finds that terms like "anticommunism," "antipathy toward Japan," "patriotism," and "march north" were the more frequently used themes by Rhee, while Park's speeches were characterized by such phrases as "national modernization," "economic development plan," "administrative reform," "change in social base values," and the like.[17] A collection of Park's speeches published in 1970 shows the symbolic distinction for the new leadership in its futurist outlook: "Efforts, "diligence," "future," "long-range perspective," 'character building," "forward-moving history," "new history," "modernization," "positive harvest," "advance," "new era," "productive politics," and "revitalization" apepared often in his speeches. The Rhee-Park contrast is further revealed in the following issues emphasized in their respective speeches:

Issues	Rhee	Park
National Unification:	1. Ultimate national goal	1. International problem
	2. Domestic problem	2. Solution in international cooperation and the South's economic development
	3. Solution in military expansion	3. Military used for "productive and constructive" projects
Foreign Exchange:	1. Important in stable economy and national budget	1. Related to domestic and international market flow
	2. Stable exchange rate as a matter of national prestige and sovereignty	2. Realistic, flexible, floating rate preferred
	3. Low, fixed rate preferred	
Economic Development:	1. Toward recovery and stabilization	1. Toward national modernization
	2. Planned economy as Communist	2. Self-supporting economy impossible by foreign aid alone

Issues	Rhee	Park
	3. Dependency on foreign (U.S.) aid but international investment as detrimental to national sovereignty	3. Planned economy needed 4. International investment preferred
Bureaucracy:	1. Hard work based on patriotism and personalized, traditional loyalty	1. As rational instrument for political, economic goals
	2. Low salaries as the main problem in bureaucracy	2. Administrative reform, elimination of corruption, rational management as solution to bureaucracy[18]

In the speeches analyzed, Rhee shows twice as much concern for national security and diplomacy as Park, whereas the latter's preoccupation with economic development is emphasized more often in the words used. The following table summarizes the contents of their respective speeches.

Themes of Presidential Speeches Compared (Unit: Number of Words)

Themes	Rhee (1955–59)	Park (1964–67)
National Security and Diplomacy	3,566 (32%)	7,700 (15%)
Economic Stabilization and Development	4,378 (38%)	25,840 (50%)
Education and Social Welfare	858 (8%)	5,973 (12%)
Government Administration	1,320 (12%)	3,182 (6%)
Others	1,000 (10%)	9,305 (17%)
Total	11,400 (100%)	52,000 (100%)

Following up the thesis that the surge of economic development in the sixties was due mainly to the different ideological outlook of the new development-oriented leadership, the speech content study further analyzed the values of the two leaders in terms of four conceptual categories that are considered critical and instrumental in economic development: (1) achievement motivation; (2) change-orientation; (3) future-orientation; and (4) overseas-orientation (extension of reality beyond one's national boundaries). The conclusion is that Rhee's values were significantly lower than Park's in all categories. Rhee employed 2.9 percent of his words emphasizing achievement compared with Park's 4.7 percent (40 versus 389 words). Rhee used the term "change" only twice whereas Park employed it 139 times. Another striking contrast is also revealed in Rhee's past-orientation and Park's future-orientation; not once did Rhee use the term "plan" and only 15 times words referring to the future, compared with Park's future-references (214 times) in which the term "plan" was consistently mentioned. Park is also differentiated in his overseas-orientation; he saw Korea in terms of international cooperation, export trade, and the like, whereas Rhee's only friendly reference was to the United States, whose foreign aid was welcome but with some degree of suspicion. The results are summarized in the following table:[19]

Values and Perceptions Reflected in Budget Speeches (Unit: Number of Words)

	Rhee (1955–59)		Park (1964–67)	
Economy	1,390	(100%)	8,270	(100%)
Achievement	40	(2.9%)	389	(4.7%)
Change	2	(0.1%)	139	(1.7%)
Future	15	(1.1%)	214	(2.5%)
Overseas	7	(0.5%)	143	(1.7%)

Scholars view development-oriented leadership as the most vital element in national development for the emerging nations. In the case of Korea, the junta leadership provided the necessary basis, psychological and structural, for the conception and execution of long-term development plans, ranging from encouraging international and foreign capital to reorganizing the administrative structure in the government to spur development.[20] Adelman and Morris, in their exhaustive study of seventy-four countries divided into lowest, intermediate, and highest levels of economic development, found that the most significant non-economic factor in economic development was the leadership committed to economic development through rational methods.

It is almost a truism to point out that the extent of commitment of the political leadership of a country to economic development is a significant determinant of its success in raising the country's standard of living. . . . Many developing nations today suffer from marked imbalances in their economies and a variety of bottlenecks that seriously impede production and distribution. Given the weakness of their private sectors, they are unlikely to move forward economically without effective action on the part of their governmental leadership.[21]

Their factor analysis shows that "the indicator of leadership commitment to economic development . . . alone accounts for close to 60 percent of cross-country differences in growth rates." On the other hand, there was no strong association between leadership's commitment to development and rates of economic growth among the low-level growth rate nations.[22]

Syngman Rhee's leadership had been based primarily on his charisma, which centered around the legacy of his anti-Japanese movement.

During the early years of the Korean nation-building, "Syngman Rhee was regarded by large segmetns of the Korean population as a Moses or a messianic leader. He was the popular figure among the Korean people, most of whom at that time believed him to be the only true patriotic leader of the country."[23] However, his "compelling personality and personal magnetism," which served him well during the nation-building phase, failed to work at all when faced with the technical, administrative tasks of government in later years.

To him, problems of contemporary life, such as economic problems, did not matter ultimately; instead of viewing the many practical problems of government as items to be solved through systematically developed policies, he tended to deal with them summarily in accordance with his limited preconceptions. . . . His image of Korea was of the country that had existed before her capitulation to Japan, and hence he felt that she had to be restored to her former integrity at the first opportunity.[24]

The painstaking hands-on demonstration of leadership in mastering facts, directing projects, and getting acquainted with operational details, characteristic of the later junta leadership, was largely foreign to Rhee's leadership style. The Nathan Plan, the first coordinated economic plan for Korea, for example, was rejected by the Liberal administration, to which "retaining political power" was the principal concern.[25]

Park, in contrast, preferred as his political style the streamlined, functionally structured hierarchic command system to which he had been accustomed during his military career. His dislike of "things political in nature" has been well documented; from it emerged his conviction that administration and politics must be separated. His function-oriented habits of mind are well revealed in the following contemporary observation: "The President is reported to take a keen interest in the details of administration, much as a general would inquire into the state of his force. He maintains his own briefing room equipped with charts showing national development; seeks his own information through his secretariat, local inspection trips, and international observation; asks searching questions of his ministers; and is known to dismiss lower officials for demonstrated ignorance."[26] According to another contemporary observer, "Within the framework of Park's government, 'less politics' has been regarded as more conducive to bringing about 'administrative' and 'economic' development," while "political" resolutions are essential for easing many social conflicts.[27] This overemphasis on functional efficiency moved another observer to warn that the preoccupation with operational improvement in the government, without a firm moral ideology, could invite increasing corruption among high governmental officials.[28] "Park was not a democrat, sharing with certain elements among his supporters a preference for authoritarian controls. He maintained more than one secret police-type organization in positions of influence." However, "his approach to political development under the new constitution (1962) was predominantly pragmatic and program-oriented, aimed at securing maximum managerial effectiveness plus maximum political stability."[29]

One example of Park's commitment to functional effectiveness in the administration was his stauch support of the vice premier, Key-young Chang, a civilian known for his individualistic and dynamic leadership in the economic sphere. Despite the strong opposition that then developed within the ruling Democratic Republican party against Chang, Park defended "the highly centralized and aggressive direction of economic policy that had . . . developed under Chang and kept that power in the hands of those primarily loyal to himself and his policies, rather than to the more diverse interests of the party."[30]

In foreign policy Rhee's view had remained rigid, aided by the Korean War fresh in memory, along the East-West ideological divide, and rarely did he forgive an enemy or one suspected of having aided the enemy. His political foes were considered "either as irritants to be eliminated or mere instruments to be exploited. . . instead of considering them as forces to be integrated into a larger framework for a common purpose."[31] Park, on the other hand, was noted for his inclination to employ a carrot-and-stick approach in dealing with domestic oppositon to his foreign policy, especially evidenced in the Korea-Japan Treaty crisis in 1965.[32]

Park increasingly found advantages in the progress of relaxing many of the authoritarian features of his regime. It reflected his desire to improve professionalism within the administration, to balance different sources of power within the government, and to take into consideration the constant demand for democracy in Korea. The foundations of such changes were laid during the treaty crisis of 1964-1965. When the crisis was over, Park found his confidence justified and strengthened.[33]

Typically, Park perceived the North-South Korea problem in terms of political and economic competition, rather than confrontation between two mortal enemies deadlocked in ideological and military struggles. To Rhee, the northern regime was an evil government that had to be destroyed. To Park, however, the North was an international competitor to be reckoned with in politics, trade, and cultural competition. He challenged the North "to a competition in development, in construction, and in creativity," instead of military conflict between the two regimes.[34] His willingness to accommodate went so far as to accept the two-Korea membership in the Untied Nations. The Park initiative with the North resulted in "(installing) a direct 'hot line' linking the two capitals, and (ceasing) propaganda broadcasts and slanderous reports against each other."[35] Realizing the trade opportunities in the Asian and

African nations, most of which had previously been ignored by the Rhee regime as communism-sympathetic neutrals, Park initiated a series of diplomatic campaigns to extend Korea's export markets to these nations, disregarding their ideological shadings.[36]

Given the managerial and rational push that the junta leadership under Park applied to the Korean bureaucracy, Lee observes that "the ascendency of the military provided an opportunity in which the military emerged and was confirmed as an important source of *development entrepreneurs*."[37] The dual aspects of the no-holds-barred commitment to international trade and the then-intensified anticommunist policy were characterized by another observer as "pragmatic conservatism."[38]

Another speech content analysis of Rhee and Park for their key ideological symbols, similar to the one quoted above, reveals the extent of their differences in commitment and world outlook. For Rhee between 1948 and 1958, the ideology of anticommunism occupied the top position of the seven major topics: communism, democracy, America, Japan, unification, nationalism, and modernization. Modernization as the national theme consistently occupied the lowest reference point. For Park between 1961 and 1969, on the other hand, the theme of anticommunism was replaced by modernization, which consistently dominated the rest.[39] The junta leaders and those who joined them later shared a similar attitude toward efficiency and functionality. Such managerial beliefs and styles were to a great degree the result of their common experience in extensive military-managerial training that had preceded their political participation.

The military, especially after the Korean War, stood out from the rest of the society in its functional and rational orientation. One study shows that 70 percent of the military respondents in the survey attributed the "negative" Korean social character responsible for its backwardness to the historical fact of poverty, as opposed to 57 percent among non-military respondents. The survey also shows that the military men tended to give little credence to the idea of "the inherent goodness of the nature of Korean population" as overwrought and romanticized. They simply thought that such sentiments were an unrealistic reading of Korean history. By contrast, the nonmilitary respondents tended to view the ability to endure hardships as a positive element in Korea's social character. When asked to name the most desirable character traits of a leader, the military group tended to prefer "decisiveness" as the most desirable, followed by "honesty." For the civilian respondents, the order was reversed.[40]

The military organization's managerial and "developmentalist" outlook was a direct outcome of the intense and extensive postwar training programs conducted jointly by the Republic Of Korea Army (ROKA) and the U.S. Army. The Korean military officers at the time of the coup d'état could be classified in three major groups, all of which contributed in one manner or another to the social conditions before and after the coup:

First, there were the "senior officers," consisting of much of the high command in the Korean military in the early phase of its buildup, mostly of Manchurian and Chinese background. Factionalism and corruption charges brought out by the later "political" officers were mainly leveled at this group of senior officers who had come "under firm political control and some of the senior staff became deeply involved in the corruption of the Rhee government."[41] (According to Rhee's and the Liberal party's scheme of things, this senior element was being gradually weeded out although it still dominated the upper echelon of the military establishment at the time.)

The military-political alliance was most clearly manifest in the way the political machinery penetrated the military ranks during elections. In determining outcomes in the results of a series of elections, the large military units were sure bets for the Liberal party candidates. Soldiers were openly encouraged by their officers to vote for the government candidates, and votes were usually delivered accordingly. In the eyes of many soldiers and younger officers, consequently, the senior officers were easily identified with civilian politicians and with their many corrupt tactics. This view was shared largely by the general public as well. To the extent that such views prevailed, the military hierarchy could not operate with any degree of effectiveness at all.[42] Indeed, one of the first acts of the military junta government was to complete the process of retiring the senior officers from the military altogether.

The "managerial" officers group, below the senior officers, was, "in relative terms, the most intellectual and managerially oriented class of the officer corps. On the whole they were politically intact at the end of the fifties."[43] These officers, just above the eighth class of the Officers Candidate School, were the main embodiment of the military establishment as a functional agent. Organizationally and managerially trained after the Koran War both in Korea and in the United States, they contributed to the junta administration as cabinet members and key political managers often under the direction of the political officers who were their military juniors.[44] When the postwar training got under way, this group was in a position most favorable to their later role as the government's workhorses. Most of them were junior-level generals by the end of the fifties and had been battalion and regiment commanders during the war. They had been much better educated as civilians than their senior officers deeply involved in political corruption. They were educated at the National Defense College as well as other staff colleges and institutions then established for their training. "Through this process they became broadly exposed to the society at large; they had ample opportunity to come into contact with civilian intellectuals, especially many university professors and senior civil servants who were invited to give lectures on the many nonmilitary subjects."[45]

Subjects taught at military schools included many social topics—not strictly of military utility—and their purely military training itself far transcended the immediate level of logistics and tactics. Between the Military Academy and the National Defense College were numerous branch schools devoted to military training, more or less on the tactical operational level. Beginning in the early fifties, selected officers were sent to the Staff and Command College at Fort Leavenworth as a part of the overall program that, over a period, reached a great number of officers in higher ranks. By the mid-fifties the Korean military reached the level of independent operation, comprising some half million personnel. It was with this postwar military buildup that the managerial officers began to receive their organizational training, whose scope and intensity matched the burgeoning size.

In 1956 the Army Logistics School was established for field and general grade officers on matters of large-scale organizational logistics. The general class officers were exposed also "to the problems of logistics and supply management, as well as planning and programming" on a large scale. At the National Defense College, "courses on foreign policy, economic policy, defense mobilization, and long-range strategic planning" were taught. Also, "interrelationships between military and nonmilitary factors—especially political and economic factors—in the process of formulation of national policy were stressed."[46] In the course of intense training, managerial and strategic, rather than tactical or operational, problems became the focus of instruction.

As the central curriculum for these officers, two critical types of knowledge and skill were stressed. On the structural level, organizational skill was taught; on the individual level, decision-making ability was enhanced. Organizational skill is essential in all phases of military operation, from the day-to-day running of companies, battalions, and regiments to the operation of larger units, such as divisions and corps. Most importantly, on the highest level, the same skill is called for in the management of national-level units such as field army and service headquarters. Such skills were fine-tuned and systematized during the training. Decision-making ability is equally essential on all levels of military operations, from the smallest to the largest. The officer-trainee was taught to arrive at a decision by a rationally conceived procedure: evaluate the situation objectively; consider alternate courses of action; and arrive at a decision on the basis of a careful and objective estimation of action. This modernistic training method was repeated until it "became a part of their way of thinking." After a decade of such intense and extensive training, the Korean military had acquired a considerable store of managerial capacity unmatched by other institutions of society and practically unnoticed by the larger society itself.[47]

Within a decade, over six thousand officers were trained in the United States; upon returning to Korea, they constituted a substantial part of the new military intelligentsia.[48] The most significant development in this managerial training program was the military's awareness of the nonmilitary aspects of national policy formulation in relation to military problems. The effectiveness of the senior officers had been compromised, and the very fact alerted the junior members to the role that the seniors played, mainly as servile political agents. The managerial class, however, remained largely outside civilian politics, thus less subject to criticisms by the "political officers," the third group, when their coalition became necessary during and after the coup.

The new military leadership, "revolutionary in tone and strongly nationalistic," but also "pragmatic and managerial, rather than ideological in its emphasis,"[49] was thus a combined leadership of the "managerial" and "political" officers, functionally blending the two distinct elements. The political officers, typically the eighth class of the OCS, its largest graduating class, bore the brunt of the Korean War— about one-half had been killed in action. The reduction of the military in 1967-1968 brought their promotion to almost a permanent freeze. As junta members, the political officers contributed fresh, imaginative policy ideas and an idealistic-futuristic thrust to the governing process, while the managerial class provided the necessary organizational functions and administrative skills to harmonize and steady the former's zeal. This combination of organizational resources and political energy was crucial to the dynamic and creative yet practical and functional administration of the junta government in the unforgettable decade of 1961-1971.

NOTES

1. Choy, *Korea*, p. 313.
2. Sohn, "Political Dominance," p. 106.
3. Ibid.
4. Kim, *The Politics of Military Revolution*, p. 65; also Morris Janowitz, *The Military in the Political Development of New Nations* (Chicago: University of Chicago Press, 1964), p. 28, 49.
5. Kim, *Military Revolution*, p. 100.
6. Robert A. Scalapino and Chong-sik Lee, *Communism in Korea* (Berkeley, California: University of California Press, 1973), p. 11.
7. Bae-ho Hahn and Kyu-taik Kim, "Korean Political Leaders: Their Social Origins and Skills." *Asian Survey*, Vol., 3, No. 7, July 1963, p. 29. "Leaders" are defined as members of the SCNR and cabinet and top liaison officers in major national agencies in both junta and post-junta administrations. The SCNR, the

Supreme Council for National Reconstruction, was the junta's political directorate.

8. Oh, *Korea*, 125.

9. Hahn and Kim, "Korean Political Leaders," p. 25.

10. In-joung Whang, "Elite Change and Program Change in the Korean Government." *Korean Journal of Public Administration*, Vol. 7, No. 1, 1969, p. 247.

11. Oh, *Korea*, p. 112.

12. Park's stubbornness and independence of mind were a constant source of irritation to the more compromising high command in the ROKA. The irritation felt by his superiors was such that between 1950, the time of commission, and 1961, he was assigned to nineteen different posts. *Korea's Who's Who* (Seoul: Hapdong News Agency, 1971), p. 58.

13. Kim, *Military Revolution*, p. 90.

14. Choy, *Korea*, p. 328.

15. Kyung-cho Chung, *Korea: The Third Republic* (New York: Macmillan, 1971), p. 71.

16. Oh, *Korea*, p. 132.

17. Whang, "Political Elite," p. 241.

18. Ibid., pp. 241-42.

19. Ibid., pp. 239, 242-44.

20. Hahn-been Lee, "Use of the Future for Development Policy." *Korean Journal of Public Administration*, Vol. 8, No. 1, 1970, p. 19.

21. Irma Adelman and Cynthia Taft Morris, *Society, Politics and Economic Development* (Baltimore, Maryland: Johns Hopkins Press, 1967), pp. 78-79.

22. Ibid., pp. 246-47.

23. Kwon Chan, "Leadership of Syngman Rhee." *Koreana Quarterly*, Vol. 13, Nos. 1-2, 1971, p. 41.

24. Lee, *Korea*, p. 80.

25. Ibid., p. 91.

26. Glen D. Paige, "Some Implications for Political Science of the Comparative Politics of Korea," *Frontiers of Development Administration*, Fred Riggs, ed. (Durham, North Carolina: Duke University Press, 1970), pp. 21-22.

27. Sung-hee Kim, "Economic Development of South Korea," *Government and Politics of Korea*, p. 224.

28. Se-jin Kim, "Moral Imperatives in Political Development: A Caveat to the Park Regime in Korea." *Asian Forum*, Vol. 1, No. 2, 1969, p. 44.

29. Cole and Lyman, *Korean Development*, p. 49.

30. Ibid., pp. 95-96.

31. Lee, *Korea*, p. 80.

32. Detailed discussion will be presented in Part Three.

33. Cole and Lyman, *Korean Development*, pp. 49-50.

34. Walter C. Clemens, Jr., "GRIT at Panmunjom: Conflict and Cooperation in Divided Korea." *Asian Survey*, Vol. XII, No. 1, 1973, p. 551.

35. Lee, "South Korea," p. 94.

36. Detailed discussion in Part Three.

37. Lee, *Korea*, p. 178 (emphasis original).

38. Sung-chul Yang, "Political Ideology in Korean Politics: Its Elements and Roles," *Government and Politics of Korea*, p. 28.

39. Sung-chul Yang, "Political Ideology, Myth and Symbolism in Korean Politics." *Asian Forum*, Vol. 4, No. 3, 1972, pp. 38-39.

40. Sung-chick Hong, "Political Diagnosis of Korean Society: A Survey of Military and Civilian Values." *Asian Survey*, Vol. 7, No. 5, 1967, pp. 234-37.

41. Cole and Lyman, *Korean Development*, pp. 36-37.

42. Lee, *Korea*, pp. 150-51.

43. Ibid., p. 151.

44. The role of the managerial officers in the junta government will be discussed in greater detail in Part Three.

45. Lee, *Korea*, p. 151.

46. Ibid., pp. 148-49.

47. Ibid., p. 149.

48. "Throughout this period of internal modernization [of the military], there was little recognition given to such development by the society at large." Ibid., p. 150.

49. Cole and Lyman, *Korean Development*, p. 37. Park Chung Hee, Chun Doo Hwan, and Roh Tae Woo, the newly elected president, represent this managerial class, whle Jong-pil Kim, a fourth candidate in the 1987 presidential election (which elected Roh), represents the political officers.

Part III

RATIONALIZATION OF THE POLITICAL SPHERE

7

General Orientation
Toward Rationality

The rationalization of the political sphere[1] is mainly observed in the following related topics: (1) the general shift toward a pragmatic and functional coalescence in the government and the ruling party; (2) the policy element directed toward the more rationalized ways of governance; and (3) the organizational changes in the government and the ruling party toward greater efficiency and rationality. These and other pertinent topics will be discussed in this and succeeding chapters.

An organization may use various available alternatives to attain its collective goal. In other words, the same goal may be attained by different means.[2] The human element necessary in the rationalization of Korean society consisted chiefly of coalescing military officers and civil bureaucrats under the leadership of political officers. While the leadership provided the overall impetus for the rationalization efforts, the managerial officers performed the vital function of carrying out such organizational tasks. The civilian bureaucrats working under the military overlords were encouraged, both by structural and personnel rearrangements, to produce new ideas and policies for the managerial echelon. Toward the end of the Rhee era, the influence of the senior officers had waned somewhat, although there remained enough of the old factional leaders in the military for the "hakuksang" incident during the Chang administration.

The extensive training of the managerial officers accompanied a new tendency in military recruitment: a tendency away from factional ties among those who joined after 1948-1949, those who graduated from the OCS as its seventh and eighth classes.[3] The extent of military organizational training was such that according to one estimate at least 300,000 soldiers had graduated from fifty institutions offering nearly two hundred different courses, military and nonmilitary.[4] The managerial officers acquired a distinctively functionalist outlook and capacity from these institutions, especially the National Defense College. "Most concluded that the civilian governments of Korea were performing inadequately. After graduation, these officers talked far more in political terms than before about the solutions to the problems around them. New management methods gave them added criteria for criticism. They became the only group outside the government seriously development-minded."[5]

One of the junta's initial actions was utilizing these vital but hitherto untapped resources of the military in the national bureaucracy. The leadership of the junta government, in its military government phase between 1961 and 1963, was concentrated in the Supreme Council for National Reconstruction (SCNR) consisting of the original coup members. Immediately below the SCNR was the "task" group, who filled the vital posts in governmental administration as cabinet members and as the junta's contact point with the civilian bureaucrats who had stayed on from the former regime. The composition of the two leadership layers, the SCNR and the cabinet, represented the extent to which the political and managerial groups were combined to create the optimum, and certainly fortuitous, human element in vitalizing the administration.

In the SCNR, the supreme power source of all three branches of the government in the early years of the junta, only seventeen out of eighty-five total members who held membership in 1961-1963 were two-stars or above, and none were civilians. The political officers as its absolute majority ruled the SCNR, which issued political directives and acted as the final repository of authority on all policies and progams. Colonels and lieutenant colonels, mostly the graduates of the seventh and eighth classes, and a few brigadier generals from the seventh class,[6] made up the core of the power elite in the SCNR. However, their numerical representation gradually declined toward the end of the military government (1961-1963). The following table summarizes the gradual shift in the direction of "task-oriented" managerial officers in the SCNR, especially during the period in which substantive policies were formulated and implemented.

	(May 20–27/61) Original membership	(May 27/61) 1st shift	(Sept/61) 2nd shift	(Jan/63) 3rd shift	(Feb/63) 4th shift
Managerial Officers	7	5	9	6	9
Political Officers	9	10	10	6	4

The original membership and the membership at the first shift, in the first hundred days of crucial governmental power consolidation, largely consisted of the core members of the coup. The main bulk of governmental actions in the first hundred days was largely defensive and destructive in nature as the junta leadership struggled to define and defend itself while trying to destroy the hold of the old political forces. The sweeping legal measures taken during this period were rather typically reflective of this posture:

May 16. Martial law; dissolution of National Assembly and local councils. Disbanding of political parties and social organizations.

May 22. Arrest of 4,200 gang leaders and 2,000 Communist suspects by this date.

May 23. Proclamation of the "Press Purification Measure."

May 25. Announcement of the Plan for Liquidation of Rural Usurious Debts.

June 10. Act Establishing the Central Intelligence Agency.

June 10. Act for the Liquidation of Rural Usurious Debts.

June 10. Act on the National Reconstruction Movement.

June 14. Act on Disposition of Illicit Fortunes.

June 15. Consolidation of three public electric companies.

June 27. Agricultural Price Support Act.

July 18. Emergency Economic Measures for Industrial Recovery.

July 22. Establishment of the Economic Planning Board and announcement of the outline of a Five-Year Economic Development Plan.

Aug. 17. Act establishing the Capital Defense Command.[7]

In this period, the radical ideology of the junta became more "systematically structured," and the generals and the colonels consolidated their political power as chairmen and working members of the committees within the SCNR. The membership created with the second shift, beginning in September 1961, was the chief workhorse of administrative tasks dealing with substantive programs. It was in this period of task and functional demand that the managerial officers were brought into the SCNR membership to push the vital tasks of long-range programs.

Soon it became evident that the period of power consolidation was over and the junta could move into a phase where pushing programs for "national reconstruction" was feasible. The membership of the SCNR was therefore revamped toward a more task-oriented composition. This was achieved by bringing in the managerially competent elements that had taken no part in the original coup d'état. These new elements were essentially outsiders, unrelated to the core SCNR group, but represented the extensive managerial training and talent that the SCNR sorely needed. In retrospect, among the various shifts in the membership this revamped, task-oriented team enjoyed the longest tenure in the government and "was mainly responsible for the achievement" that is normally associated with the military junta in its early years.[8]

The ratio of political officers to managerial officers in the months of January and February 1963, when the junta's transfer to a civilian government was the crucial issue, shifted in favor of the former to meet the primarily political task. The last membership that began in February 1963 was once again a task-oriented group, generally dominated by the managerial officers for the task of governmental turnover.

On the cabinet level, the actual functionaries of the junta government, the functional and task-oriented intention of the leadership is more apparent. The 57 cabinet members during the military administration, 1961-1963, included thirty who were two-star generals and above and thirteen civilians whose number increased toward the end of the period. The following summary indicates the membership composition that was chiefly function-oriented.[9]

	May–June 1961	July 1961–1962	1963
Managerial officers	12	11	6
Political officers	3	1	1
Civilians	0	3	10

None of the original coup members ever joined the cabinet. The actual working members of the government—as cabinet ministers and heads of governmental agencies—were selected for their managerial talents. The majority members of the three main cabinets during this period consisted of generals, retired and active. Most of the generals had taken no part in the coup but later joined the junta government on the basis of their managerial knowledge and training. They had been the main beneficiaries of the intensive training programs that gave them a fundamentally "developmentalist time orientation." As a whole, they were better equipped to deal with the day-to-day affairs of government than their political superiors, the SCNR members, who were actually their military subordinates.[10]

Having been a member of the better trained managerial class and also of the junta force, Park became the major link between the two groups, military seniors but political subordinates and military subordinates but political seniors, or between managerial generals and political colonels. "In this role he continued to place emphasis on managerial skills and on the drafting of senior military men, as well as trained civilians into both the military and, later, into the civilian government."[11]

Streamlining the bureaucratic system was consolidated under Prime Minister Yo-chan Song, a lieutenant general who had not participated in the coup. He put his military skill to good effect in integrating central and local governments, and in formulating and implementing economic development plans, both long and short term. Through these program initiatives, Premier Song attempted to maintain some measure of balance between the SCNR (the power elite) and the cabinet (the task elite). However, drafted into the government for his talent and influence, Song nevertheless remained primarily a functionary in the administration. He and other managerial officers who had participated in the junta bridged the gap between SCNR members and civilian bureaucracy.

The political officers in the SCNR were generally suspicious of the civil bureaucrats "as having partaken in the corruption of the previous regimes, although they recognized the instrumental importance of the bureaucracy in task performance."[12] Because of this built-in bias and suspicion, often causing tension, it fell on the managerial members in the government to build a close working relationship with the civilians by smoothing their ruffled feathers. The placement of these managerial officers in strategic positions in the government accomplished that very objective. The military superiors imposed new expectations on the civilian bureaucracy after some positive changes had been made within the governing organs. The government bureaucracy had certainly lagged behind the functionalist outlook of the military overlords in the cabinet. The generals cleared away many remnants of the old mentality by promoting younger officials to positions of responsibility. Sometimes this change was accomplished by the arrival of a liaison officer from the military to assist the civilian official. Undoubtedly there was a period of confusion and uncertainty while many changes were put into effect in haste. The end result of all this, however, was considerable rejuvenation that affected the top levels of government bureaucracy.[13]

As a great number of military personnel "invaded" the civil bureaucracy, the more merit-oriented younger civil servants and their new military superiors struck upon an alliance in the reformist outlook both shared in the new administration. Many of the policies, including emergency economic relief programs and various long-range economic development plans put into effect after the first hundred days of the junta government, were products of this cooperation between the progressive segment among civil bureaucrats and their military managers. "In this respect, the cabinet played a kind of mitigating role between the military power elite in the SCNR and the professional bureaucracy."[14] Preliminary to the more extensive form of civil-military convergence to come, this initial phase of military inroads into the governmental sector introduced a vigorous managerial approach in organizational affairs. A far more extensive coalition of miitary and civil human resources was manifest, however, in the willingness with which the civilian and non-coup military groups joined the junta government.

The gradual stabilization of the SCNR membership toward the "managerial" emphasis during the junta period is also revealed in their age shift. Those members between forty and forty-four years of age gradually increased from 18 percent in June 1961 to 25 percent in December

1962, and to 30 percent in December 1963. Correspondingly, the younger political officers, those between thirty-five and thirty-nine years of age, declined from 67 percent in the beginning of the period to 50 percent in December 1963. Even with the increasing representation of the managerial class in the SCNR, the average age was still far lower for the leaders in the junta government than those of the previous two regimes. The majority of the political leaders in the Rhee and Chang governments belonged to the fifty to sixty-nine group, while the junta government had 77.5 percent of its key members under thirty-nine, and none over fifty.[15]

Many of the junta members returned to active service at the end of the military government. The fusion of the military and civil sectors in the administration did take into account the possible harmful effects resulting from indiscriminate personnel management in the government. To be sure, many retiring generals received preferential treatment from the government when they were assigned to positions in state-owned corporations, to provincial governorships, and sometimes to cabinet posts. But they were so treated largely to avoid internal frustration in the military, which had, in 1961, resulted in the initial overthrow of government by military men. In most cases, the posting of exgenerals had no disruptive effect on the ongoing institutional programs and objectives. Thus the government largely succeeded in balancing the military personnel with their civilian counterparts.[16]

After the formal return to civilian rule in 1963, participation in the government by the military officers, especially the managerially trained generals, continued to be extensive. The continued military involvement was absolutely necessary in the civilian phase of government for two main reasons: (1) the administration needed the talented and well-trained managerial officers; and (2) in order to ward off any further internal conflict within the military, its continuous participation in power politics was made a basic condition for stability in Korea.[17] Toward the end of the decade, most of the highly placed positions in the Korean government continued to be held in the hands of military men. The following list, compiled in 1970, shows the extent of this military participation:[18]

Title	Name	Military Origin
President (Head of State):	Park Chung Hee	General, Army
Presidential Secretariat:		
Political Affairs:	Sang-bok Kim	Lt. General, Army
Civil Affairs:	Sung-won Yu	Brig. General, Army
Public Information:	Sang-uk Kang	Brig. General, Army
Protocol:	Sang-ho Cho	Colonel, Army
General Affairs:	Won-hee Kim	Brig. General, Army
CIA Director:	Kye-won Kim	Lt. General, Army

Title	Name	Military Origin
Prime Minister:	Jong-pil Kim	Brig. General, Army
Minister of Defense:	Nae-hyuk Chung	Lt. General, Army
Minister of Home Affairs (National Police and Internal Security):	Kyung-won Park	Lt. General, Army
Minister of Transporation:	Sun-yup Paik	General, Army
Minister of Agriculture and Forestry:	Si-hyung Choi	Maj. General, Army
Chairman, National Assembly's Committee on Agriculture and Forestry:	Chong-gun Lee	Brig. General, Army
Chairman, National Assembly's Committee on Commerce and Industry:	Chong-sik Kil	Colonel, Army
Chairman, National Assembly's Committee on Foreign Affairs:	Chi-choi Cha	Colonel, Army
Chairman, National Assembly's Committee on Home Affairs:	Sang-mu Yu	Colonel, Army
Chairman, National Assembly's Judiciary Committee:	Chee-pil No	General, Army
Chairman, National Assembly's Committee on National Defense:	Pyung-kwon Min	Lt. General, Army
Chairman, Naitonal Assembly's Committee on Steering and Planning:	Pyung-whi Lee	Colonel, Army

With the senior officers out of the service, Park was presently elevated to the status of highest seniority, a point of great honor in the Orient. The seniority placed him in a highly fortuitous position both in the government and in the military to further strengthen the civil-military coalition. The second class of the OCS—Park's classmates, as much as Jong-pil Kim's eighth class, was assigned to the posts of strategic confidence. In 1969, for example, all five corps commanders in the Republic of Korea Army were from the second OCS class. Kim's classmates meanwhile were occupying important positions at the division level as commanders and staff officers. Park used his influence to attract his former military superiors to administrative positions in the new government. Among them, more noticeable were General Sun-yup Paik, Minister of Transportation, and Han-rim Lee, Minister of Construction, who had almost foiled the coup as the First Field Army commander by refusing to support it in its early days. They were some of the managerial generals who were persuaded into the junta government. One contemporary observer commented: ''This highly convivial state of affairs seems to be a result of two principal factors: President Park's earnest desire to create an atmosphere of consensus within the military and the willingness of the former rivals to bury their hatchets and join the mainstream of politics. Whatever is the governing reason for this harmony, President Park deserves a high mark for his statesmanship."[19]

As a result, many key governmental positions were filled by the military officers who had nothing to do with the coup. "Even if some of these officers were appointed to the higher civil service jobs for reasons other than their qualifications, the result was an injection of new blood into these stagnant elements of the Korean government."[20] Thirty-three directorships of 42 major state-owned industrial establishments, 40 out of 95 cabinet-level posts, 10 out of 11 regulatory commissioner-ships, 32 out of 59 ambassadorial assignments, and 36 out of 174 National Assembly seats were held by those exgenerals.[21] As of 1968, half of the cabinet posts were held by generals (not including those of other ranks) and all of the eight surviving four-star generals were in the government, including the presidency and premiership. Toward the decade's end, the government was still "clearly a lineal successor to the military government of 1961-1963."[22] However, especially after the formal transfer of power, the seeming dominance of government by the military officers was being counterbalanced by the civilians whose participation was strongly encouraged.

The power base was expanded by including civilians as a prelude to the formal termination of military government. In fact there had always been some civilians associated with the revolutionary government; for example, those who provided financial support to revolutionary activity prior to the seizure of power. Some civilians had been persuaded to participate in cabinet positions or key bureau-cratic or advisory positions once the military came into power; their skills were useful to the regime, and their presence added a certain aura of respectability which would otherwise have been lacking.[23]

The Democratic Republican party (DRP), the ruling political party taking shape in 1963 under Jong-pil Kim's direction, was established as the organizational outlet for the exmilitary officers now in civil politics. The military element naturally took control of the party as "the dominant political force."[24] But to the extent that the DRP remained a special channel for military influence, the party weakened its ability to establish itself as a predominantly populist institution responsive to popular control and direction, as the party undoubtedly perceived itself. In spite of such misgivings, however, the party functioned as an open channel of communication with the exgenerals now in charge of the government by providing stability and by supplying managerial talent. By involving the exmilitary officers in the affairs of its political party, the government made possible a smooth transition from military control to civilian government.

Power consolidation following the junta days was attempted on many different fronts. The coup leadership, born of a campaign against factionalism, among other issues, strongly favored balance on the top levels of government, such as the SCNR membership. On the other hand, they worked on a gradual shift, structurally and constitutionally, toward a strong centralized government and streamlined leadership structure. Two main counterbalancing actions were considered important: (1) regional balance among competing and often feuding provinces, and (2) urban-rural balance, which had been a chronic difficulty in Korean society.

The political leaders of the Rhee and Chang regimes had been mainly urban-educated and Seoul-born, while a considerably smaller number of those was seen in the leadership element of the junta government. "Critical of provincial or other forms of factionalism in Korean politics under previous regimes, since it represented to him the backward, traditional ways of the past which had to be reformed," Park remained committed to balancing the membership within the SCNR.[25] In comparison with the previous regimes in which more than three-fourths of both regimes' leaders had been born in southern provinces, for example, less than half of the SCNR members were southern-born.[26] Wherever there was no direct threat posed to the power structure itself, the junta leadership sought political and personnel balance in the government, although in the early phase a certain degree of favoritism, for example, to the OCS classmates loyal to Park and Kim, contributed to solidarity within the government.

Adelman and Morris found that economic development in the emerging nations is "typically accompanied by greater centralization of political power in the sense of the firmer establishment of an effective nation-wide network of government authority."[27] The Korean political structure after the coup predictably followed the path of strong centralization. This began with the dissolution of the two-chamber National Assembly, elected local governments, and provincial councils, highly ineffective as a functioning structure if somewhat responsive to popular will. Instituted under the Chang regime, the self-government concept on the local level was often overwhelmed by the frequencies and volumes of elections and, once formed, the system proved sluggish while the national needs called for efficient and prompt responses from below. Commenting on Kim Ilsung's successful political stature in North Korea, Henderson suggested that "a consistent, unwavering autocratic policy operating in an otherwise fluid social context" may be suitable to the Korean situation as a whole.[28] On purely organizational grounds, another observer commented similarly that "authoritarian and oligarchic forms may be superior to democratic forms in the earlier stages of political development, if the quality of leadership is held constant."[29]

Whether centralization is superior to decentralization in the national government has varying answers, for different sociopolitical and economic conditions determine the desirable collective goals and the method by which such goals are attained. In the Korean case, however, the junta leadership desired a centralized governing structure as superior to other forms of government. The result was a gradual shift of the governmental structure toward a strong presidency and its executive branch at the expense of an ever-weakening National Assembly and certainly of "competitive politics." Although the 1962 constitutional amendment made the presidency stronger than ever, by 1972 it was considered not strong enough, for it had defined the presidency merely in terms of heading the executive branch, not "as a national leader who may act, if necessary, as the arbiter among the administrative, legislative and judiciary branches of the government."[30]

The 1972 amendment, ratified by 92 percent of votes cast, enormously fortified the presidency, perhaps to the very limit of constitutional legitimacy. The presidential term was extended from four to six years; Article 53 provided that "when in time of national calamity or a grave financial or economic crisis, and in case the national security or the public safety and order is seriously threatened or anticipated to be threatened, making it necessary to take speedy measures, the President shall have power to take necessary emergency measures in the whole range of the State affairs, including internal affairs, foreign affairs, national defense, economic, financial and judicial affairs."[31] The provision left the definition of calamity or crisis to the president. In addition, the new constitutional amendment gave the president the power to dissolve the National Assembly at will.

Since "the partisan and incremental approach toward parliamentary bargains was considered to be detrimental to the undisturbed pursuit of his own vision of all-embracing national priorities," Park was determined to cut down the participation by what he regarded as a bungling and wasteful National Assembly in the otherwise streamlined national administration.[32] The major ingredients of civil politics such as debate and bargaining were never part of the military conception of efficiency in organizational management. In consequence the 1972 amendment made the Assembly entirely dependent on the executive branch, or more specifically the president.

The mechanism central to undermining the National Assembly was the amendment-created National Conference for Unification (NCU), a supernational assembly of sorts, for which a membership of 2,000 to 5,000 deputies was to be locally elected, administered by local governments. It was to be a grass roots national organization, purported to solidify the presidential powers in electing the president and one-third of the seats in the National Assembly. The president, as chairman of the NCU, "through secret ballot, without conducting debate" (Article 39), was to submit a list of candidates for one-third of the Assembly seats.

The NCU was to consider the candidates as a slate. If the initial slate as a whole was not approved by the NCU, "the president shall again prepare a list of candidates with all or part of the candidates changed and submit the same to the NCU, requesting their election, until a slate of candidates is decided upon" (Article 40). The president would also prepare for the NCU's approval a list of reserve candidates who would fill the seats vacated by the NCU-elected members of the National Assembly. In short, the 1972 constitutional amendment guaranteed the president at least one-third of all National Assembly seats at all times. "Viewed from the perspective of general democratic norms," Lee commented, "the entire sequence of South Korea's domestic political development during 1972 was an unfortunate step backward." But he also recognized the necessity of such an unfortunate step.

The legitimacy of this sweeping enhancement of presidential powers hinged on the legitimacy of Park's perception of Korean needs itself. President Park basically perceived his country as being at a critical crossroads in its struggle for survival and prosperity. The president had maintained a fairly negative view (obviously strengthened by his military authoritarian preference) of the factionalism in Korea's political habits as detrimental to and incapable of dealing with the critical turning point. If one agreed with this perception of Korea in need of the sweeping political restructuring toward greater productivity and efficiency, President Park's constitutional amendment "might be appreciated."[33]

This built-in advantage of the sitting president was not lost on the Korean electorate. In the 1972 general election after the above amendment had been ratified by a 92 percent approval in a plebiscite, the Korean voters sent only one-third of the ruling DRP members to the National Assembly. This one-third, together with the NCU-elected one-third, gave the government force a comfortable majority in the Assembly, but not an overwhelming dominance in the Assembly that the opposition had feared. Yet, as the president remained reasonably popular, the new constitution continued to strengthen his hand in the governing process.

NOTES

1. It is difficult to distinguish what is "political" from what is "economic," especially in a nation where the two spheres are intimately intertwined on every level and in every dimension of its society. For convenience, however, the classification will follow what could be discerned in the motives of policy formulation and in the consequences of its implementation. In this, the terms "rational" and "functional" will be used somewhat interchangeably, although the former tends to connote the means and the latter the ends in organizational performance.

2. Robert E. Cole, "Functional Alternatives and Economic Development." *American Sociological Review,* Vol. 38, No. 4, 1973.

3. Henderson, *Korea,* p. 351.

4. John Lovell, "The Military as an Instrument for Political Development in South Korea," *Studies in the Developmental Aspects of Korea*, Andre Nahm, ed. Kalamazoo, Michigan: Western Michigan University Press, 1969), p. 17.

5. Henderson, *Korea*, p. 354.

6. Few of the graduates of the seventh and eighth classes, the so-called non-factional recruits beginning in 1948, had attained the general ranks by May 1961. The overwhelming majority of them remained colonels and lieutenant colonels.

7. Lee, *Korea*, p. 155.

8. Ibid., p. 165.

9. The tables for the SCNR and cabinet members have been rearranged from Lee, *Korea*, pp. 164-68.

10. Ibid., p. 167.

11. Cole and Lyman, *Korean Development*, p. 41.

12. Suk-choon Cho, "The Military Government of Korea and the Reorganization of Bureaucracy." *Koreana Quarterly*, Vol. 6, No. 1, 1968, p. 223.

13. Lee, *Korea*, p. 169.

14. Ibid., p. 140.

15. John Lovell, ed., *The Military and Politics in Five Developing Nations* (Kensington, Maryland: Center for Research in Social Problems, 1970), pp. 182-83.

16. Cole and Lyman, *Korean Development*, pp. 47-48.

17. The new regular four-year graduates of the Korean Miliitary Academy, some of whom advanced to the rank of lieutenant colonel, had become a force to be reckoned with within the military. See Chong-what Yoon, "A Study on the Role of the Army Elites and the Education at the Military Academy." *Korean Journal of Public Administration*, Vol. X, No. 1, 1972, pp. 316-32. Most of the graduates were absorbed into the government, thus preventing any accumulation of internal frustration within the military elite.

18. Kim, *The Politics of Military Revolution*, pp. 162-63.

19. Ibid., p. 157.

20. Chang-hyun Cho, "Bureaucracy and Local Government in South Korea," *Government and Politics of Korea*, p. 98.

21. Kim, *Military Revolution*, pp. 161-62.

22. Jungwon Alexander Kim, "The Military as Modernizer." *Journal of Comparative Administration*, Vol. 2, No. 3, 1968, pp. 357-58.

23. Lovell, *The Military and Politics*, p. 187.

24. Han, "Political Parties," p. 132.

25. Cole and Lyman, p. 249.

26. Lovell, *The Military and Politics*, p. 182.

27. Adelman and Morris, *Society*, p. 57.

28. Henderson, *Korea*, p. 329.

29. Robert E. Ward, "Epilogue," *Political Development in Modern Japan*, Robert E. Ward, ed. (Princeton, New Jersey: Princeton University Press, 1968), p. 590.

30. *Draft: Amendments to the Constitution of the Republic of Korea* (Seoul: Korean Overseas Information Service, 1972).

31. Ibid.

32. Lee, "South Korea," p. 99.

33. Ibid., p. 101.

8

The Policy Element

A truism holds that administrative efficiency is strongly related to economic development, especially in the emerging nations. Adelman and Morris noted that, "Rationally organized administrative services can help establish and strengthen the legal and public service facilities necessary for steady growth; they can help create financial institutions and tax instruments favorable to the expansion of private economic activity, or they can take direct responsibility for initiating development projects and plans."[1]

The administrative apparatus in South Korea, as the practical instrument of national governance and development, had not previously received recognition of its importance. Politics and public administration continued to be unproductively mixed, and the technical and instrumental aspects of organizational performance were generally ignored. Recognizing this historical gap in the functional conception of organization, the military leaders were anxious to impress upon the civilian sector of the bureaucracy the paramount importance of managerial techniques.

Cole and Lyman observed that the military and the ruling party failed "in creating complete national discipline and solidarity" through coordinated action.[2] Many circumstantial factors in Korea's past worked against the creation of an effective and disciplined national administration on short notice. First, contrary to the professional, nonaffective requirements for bureaucratic administration, in Korea emotive foundations had always influenced the workings of such systems and institutions. Emotion and personality freely interfered with the bureaucratic process, causing corruption and waste. Second, the objective and universal standards necessary for bureaucratic administration were too often bungled by such "ascriptive" factors as clanship, provincialism, school ties, and military career, especially in the area of personnel administration. Third, good administration was too often undermined by political and irrational motives and values. Professionally neutral and effective coordination was not given fair consideration. Fourth, the Korean bureaucracy rarely recognized the desirability of universal truths and standards, giving way to the Confucian practice of "personal relations" and "irregularities." Also, the historical conditions that discouraged the development of egalitarianism in social relations maintained bureaucrats at a below subsistence level and failed to provide them with a sense of job security and satisfaction.[3]

While such conditions in Korea's past adversely affected an efficient national bureaucracy, the need and potential for a dynamic and authoritative administrative apparatus were also of paramount importance in the national development of Korea. Because of those very conditions, the administrative branch of government had always been the most powerful segment in Korean society:

1. Historically and traditionally, administration in this country has exercised supreme power and authority. The people had no opportunity to know of the merits of parliamentarism or the importance of an independent judicature. This was true during the Japanese rule over their country, also. In their eyes, there was no difference between government and administration. 2. The status of a politician or a National Assembly member has been less secure than that of a high-ranking government official. 3. The administration's control over economic circles has been exceedingly powerful. The bulk of private capital in this country has been accumulated thanks to government assistance.[4]

There were other factors in establishing the bureaucracy's all-powerful significance in Korean life. The representative system had never fully developed to allow adequate reflections of popular will in public policies, via electoral representation, which only enhanced the power of administrators by default; also, the politicians had always relied on bureaucracy for political repression, election rigging, and other purely political matters.[5] In the economic sphere, the government's intervention was vital and essential to regulate licensing, allocation of foreign funds, and investment of national resources. "Businessmen were forced to rely on the government," and as a result, "in contrast to Japan, the business giants of South Korea do not wield independent political power. They are subject to the pressures of politics as the government sees them."[6]

Strengthening and utilizing a powerful bureaucracy to be expanded and streamlined and made autonomous obviously became the top priority for the junta government. As a band of military men who had overthrown a constitutional government, the junta keenly needed public support, moral legitimacy, and sterling political performance as the new force in power. The propaganda work that had started in self-defense of the junta gradually became a regular feature of its government, now enormously expanded.[7]

One obvious aspect of an organization's effectiveness consists of its broad communication with its constituent population. The junta government effectively deployed the communication network in electioneering, holding national referenda, soliciting mass support, and so on, rather than relying on cloak-and-dagger maneuvers or personality-based appeals. The massive propaganda campaign launched soon after the coup succeeded in presenting the following contrast between the old and new, rather convincingly, aided to a considerable degree by the now-widespread recognition of the old regimes' failures:

Issues	Image of the past (under civilian rule)	Image of the future (to be developed by military rule)
National security:	Nation weakened to external threat through factional strife and inadequate leadership; susceptible to communism.	Nation strong before its enemies under strong leadership.
Economy:	Subsistence economy, heavily dependent upon the United States, oriented to lavish consumption items.	Self-sufficient economy providing for welfare of all, through planning; emphasis on primary industry, and expanded base of trade.
Social values and ideals:	Continued prevalence of decadent Confucian ideas and customs.	Prevalence of modern ideas; achievement-oriented society.
Social and political structure:	Factions, parties, and cliques feuding with one another and pursuing their own self-interest under the guise of democracy.	National solidarity; "administrative democracy."
Governmental leadership:	Those in power committed to self aggrandizement, profiteering at the expense of the people. Rulers incapable as well as irresponsible.	Those in power committed selflessly to building the nation and promoting welfare of the people. Rulers wise and efficient.[8]

Hitting upon this broad outline of propaganda, the junta government waged an intense public relations campaign, especially aimed at convincing the farmers and underprivileged population, in a way the previous governments had never attempted. The Rhee and Chang administrations had rarely recognized public relations as an administrative means or resorted to the effective mechanisms of mass persuasion in modern government. The junta's public relations campaign had two major purposes. (1) Having come to power unconstitutionally, the junta leadership appreciated, as its coercive phase had passed, the urgent need for legitimation through mass persuasion. Coercion was perceived as necessary in the earlier contingencies but undesirable in the ensuing period. (2) The junta leadership, well aware of the necessity of mass mobilization for economic and political ends, was determined to bring about certain attitudinal changes in the general population. It saw the prevailing pessimism and cynicism as critically detrimental to the image and intention of the new government. To wage the campaign, every existing governmental organization was called upon and expanded, and new agencies established. The Korean population had never been subjected to such a barrage of persuasion by their government.

Fifteen million copies of the *New Nation Weekly*—containing various pieces of information on agriculture, current events, and the weekly accomplishments of the junta government—were distributed in the first two years at nominal costs. In addition, millions of copies of national mottoes, anti-communist and anti-foreign slogans, pamphlets containing Park's speeches, and listings of government accomplishments were distributed free of charge. Loud speakers and radio transmitters were also widely employed. In the first two years, the junta government distributed over 20,000 transistor radios and over 1,000 speakers. Eleven new transmitting stations were constructed and a tremendous increase in the number of government broadcasts followed. Furthermore, from May 16, 1961 to September 30, 1962, 237 films were made and shown to culturally deprived rural audiences free of charge.[9]

The political rationalization launched by the junta government in the area of public relations was reflected foremost in the organizational adaptation of the Ministry of Public Information. During the Rhee and Chang eras, the main governmental organ for public relations through mass communication remained the Bureau of Public Information. The junta government, realizing the need and importance of mass persuasion, upgraded the bureau to a cabinet ministry with the enactment of the Government Reorganization Law in June 1961 which resulted in a radical reorganization and expansion of the national bureaucracy. The Bureau of Public Information under Rhee and Chang had 15 divisions and subdivisions; with the 1961 reorganization the bureau became a ministry with 28 divisions and subdivisions, which again expanded into 33 by 1971. With the expansion of organization, the budget also increased for the increased task. In 1957 the entire budget for the bureau was 150 million won, about 6 percent of the entire government budget; this increased to 730 million in the first year of junta government, about 8 percent of the entire government budget. The allocation of funds for public relations continued to increase with the increased size of total governmental expenditures: 1.1 billion won in 1966; 1.6 billion in 1968; 2.6 billion in 1970; and 3.1 billion in 1972.[10]

In the first five months of the junta government, over 854,000 copies of ten major periodicals, ranging from the *New Nation Weekly* to the pictorial *Facts about Korea*, were distributed free of charge. Toward the end of the decade the number of such publications reached 121, including English and Japanese versions. Exhibitions for government propaganda in 1969 alone drew 11 million people on 127 occasions.[11] Other media—television, radio, and motion pictures—were also expanded and enlisted by the government in public persuasion. The 1972 campaign for the national referendum was an example of how the government's mass persuasion brought about positive results. The government's propaganda, aided by the dissent-silencing martial law, succeeded in inducing ''a sense of crisis among the general voters.'' Not surprisingly, nearly 92 percent of eligible voters turned out, braving cold weather, to cast their ballots, and an overwhelming majority of them, 92.3 percent, approved the constitutional revision.[12]

Naturally the extensive use of modern public relations was accompanied by the reduction in the need for or actual use of violence for mass repression or outright coercion. The junta government, it was generally observed, resorted more emphatically to the means of persuasion and public relations campaigns than to manipulative or repressive politics. Firmness and persuasion continued to characterize the junta government's public relations. Yet when a show of force was necessary, as in the Korea-Japan Treaty crisis in 1964-1965, it did not hesitate to use troops.[13]

One of the clearest indications of the junta government's rationalization in the political sphere may be observed in its disposition toward, and its capacity in mass mobilization. In this also, the junta's efficiency was prodigious. The new government immediately embarked on national mobilization, creating organizations and public works projects. The government's ability to mobilize the nation was convincing in its demonstration and beneficial in its significant economic dividends. The National Reconstruction Movement, the first to be nationally organized after the coup, registered nearly four million members in 1963 when it was transformed into a voluntary organization with the formal transition of government into civilian form. The movement eventually expanded into some 30,000 branches throughout the nation.[14] The 1961 Agricultural Cooperation Law organized the Land Reclamation Movement for which in 1965 alone over 45 million worker-days of employment were provided by the government.[15] Draft dodgers, recalled through voluntary surrender, were mobilized into the National Reconstruction Corps. While receiving military training, they performed tasks in highway construction, dam building, and railroad construction, and were frequently dispatched to aid emergency flood recovery projects.[16] Medical doctors were mobilized and dispatched, 700 initially, to doctorless villages, in which the Seoul-born were assigned to especially remote areas for two years of public service. (The mobilized M.D.'s were those who either did not complete military service, were discharged within six months of induction, or avoided the draft.)[17]

Rural organizations mushroomed under the junta government's determination to mobilize the nation. The National Reconstruction Movement was active in the rural areas, but other organizations were also established: the Cooperative Association, Offices of Rural Development, Irrigation Association, Livestock Association, 4H Club, Offices of Regional Construction, Veterans Association, Forest Cooperative, and others.[18] The rural administrative system was expanded and strengthened to facilitate mass mobilization on the county, township, and village levels with extensive financial support from the central government especially for communication and transportation.[19] One study indicates that 64 percent of villagers surveyed belonged to at least one organization.[20] Early in 1972, the ambitious decade-spanning New Village Movement was launched; the government earmarked $1 billion in foreign funds as part of its costs.[21]

Conceived as an experiment for "balanced economic development" in rural areas, the New Village Movement, which President Park called a "big leap forward movement" for the twin national goals of modernization and unification, was greatly expanded during 1972 to increase farmers' incomes and to improve their environments. A vast number of urban-dwellers—students, civil servants, white-collar workers, and the like—were mobilized to assist the Movement. It was basically a government-managed endeavor, but it promises to be a solution to the problems of rural underdevelopment provided the farmers, especially indigenous rural leaders, can see its economic merits and are persuaded to take active part in its developmental projects.[22]

By the early seventies, the New Village Movement would be hailed as a model project for the emerging nations to emulate.

Within a year of the military takeover there materialized a telling opportunity to showcase national mobilization that left a lasting impression and foretold the power of military-civil coalition: the infamous Korean drought. The drought, an almost annual event, had been terrorizing the nature-dependent farmer since time immemorial. The year 1962 was no exception. One travelling Anglican priest recorded the age-old problem of drought in the rural areas, usually in May and early June when the rice shoots are transplanted to regular paddies well stocked with water:

The farmers are bitterly complaining that they require rain badly so that they can finish transplanting the rice, but they vary in their estimates of how long the crop can wait. Farmers are professional complainers, and the nonfarmer is puzzled to know exactly how difficult their situation is. However, a few are busy again shifting water from the lower to the higher paddies. . . . So much summertime conversation seems to be about rain, especially when, as now, there is a lack of it. By proverbial tradition we cannot expect it because the tiny white roses are smothering the briars in the banks and copses, and they say, "It never rains while the wild rose blooms."[23]

Although rain was always of utmost importance in determining the year's rice harvest, very little mechanical effort had been made to over- come the almost annual visit of drought when the transplanting had to be delicately timed. The harvest was thus entirely dependent on the timely (or untimely) rainfall in the early summer. The summer of 1962, the second year of junta government, however, was an exception. For the first time in Korean history, the government committed itself to solving the natural problem by mechanical and human efforts in which the military played an important part. The following chronicle describes the government's epic battle with drought:[24]

May 22: The Central Weather Station announces that an "unusual dry spell" is in the making, and that the rainfall is far below the annual average, warning of both fire hazards and drought. Park Chung Hee, chairman of the Supreme Council for National Reconstruction, orders the cabinet to prepare a plan to fight drought in the coming days, pointing out that drought-fighting must be a government-civilian joint task. Stressing the need for purchasing water pumps en masse, he observes that "although drought is a natural event at times beyond human power, it is the responsibility of the government and citizenry to fight it, for to some extent human efforts can overcome natural disasters."

May 23: The SCNR under the order of its chairman calls an emergency session to form a drought solution committee for an overall plan; director of the National Weather Bureau is dispatched to Japan to study "the artificial means of rain inducement"; the Ministry of Agriculture announces that the paddies minus water are ready for rice transplanting; Chairman Park states at a meeting with the committee that "it will be our responsibility to overcome the drought by human efforts"; he also attends a conference with the director of the weather bureau as the latter departs for Japan with a group of technicians.

May 24: It is reported that the fall harvest would be "seriously damaged" if no solution can be found within two or three days; the impact of drought is reported to be nationwide and "more serious than suspected."

May 25: Chairman Park issues an emergency order to all branches of the military "to mobilize all available personnel and equipment to aid the drought- stricken areas"; the Ministry of Defense immediately announces that the three branches and the marine corps, with the help of the Eighth U.S. Army, would utilize all the pumping equipment and personnel; the Army Headquarters orders all units to mobilize their power equipment for the rescue mission; the Second Army announces that it would dispatch the Corps of Engineers equipped with pumps and fire engines to the needy areas.

May 26: The SCNR ratifies a plan drawn by the drought solution committee, which includes purchasing 10,000 pumps immediately, setting aside 43 million won for the drought-fight expenditures, and initiating a pannational drought-fight movement mobilizing the military personnel, students, and civil servants; the director of the weather bureau reports that testing of artificial rain induce-ment would be conducted in July or August; a provincial governors' conference is convened to discussed local solutions for the drought-fight movement.

May 27: Some signs of rain are announced; provincial governors meet and discuss the situation with representatives from the two armies, cabinet ministries, three service branches, and local military district commanders.

May 28: "Let's Beat the Devil Out of Drought" reads one news headline with an article featuring a military-governmental-civilian joint project on drought-fighting; Hwasung County's situation is being countered by soldiers who dig wells; local school teachers join the soldiers; other nationwide participation by military personnel is also featured.

May 29: Nationwide, fire stations and voluntary fire companies announce that five million gallons of water are distributed into 360,000 pyungs of paddies, involving 680 fire engines and 7,600 personnel; one village in Kyung-sang province announces that it succeeded in diverting a nearby river flow by a massive human effort.

June 1: The weather station announces that some rainfall is expected tonight; the headline reads "Military-Civil Cooperation in Drought-Fighting Continues Nationwide"; there are reports on fire companies involved in water supply with their fire engines; in Changwon County the 39th Infantry Divison organizes a drought-fighting rescue corps that is dispatched to the adjacent drought areas; similar nationwide participation is reported.

June 2: "Drought-Fighting Soldiers Continue Their Effort" reads the headline; General Jong-oh Kim, army chief of staff, flies to Taejun to inspect soldiers and civil servants at work; General Kim later states that "the siutuation is more serious than I suspected. So far military involvement has been mainly machine-oriented. But if the situation continues, foot soldiers will be dispatched where machines cannot reach. However, the farmers should not rely entirely on the military"; rain starts in some areas.

June 3: Enough rain is reported for rice transplanting; "Solution Lies in Human Effort" reads the editorial; "We should not rely on nature. Local villages must be organized in the future to fight any contingencies without relying too much on the aid of the government"; provincial governors are instructed to aid the farmers in rice transplanting. (Translation by the author.)

This episode shows that military participation in "civic action" was strongly stressed by the junta government as its program "for the utili-zation of military units in activities such as agriculture, construction, public education, public health, and the like."[25] The military's civic action program was extensive in many dimensions. The military person-nel participated in the program in a variety of ways: they helped farmers in planting and harvesting rice; they constructed dams, roads, and schools; they worked to distribute food, medical supplies, machinery, and equipment to civilians in need; they donated transistor radios to remote villages; and they established fraternal relationships with many communities and schools and assisted youth groups.[26]

As the central government assumed an increasingly effective role in national life, its sheer size grew correspondingly, accompanied by the growing sense of confidence and positive prospects. The governmental budget increase in the first ten years of the junta regime testifies to its growth. The meager 24 billion won in 1957's government budget rose to 88 billion in the first year of the junta, 1962, and continued to rise to 180 billion by 1967 and finally to 660 billion in 1972.[27] Decentralization was briefly attempted "as a method of guaranteeing strong executory capacity for central programs . . . (and) of achieving administrative efficiency," but it was soon withdrawn as its response to central authority proved not to be vigorous enough to satisfy the military overlords.[28] The government's capacity in task performance increased steadily over the years, covering virtually every aspect of life in Korean society.

The show of governmental powers was more clearly manifest in the early years of the junta in which punitive measures characterized many of the policies enacted and put into effect. With the self-defining Extraordinary Measures for National Reconstruction Law, civil rights were suspended overnight and those charged and suspected were also arrested. In what was called "one of the greatest purges in Korean history," 2,000 military officers, including 55 generals, were summarily dismissed from the service on charges of corruption and factionalism.[29] Within a few days of the coup, over 4,000 civil servants were dismissed or arrested on various charges. The junta's Revolutionary Tribune was established in July 1961 and, within its first ten months 551 cases involving 1,474 persons were prosecuted in 901 trials, consuming nearly 8,200 staff hours. Crimes that could be prosecuted by the tribune ranged broadly from murder and smuggling to vaguely defined, yet sweeping, antistate offenses. It sentenced 268 persons to terms ranging from one to 20 years, 17 persons fo life, and 18 persons to death.[30]

The business class, never a powerful segment in Korean society, was also hit by the enactment of the Illicitly Accumulated Wealth Disposition Law, which defined the offenses in broad terms, ranging from profiteering on state-managed property and foreign capital to evacuation of money to foreign locations. The fines on thirty-two convicted individuals ranged from 50 million to 2.2 billion won, from persons including renowned politicians, provincial governors, and military generals. The top thirty corporations were also punished for various violations, receiving penalties ranging from 50 million to 12.5 billion won.[31] By 1964 the government collected 404 billion won from individuals and 3.7 billion from corporations in which the latter received clemency.[32]

Nearly 14,000 thugs and gangsters were rounded up and marched through the streets with signs around their necks that read, "I am a hoodlum, I am waiting for your punishment." This apparently delighted the public, which had suffered the hoodlum-Liberal party collusion in terrorism and election rigging. One of the gangsters rounded up, Wha-soo Yim, had even been considered for Minister of Education under Rhee.

The signs of a new powerful government were everywhere. In a sweep, the new Public Information Ordinance clamped down on the then-mushrooming news media, for some of which extortion and blackmailing were their main business without publishing one single edition. With the general liberal tendencies under Chang, the previously existing 600 printed media had increased to 1,600 by the eve of the military coup. The junta government ordered the dailies reduced from 115 to 39, news services from 317 to 11, weeklies from 480 to 32, monthlies from 464 to 223, and other similar publications from 203 to 98.[33]

In April 1962, the government passed the Resident Registration Law by which every citizen could be accounted for or tracked down by the government. The law stipulated a centralized file, sweeping and comprehensive, on every citizen. The file was to follow one's places of new residency—registration at new localities within 30 days of move was made mandatory. The penalty was set at 3,000 won for failing to register so that the government could "better manage the population migration patterns and simplify the administrative procedures."[34] A similar governmental show of functional authority was its swift disposition of the draft evaders, in which firmness and clemency were judiciously mixed. In January 1963, the government set aside a period, from January 20 to February 20, for a voluntary surrender of (1) those AWOL while on active duty before the coup; (2) those who had not responded to induction notices; (3) those who had failed to register at local offices for selective service; and (4) others who had failed to respond to previous clemency offers.[35] The voluntary registration period was offered several more times, and by the decade's end, the re-registration of the wayward was announced to have been completed.

The new government resolved to bring about law and order in society; thousands of traffic and curfew violators were retained in great discomfort at police stations, and the government announced its willingness to continue its present policy of strict pursuance of order. The public—terrified, puzzled and somewhat delighted—complied. Demonstrations by students, workers, and civil organizations, hitherto numerous in frequency and paralyzing in effect, disappeared under the new legislation against such demonstrations and strikes.

In March 1962, the feared and much debated Political Purification Law was put into effect, barring some 4,200 persons, mostly former politicians during the Rhee and Chang eras, from political activity. Further political activity of the listed persons had to be cleared by the junta authority. The former political leaders were outraged but remained powerless. There were cautious but positive speculations as well as criticisms from the press, but the public seemed to take it in stride; there had been numerous stunning changes following the junta's takeover. Over 3,000 persons eventually applied for clearance, but Chang and other key political leaders of the former regimes remained silent; the general feeling was that their clearance would not be granted by the junta government and they obviously wished to avoid further public humiliation. Charges against the former political leaders (hence the need for the new law) were, in common with other junta enactments, broad and sweeping: (1) involvement in the rigging of elections; (2) aggravating political factional strife; (3) commission of political mistakes or deeds to mislead public opinion; (4) pursuit of selfish interests; (5) indulgence in improper or irregular activities; and (6) accumulation of illegal fortunes or conspicuous responsibility leading to political corruption, and so on.[36] The Purification Act ultimately served, as intended by its framers, the function of establishing the "authority of the Military Government."[37] In this also the junta government showed a remarkable mix of authority and judiciousness. Under criticism from the former politicians and pressure from the public in general, however, the junta government eventually released all but four persons from the blacklist by the early part of 1964. Nonetheless, the clearance was timed to maximize confusion in the opposition camp for the elections in 1963. The opposition never stopped complaining thereafter that the junta government had deliberately calculated the timing of the clearance to weaken the opposition forces and to unfairly strengthen the ruling Democratic Republican party's hands.[38]

"The most serious crisis" the military leadership faced undoubtedly was the 1965 Korea-Japan Normalization Treaty, which inspired nearly three million people, pros and cons, to participate in open demonstration.[39] The treaty crisis, two years after the formal transfer to civilian rule, "provided a great political opportunity for the opposition to exploit against the government, as well as a severe test of survival for the government."[40]

Diplomatic relations between Korea and Japan had not existed following the termination of Japanese rule over Korea in 1945. The Rhee regime's posture was so anti-Japanese that virtually no diplomatic attempt had been made between the two Asian nations although international viewpoints and economic circumstances strongly favored an early reopening of their diplomatic relations. For the majority of Koreans, South and North, the normalization issue with Japan was fraught with emotion stemming from the memories of colonial rule between 1910 and 1945. Japanese "atrocities" were dramatized, and during the Rhee era anti-Japanese ideology was made a national theme. When the junta government announced its intention to bring the issue to a swift and final conclusion, the nation exploded. The following is a brief chronicle of the events between March 1964, when the negotiation between the two nations began, and September 1965, when the treaty was ratified by the National Assembly amid stormy protests from the opposition:[41]

March 6, 1964: Negotiations between Korea and Japan resume; the opposition members of the National Assembly form a Struggling Committee (SC); over 200 prominent national leaders join to demand an immediate suspension of the negotiation talks.

March 15-21: The SC conducts nationwide speech campaigns against the talks, some of which attract as many as 35,000 people at one gathering, and the speech tour involves a total of 120,000 persons; President Park counters the opposition by declaring the government's intention to carry out the negotiations; Assembly-man Po-sun Yun, the opposition leader, threatens to resign if the treaty is concluded; Jong-pil Kim and the Japanese foreign minister agree to work toward a speedy settlement.

March 24: Student demonstrations, initially involving 5,000 in Seoul, spread nationwide to 80,000 students; the government introduces military troops for crowd control.

March 28: Kim is recalled from Tokyo.

March 31: President Park meets with student representatives; soon negotiations are suspended under Park's order.

May 20: New Prime Minister Il-kwon Chung announces the government's resumption of talks, which ignites student demonstrations spreading nationwide; among student demands is the resignation of Park.

May 29: Demonstrating students present the government with an ultimatum; more demonstrations follow.

June 3: 15,000 demonstrating students clash with combat troops called in under martial law declared on the same day; colleges and universities are ordered closed; students and citizens are arrested and charged with martial law violations; martial law continues through July 29.

June 18: Jong-pil Kim resigns under pressure and leaves the country for the United States.

February 17, 1965: The Japanese foreign minister arrives in Seoul to sign a preliminary draft of the treaty.

February 19: The SC stages a rally; over 10,000 persons led by Po-sun Yun and others are dispersed by the police; in the scuffle with the police Yun receives a slight head injury.

March 20: The SC stages a protest rally, attracting some 30,000 persons.

March 27-April 15: The SC makes nationwide speech tours.

April 17: 45,000 protesters stage a rally, 5,000 of whom subsequently clash with police; 227 arrests are made from the clash; the government announces that the SC is an "illegal and subversive" organization; similar demonstrations take place throughout the nation.

June 21: The government orders an early summer recess for thirteen colleges and universities, and fifty-eight high schools.

June 22: The treaty is signed by the two governments; the SC calls it null and void: 10,000 students demonstrate against the treaty; opposition leaders and about 800 students start a hunger strike in protest.

June 23: All opposition National Assembly members and leaders of the SC join the hunger strike for twenty-four hours.

July 5: The SC stages a massive rally in Seoul denouncing the "treacherous treaty," and promises continuous struggle; the summer is marked with less intense student and SC demonstrations; however, the Korean Federation of Educators, Christian leaders, and professors protest the treaty and appeal to the National Assembly to reject it.

July 13: Eleven prominent citizens advise the government to respect public opinion on treaty matters.

July 14: Eleven former generals, some of whom were cabinet members under the SCNR, voice opposition.

July 22: Thirty-eight persons representing students, lawyers, retired generals, former politicians, writers and artists, professors, Christian leaders and Confucian scholars, and leaders of other patriotic organizations meet for unified strategy to defeat ratification; the treaty bill is placed on the National Assembly agenda for debate.

July 28: Yun and the militant faction of the opposition resign from the National Assembly in protest by resigning from the party, which results in statutory loss of seats in the Assembly.

August 11: The Special Committee for the treaty bill, dominated by the ruling DRP members, endorses the bill to the floor.

August 12: All fifty-nine opposition Assembly members resign, protesting the endorsement.

August 14: The bill is ratified in the Assembly with 110 DRP members and one independent present.

August 26: The newly returned students stage a mass demonstration but it is crushed by soldiers; organized opposition gradually comes to an end.

During the treaty crisis the government made concessions to the opposition and twice discontinued the negotiations with Japan as a gesture of compromise. But at the same time it was determined to bring the normalization treaty to a conclusion. Its commitment to reopening relations with its closest and increasingly powerful neighbor had run into the violent emotions of the past.

Opposition to the government's treaty attempt was as united as it was vocal. Leaders of the opposition and the press labeled the government's action "unconstitutional, cruel, and undemocratic." Even the Democratic Republican party-dominated National Assembly unanimously asked the government to relax its reaction to the protesters, especially the professors and students who had been expelled for their opposition to the treaty. The government firmly ignored the appeal. A year or so later, the National Assembly once again called on the administration to consider reinstating them. Once again, the government stood firm on the issue. The administration had resolved in 1965 that it would "not allow student demonstrations to dictate the course of political events, particularly to threaten the government itself." The government had felt that it had enough public support on the treaty issue—as public opinion polls indicated at the time. In view of both the historical and geopolitical necessity and the domestic need and support for the treaty, the government did not hesitate to use force against dangerous and continually disruptive demonstrations to the extent that they would threaten the very functioning of government itself.[42]

The main issues in the treaty that caused fierce determination by both the opposition and the government, each one loaded with explosive emotion, were as follows:

1. The basic relations issue: Critics questioned the validity of past treaties, especially the 1910 annexation, conducted under duress.
2. The Dokdo issue: Dokdo, the small uninhabited rocky island off the eastern coast of Korea had changed hands a few times between the two countries but was currently controlled by the Korean navy; Japan claimed it as its sovereign territory.
3. The property claim issue: Some Korean critics argued that material loss Korea suffered during Japanese rule alone amounted to nearly $3 billion, whereas Japan argued that at the time of their withdrawal in 1945 the Japanese residents left a significant portion of their property in Korea, which was subsequently turned over to the Korean government.
4. The Korean residents in Japan issue: Nearly one million Koreans settled in Japan during the colonial period, but their legal status in Japan had remained uncertain.
5. The Peace Line issue: Called the "Rhee Line" by the Japanese, the line had been drawn unilaterally by Rhee after the Korean War, ostensibly for security reasons but in reality to protect Korean fishing territory from the more technologically advanced Japanese fishing industry, and it had been a bone of contention ever since.

Since the issues at stake were such, the opposition to the treaty evoked nationalism and questioned the basic motives of the current government. The opposition in general agreed on the necessity of resuming normal relations with the powerful neighboring nation, obviously beneficial politically and economically, but disagreed on the terms of negotiation that the government was prepared to accept. Determined to settle a speedy treaty with Japan, the government proceeded to produce the controversial Kim-Ohira Memorandum, which Jong-Pil Kim had almost single-handedly concluded in Japan with his Japanese counterpart. This high-handed method of negotiation triggered the initial phase of opposition that, among the critics, was viewed as Korea's sellout to Japan on unfavorable terms. The government claimed that the $800 million settlement was the best it could negotiate with Japan and that "the important matter was the substance, not emotionalism."[43] The opposition suspected the government of having reached a secret settlement in order to perpetuate its power at the expense of sovereign pride and historical lessons. The government considered the opposition (consisting largely of the politicians under the Rhee and Chang regimes) to be emotional and outdated nationalists, irrational and backward looking, with little understanding of contemporary international politics and economics.

Among the more vocal critics outside the National Assembly were intellectuals, mainly professors, journalists, and students. One survey indicates the extent of their suspicion of Korean dependency on the Japanese economy as a possible consequence of the treaty. When asked "What results do you think the reopening of diplomatic relations between Korea and Japan will bring to the development of the Korean economy?" 38 percent answered that it would help Korean economic development to some degree, but 58 percent answered that the Korean economy would become dependent on Japan in general.[44] The normalization of relations was especially a bitter issue among older nationalists who had experienced the colonial rule first-hand, and to a lesser extent among the younger generations brought up anti-Japanese, although they were considerably softened by the postwar cosmopolitanism. A former prime minister under Rhee, for instance, expressed an opinion that was rather typical of the old generation's opposition to the treaty: "It seems that there are some people who believe that we can live better only by opening diplomatic relations with Japan. It is the story either of the fools or of those who want to prolong their political power by Japanese financial resources. . . . Think what Japan did to us. Think what today's Japan is. It is all clear that Japan will again invade and dominate us, this time by cultural, political, and economic means, even if its forms of rule might be different."[45] The opposition was highly suspicious of the government's "underhanded method" of settlement that was bringing fourteen years of negotiations to a final conclusion so swiftly and with such military efficiency.

Fear of Japan, one of the main ingredients in the violent and emotional confrontation, was genuine in those who opposed the treaty. Japan had struck an ambivalent chord in the Korean mind, evoking envy and admiration on one hand, and jealousy and fear on the other. Following 1945 Korea had seen Japan reclaim its preeminence among the nations of Asia, while Korea suffered through war and poverty. This fear and ambivalence made the treaty difficult to conclude, for any terms of settlement were bound to arouse dissatisfaction. As the sums involved in the negotiations grew large, the Korean fear of Japanese inroads into the Korean economy saddled with outdated machines and cheap local labor also grew large.[46] The process of negotiation under complicated emotive and political circumstances had been difficult and sporadic under Rhee and shaky under Chang. In the previous twenty years, delegates from the two nations had met intermittently and at times had parted exchanging shouts and insults. The government's speedy conclusion of the treaty naturally aroused fear and suspicion—not entirely without envy among the opposition at such power and efficiency displayed by the junta government. Subjugation of South Korea to Japan through the later's "economic invasion" was the major theme of those who opposed it.

Behind the determination of the government to end the long overdue diplomatic normalization stood the generally favorable conditions that had strengthened the government's hands: the military was firmly under control; the ruling DRP had a solid majority in the National Assembly; and the United States, always a significant force in Korean politics,[47] strongly encouraged Korea to reopen diplomatic relations with Japan. The most encouraging sign of all for the government force, however, was the public response to the Korea-Japan rapprochement issue: a *Dong-A-Daily* survey in December 1964, in the midst of the treaty crisis, revealed that 45 percent of those surveyed favored normalization, while 28 percent opposed it, with another 28 percent undecided. The survey also revealed a favorable overall rating of the government's foreign affairs performance. While the government was solidly equipped to handle the issue head-on, the opposition was burdened with its usual internal strife and disagreement on strategy, although the opposition had never been so united around one specific issue since the fall of Rhee.

All opposition parties in Korea had been formed almost without exception as a result of either factional grievance against the original party or having been eliminated through power struggle and therefore resolved to form their own party. In almost none of these opposition parties was programmatic or ideological difference ever the reason for their initial formation as a political group. In general, opposition parties were formed whenever a faction failed in its struggle for party hegemony or control of the government; the losing faction simply separated from the main body to form a new party in opposition either to the original opposition party or to the ruling party.[48]

The split between the Democratic party's Old and New factions under the Chang regime (the New faction) genealogically goes back to 1896 when the Independence Club, of which Rhee was a member, was formed as the first modern political group in Korea. Different factions splintered from Rhee's (which later became his Liberal party) and established the now-crippled Democratic party in opposition once again. Since the junta toppled Chang's New faction from power, opposition groups had suffered heavy defeats at the ballot box against the better organized Park-military-DRP alliance. The opposition's emotionally urgent task of fighting the Korea-Japan treaty suffered a similar setback from internal dissension. The Old faction of the Democratic party now became the Civil Rule party, from which another new party, the People's party under Posun Yun was being forged. Soon the dispute over strategy followed; the more moderate Democratic party majority favored a National Assembly–based struggle against ratification while the Civil Rule party and Yun insisted on more radical means, including a mass resignation from the Assembly. When the fifty-six opposition Assembly members tendered their resignations and were refused by the DRP majority, the moderate members simply went back to the National Assembly, breaking away from the united front. Unfortunate as it was, this style of infighting within the opposition party was fairly typical. Neither effective nor constructive, it predictably degenerated into a personal contest between factional leaders. The opposition's failure to block the ratification and discourage return of the moderate members to the Assembly created renewed tension within the new party. This failure (most dramatically shown in the 1988 presidential election in which the split of two opposition leaders enabled the military's Roh Tae Woo to win the presidency) was widely lamented in the capital, especially in view of the cohesion shown by the ruling DRP.[49]

Political opposition had almost always been directed "almost exclusively to changes in the personnel of government rather than in specific policies or in the structure of the political system."[50] The solid capacity of the government in presenting a seemingly undebatable rationale for the need for rapprochement, on the other hand, appeared quite formidable. The geopolitical necessity of alliance with Japan, the closest non-communist neighbor, and the implication of economic cooperation that would follow the normalization (although Korea's Second Five-Year Economic Plan did not include this possible revenue source), among other reasons, were simply too good to ignore.

The chronicle above shows that the opposition was effective in street demonstrations and rallies able to attract dissatisfied intellectuals and particularly students. The opposition had always counted on students for support since the days of the Rhee regime, and the most effective coordination between the two forces was demonstrated during this crisis. One poll taken in May 1965[51] indicates the determination of the students to oppose the treaty: 50 percent of those polled stated that the government should not compromise with Japan on the issue of property claims, while 45 percent thought compromise possible. Nationalism had been the most manifest and persistent ideology of the student movement since the fall of Rhee, followed by anti-Americanism inspired by incidents of violence between Koreans and some American soldiers, expressed sporadically during the antitreaty movement for tacit American support of the normalization.[52] They strongly suspected a sovereign weakness in the government's diplomatic stance with Japan, in concluding the twenty-year-old problem so efficiently and rapidly; at the same time, they suspected that the government had unnecessarily sacrificed its advantages for the purpose of a speedy conclusion. In one posttreaty survey of university students in Seoul on the treaty demonstrations, "fear that Korea would be subjected again to Japan's economic and political exploitation" was the reason for their activity preferred by 31 percent, while 20 percent gave "distrust of the present regime" as the reason.[53]

The memory of Japanese thoroughness and ruthlessness, amply demonstrated during the colonial era, was so vivid and had been so strongly ingrained in the Korean mind, and the intention of the government in bringing the treaty to a prompt conclusion was so preemptive, that the opposition leaders called for "fighting to the death the humiliating negotiation with Japan by an anti-national government." Emotionalism and fear predominantly characterized the psychology of the antitreaty forces. President Park, in apparent exasperation, responded in June 1965:

If their assertions came out of a genuine fear that we might again be invaded by Japan or be economically subjugated to Japan, I wish to ask them: Why are they so lacking in confidence, so unreasoningly afraid of Japan, and so enslaved by a persecution mania and inferiority complex? Such timid mentality is in itself humiliating! We should first of all discard the inferiority complex, the defeatist feeling that we are bound to be defeated by the Japanese whenever we confront them. The biggest factors obstructing our modernization are defeatism, inferiority complex, and retrogressive inactivism which occupy one corner of our hearts.[54]

The government had tried to involve students in the negotiation with Japan and showed (for whatever motive) considerable interest in persuading the activists. Park met with their representatives, and cabinet members made separate efforts to explain the status of negotiation to student audiences. "When all this failed to hold the student demonstrations, the government sent troops to effectively crush the demonstrators even following them to their campuses, hitherto sanctuaries for the students, and the lesson was learned."[55] By the end of 1965, however, the treaty crisis was largely over. "By the time of the national elections in 1967, Japan was no longer even an issue."[56]

Along with the reopening of normal diplomatic relations with Japan, the junta government initiated a radically different diplomatic front at the international level. In its new drive for world diplomacy, the government drastically altered its previous emphasis on ideology and nationalism as criteria for its international relations. Normally the most conservative institution in society, the military government in Korea at the time, however, was the most progressive of social institutions.

Foreign policy under Rhee, especially concerning the new nations in Africa and Asia, had been governed by the so-called "Hallstein Doctrine" in which the Republic of Korea would have no diplomatic relations with nations that recognized, or were suspected to be sympathetic with, North Korea. It was a policy based on narrow sovereign pride and rigidly emotional principle that forced South Korea to paint itself into an international corner.

Rhee, who was an anti-communist crusader, pursued a policy of opposing any diplomatic relationship with the so-called neutral countries, as he was severely critical of their non-alignment policy. He branded them as pro-communist and accused their foreign policies of assisting the cause of communism. Rhee ardently opposed not only diplomatic ties but any dealings whatsoever with the neutral nations. In brief, his policy not only alienated the majority of the neutral nations but generated unfriendly responses from them.[57]

Rhee's rigidity was not helped by the cold war atmosphere of the fifties in which the feeling of anticommunism ran unusually high. Consequently, this friend-or-foe foreign policy significantly reduced the field of diplomacy for his administration with the growing loss of support for South Korea at the United Nations. The numerous nonaligned or neutral nations were considered communist or procommunist, and, thus, Rhee preferred to have nothing to do with them.

Upon its ascent to power in 1961, the junta government immediately saw political and economic merits in opening diplomatic relations with the neutral nations, mainly for the pragmatic and rational benefits. The junta government promptly abandoned the Hallstein Doctrine by opening diplomatic relations with twelve nonaligned nations. While repeating its pledge of anticommunism and paying lip service to the die-hard antagonism against the North, the junta government was quietly receiving trade delegates from Eastern European nations and sending a mission to Yugoslavia—a long-taboo area for Korean diplomacy. Soon Korean diplomats and trade delegates were in every corner of the world and the junta government was tackling the new global mission with its characteristic energy and determination.

Accordingly, the government budget for overseas propaganda rose from 4 million won in 1962 to 46 million by 1965, and its steady annual increase reached 250 million by the decade's end as testimony to intensified diplomatic action by the Ministry of Public Information alone.[58] Before the junta government came to power Korea had maintained diplomatic relations with only twenty-three nations, for which thirteen had resident embassies and six had consulates. Within a year under the junta government, the number rose to forty (twenty-eight embassies, three missions, and nine consulates). By 1966 the number of nations reached eighty-seven, including the consulate in Indonesia, thus establishing a precedent of coexistence with North Korea, which had already been maintaining a permanent mission. This marked a radical turn in South Korea's foreign policy.[59] As of early 1969, Korea opened diplomatic relations with seven nonaligned nations, and in five of them South Korea negotiated the status after North Korea had already positioned itself.[60]

By 1972, the number of embassies increased to eighty-four, consulates to thirty-one and honorary consulates to twenty-three, with six more nations having agreed to open diplomatic relations with South Korea. Concurrently with the diplomatic drives, twenty-two trade centers were established in various nations to promote economic activities.[61] Early in 1965, a seven-person goodwill mission was sent to Senegal, the Ivory Coast, Niger, Dahomey, Cameroon, Central Africa, Nigeria, Gabon, and Chad. In March and April of the same year, a six-person team visited Uganda, Malawi, Kenya, Somalia, Tanzania, Ethiopia, and the Sudan, all African nations. The diplomatic emphasis on neutral nations stepped up further when in August and September another goodwill mission visited India, Pakistan, Ceylon, and Malaysia for political and economic purpose; two more missions visited other African nations in October. In 1968, four goodwill missions toured thirty African, Middle Eastern, and Latin American nations to solicit political support at the United Nations on the Korean question and to explore trade possibilities. The year 1967 saw the "invitational diplomacy" in which many state chiefs visited Korea at the government's request. Bursting with new confidence, South Korea's exclusive concentration on the emerging nations also offered technical assistance as well. More than 100 doctors were sent to Africa with $100,000 in medical assistance while the dispatch of a Korean peace corps was also scheduled.[62]

Many considered all this diplomatic activity nothing short of a stunning reversal of Korea's traditional foreign policy.

The foreign policy of the Republic of Korea under President Rhee was negative in nature and unrealistic in terms of achieving national interests; it contained irrationality, emotionalism and isolationism. It seemed as though the government had no foreign policy except to follow the policy line of the United States. Its dealings with Japan since 1951 to settle various problems and to establish normal relations between the two countries clearly demonstrated an emotional nature while its attitude toward the nonaligned nations unmistakably reflected the moralistic character of its foreign policy.[63]

If the nationalist strain of Rhee's emotionalism and rigidity was manifest in limited foreign contact and the consequent isolation of Korea from the world's economy and politics, Park's new diplomatic direction also served as an unmistakable mark of his intentions. For Rhee, countering North Korea's diplomatic expansion took the form of having nothing to do with any nation doing business with North Korea. The junta leaders, on the other hand, were thoroughly alarmed at the aggressiveness demonstrated by its northern competitor. Economically, the leadership also recognized the potential overseas markets in those emerging nations. Thus, the military competition between the two Koreas began to turn, however subtlely, into diplomatic and developmental competition.

NOTES

1. Adelman and Morris, *Society, Politics and Economic Development*, p. 76.
2. Cole and Lyman, *Korean Development*, p. 8.
3. Dong-suh Bark, "An Ecological Analysis of Korean Administration." *Koreana Quarterly*, Vol. 9, No. 4, 1967, pp. 62-64. A survey on the attitudes of Korean intellectuals (professors and journalists) reflected their positive inclination toward rationality and materialist perspective. The majority identified modernization with technology, industrialization, high living standards, large middle classes, and rational and scientific control of life patterns. Sung-chick Hong, "Intellectuals' Attitudes toward Economic Development in Korea." *Korean Observer*, Vol. 1, No. 2, 1969, p. 305.
4. Bark, "Ecological Analysis," p. 57.
5. Ibid., p. 60.
6. Cole and Lyman, *Korean Development*, p. 253.
7. On the junta government's effort to create a more effective administrative apparatus (bureaucracy), Cho proposes two premises: (1) "The greater need for legitimation by the ruling organization, the greater reflection of the popular desires by the organization"; and (2) the military coup was a reaction against ineffectiveness and inefficiency, and therefore the junta government tended to emphasize efficiency and effectiveness. Cho, "The Military Government of Korea," p. 221.
8. Lovell, *The Military and Politics*, p. 170.
9. Kim, *Military Revolution*, p. 110.
10. Hee-joung Yoon, "A Study on Overseas Public Relations of the ROK Government," *Theses Collections*, Vol. 19 (Seoul: Ewha Women's University, 1972), pp. 23-32.

11. Hee-joung Yoon, "A Study of ROK Government Public Relations," *Theses Collections*, Vol. 17 (Seoul: Ewha Women's University, 1971), pp. 196-201.

12. Lee, "South Korea," pp. 99-100.

13. Cole and Lyman, *Korean Development*, pp. 73-75.

14. *History of Korean Military Revolutionary Tribune* (Seoul: Publications Committee, Supreme Council for National Reconstruction, 1962), pp. 1712-13.

15. Cole and Lyman, *Korean Development*, pp. 145-46. Details of the Reclamation Movement and other related agricultural projects will be discussed in Part Four.

16. *History of the Korean Military Revolution* (Seoul: Publications Committee, Supreme Council for National Reconstruction, 1963), pp. 1000-1003. By 1970, the government closed its book on draft dodgers, a hitherto chronic segment in Korea, by announcing that "all draft evaders had been registered and would be required to serve in the armed forces." Kyung-cho Chung, *Korea*, p. 131.

17. *Dong-A Daily*, May 9, 1962.

18. Won-tai Kim, "People's Communication and Consciousness in Regional Development." *Koreana Quarterly*, Vol. 10, No. 2, 1968, p. 148.

19. Hae-kyun Ahn, "Rural Social Change and Administrative System in Korea." *Korean Journal of Public Administration*, Vol. 9, No. 2, 1971, pp. 135-42.

20. Heung-yul Do, "Participation in Cooperative Movements in Korean Agricultural Villages," *Aspects of Social Change in Korea*, Eugene Kim, ed. (Kalamazoo, Michigan: The Korean Research and Publications, Inc., 1969),. p. 102.

21. For details see *The New Village Movement* (Seoul: Ministry. of Home Affairs, 1972).

22. Lee, "South Korea," p. 98.

23. Richard Rutt, *Korean Works and Days: Notes from the Diary of a Country Priest* (Rutland, Vermont: Charles E. Tuttle, 1964), pp. 80-84.

24. *Dong-A Daily*, May 22-June 3, 1962.

25. Lovell, "The Military as an Instrument," p. 20.

26. Ibid., pp. 21-22.

27. *Dong-A Daily*, December 12, 1972; also Yoon, "A Study on the Role of the Army Elites and the Education at the Military Academy." *Korean Journal of Public Administration*, Vol. 10, No. 1, 1972, p. 32.

28. Suck-choon Cho, "Administrative Decentralization: A Case Study in the South Korean Military Government," *Aspects of Administrative Development in South Korea*, Byung-chul Koh, ed. (Kalamazoo, Michigan: The Korean Research and Publications, Inc., 1967), p. 79.

29. Henderson, *Korea*, p. 183, 357.

30. *History of the Korean Military Revolution*, p. 1834.

31. *History of Korean Military Revolutionary Tribune*, pp. 992-93.

32. *Hankook Nyungam (Korea Annual)* (Seoul: Hapdong News Agency, 1965), p. 312.

33. *The Military Revolution in Korea* (Seoul: Dong-A Publishing Co., 1961), p. 29.

34. *Dong-A-Daily*, May 8, 1962.

35. *Hankook Nyungam*, 1963, p. 401-2.

36. United Nations Commission for the Unification and Rehabilitation of Korea (UNCURK), *Report to the General Assembly* (New York: United Nations, 1972), p. 5.

37. Cole and Lyman, *Korean Development*, p. 38.

38. Kim, *The Korea-Japan Treaty Crisis*, p. 131.

39. Chong-sik Lee, "Korea: Troubles in a Divided State." *Asian Survey*, Vol. 5, No. 1, 1965, p. 25.

40. Myung-whai Kim, Eui-yung Ham and Hyoung-sup Yoon, "Korean Voting Behavior and Political Orientation." *Korean Observer*, Vol. 3, No. 2, 1970.

41. The following is summarized from Kim, *Korea-Japan Treaty*, pp. 109-16.

42. Cole and Lyman, *Korean Development*, p. 74.

43. Kim, *Korea-Japan Treaty*, p. 97.

44. Hong, "Intellectuals' Attitudes."

45. Kim, *Korea-Japan Treaty*, p. 103.

46. Cole and Lyman, *Korean Development*, p. 106.

47. It was this mounting American pressure for a speedy Korea-Japan Treaty that triggered a strong anti-American feeling among students and the general public, a rather rare occurrence in Korea, which resurfaced briefly during the 1988 Summer Olympics in Seoul. Concerning the treaty, they felt that the United States, anxious to shift its defense burden of Korea to Japan, was unduly interfering with Korea's domestic issue. J. Maru Mobius, "The Japan-Korea Normalization Process and Korean Anti-Americanism." *Asian Survey*, Vol. 6, No. 4, 1966, pp. 241-48. Korea's attitude toward the United States—and things "American"—is an intriguing and complex phenomenon worthy of pyschoanalysis. The closest analogy may be that of Korea's feeling is that of a son, previously overshadowed by his hero father, who has come of age.

48. Kim, *Korea-Japan Treaty*, p. 227.

49. Kim, *Military Revolution*, p. 36.

50. Byung-kyu Woo and Chong-lim Kim, "Intra-Elite Cleavages in the Korean National Assembly." *Asian Survey*, Vol. 2, No. 6, 1971, p. 560.

51. *Chosun Daily*, May 8, 1965.

52. Oh, "University Students," p. 16.

53. Kim, *Military Revolution*, p. 37.

54. Quoted in Cole and Lyman, *Korean Development*, p. 105.

55. Oh, "University Students," p. 17.

56. Cole and Lyman, *Korean Development*, p. 18.

57. Seung K. Ko, "South Korea's Policy toward the Non-Aligned Countries." *Asian Forum*, Vol. 3, No. 2, 1971, p. 111.

58. Yoon, "Overseas Public Relations," p. 32.

59. Andrew C. Nahm, "Korea's Search for New Status," *Studies in the Developmental Aspects of Korea*, Andrew C. Nahm, ed. (Marquette, Michigan: Western Michigan University, 1969), p. 61.

60. Ko, "South Korea's Policy," p. 115. In India, one of the seven nations, South and North Korea opened their missions on the same day, March 1, 1969.

61. *The Democratic Republican Party (DRP)* (Seoul: Publicity Department, The Democratic Republican Party, 1972), p. 59.

62. Ko, "South Korea's Policy," pp. 115-17.

63. Nahm, "Korea's Search," pp. 57-58.

9

The Organizational Element

One of the more pronounced features of streamlined politics (a contradiction in terms, but not in the Korean context) since the junta force came to power was the structural reorganization and professionalization of the national government and the ruling party organ, the Democratic Republican party. Both the national bureaucracy and the party underwent a structural adjustment toward professionalism and efficiency, away from personality, adopting technical competence as the sole criterion in the management of organizational affairs.

The national bureaucracy was expanded as an instrumental organization, its structure further differentiated and specialized, and personnel management was given the emphasis of professional qualification. The Democratic Republican party, created at the time of power transfer in 1963 to civilian rule, was designed to be a functional and professional organization, rather than a boss-oriented poltical arm. The reorientation of both the national government and the ruling party was a result of the leadership's managerial emphasis, manifest in other areas as well, that stressed the importance of rational management and organizational efficiency.

During the colonial days the top-ranking bureaucratic positions had been occupied by the Japanese: 80 percent of the highest positions, 60 percent of intermediary ranks, and 50 percent of the clerical positions. Although some Koreans advanced up the ranks, they were fairly limited both in number and importance.[1] As a result of the restriction, the First Republic under Rhee faced many of the modern managerial difficulties of the U.S. military government before it and had to operate without the benefit of an adequate management system. Because of Rhee's rather personalized view of the bureaucratic function and the generally emotional atmosphere of nation-building, little attention had been paid to the need for revitalizing central administration.

Between 1948 and 1959, however, the composition of civil service in the Rhee regime slowly shifted from politicians to professionals. The occupational backgrounds of cabinet members during the period attest to the shift. An "amateur political elite" (mainly of educators, doctors, anti-Japanese nationalists, and businessmen) outnumbered career bureaucrats (former colonial civil servants, police officers, bank managers, and legal practitioners) 77 to 23 percent in the initial nation-building period. The ratio gradually shifted in the postwar recovery period in favor of professionals, 46 to 54 percent, and toward the end of the fifties the ratio had become 25 percent "amateur politicians" versus 75 percent professionals.[2] But this did little to professionalize and revitalize the national bureaucracy. The bureaucrats under Rhee and his Liberal party, by and large former colonial civil servants, were now made "docile agents" of those in power. "The bureaucracy as a whole became subservient to the demands of Liberal party machinery. . . . In this atmosphere it retreated into the strictest kind of ritualism and routine. Innovations were not only rare but 'viewed with suspicion.' "[3]

One of the more serious defects of the bureaucracy during the Rhee era was the limited formal education among bureaucrats. Nearly two-thirds of the Grade III-Bs, the main functionaries as subsection chiefs in the central government, had not attained a formal education beyond the secondary school level, and there was virtually no in-service training in place during the Rhee regime. Grade IIs and Grade III-As, bureau directors and section chiefs, had slightly better, but not sufficient, education. Such general limitations in basic preparation had also contributed to the bureaucracy's essentially narrow social outlook.

Also noticeable for its serious defect was the bureaucracy's persistent tendency toward inbreeding, especially for the crucial ranks mentioned above. Over 81 percent of incumbents in the three ranks had been promoted from the clerical level, mainly through complacent seniority and clerical routine. "Innovations and reformist initiatives were jealously checked."[4] Rhee's higher civil service remained untouched by the decade's remarkable expansion in university education and its potent influence on social change. A small group of university graduates found their way into the civil service, but even this channel suffered from two major shortcomings: one was the extremely small number of those allowed to join the government (less than 5 percent at the Grade III-B level); the other was the traditional legalistic emphasis of the examination, which severely discouraged those candidates with modern outlooks and habits.[5]

"Overall effect of these conditions in the bureaucracy," Lee observed, "was the isolation of the bureaucracy from the society. . . . Mere ritualism, which is the safest and most elegant way of accumulating seniority, was the accepted mode of conduct. Routine was the norm of operation."[6] Individual initiatives and innovative outlooks among the bureaucrats were in short supply. A study of high civil servants on their attitude concerning administrative programs reveals that the pre-1960 bureaucrats (79 percent) "preferred that new programs or program change be initiated only by political leaders. Even in the case that new programs were initiated by bureaucratic elite members, the formulation of program change tended to be motivated by the preservation of their bureaucratic power under the conditions of changing government and to the bureaucratism in order to obtain more power."[7] Likewise, the main thrust of governmental reorganizations under Rhee was toward obtaining "frugality" and maintaining a "smallest possible structure." Reduction in administrative capacity and personnel was Rhee's constant emphasis.[8]

The junta government, however, took radical steps to overhaul the administrative apparatus, beginning with the wholesale dismissal of 35,684 bureaucrats on various charges ranging from "evasion of military service," "irregularities," and "complacency" to "violation of rules" and peddling "political influence." More than 10 percent of all personnel were dismissed before the military overlords became direct participants in the bureaucracy.[9] The bureaucratic forms were at the same time drastically reduced for simplification and efficiency from 4,500 to 305, and for the first time an in-depth staffing survey was conducted in the governmental organizations.[10] The insertion of a great number of military personnel into the civil bureaucracy brought about dramatic changes in its otherwise stagnant habits. These changes opened up a new channel of opportunity for those trained in Korean universities in the preceding decade, who had gone previously untapped. The government bureaucrats who had received modern training abroad but had been frustrated by their superiors were also encouraged by such changes. Rational-functional techniques of organizational management—called the "Fort Leavenworth style," named after the place in the United States where most of such training had taken place—were introduced in all levels of government administration.[11]

The changing composition was most immediately manifest in the age distribution on the higher levels of administration. As a result of massive promotion of the university graduates to the level of bureau directors, the Grade II-A civil servants became the youngest, at an average age of forty, even younger than their immediate subordinates, Grade II-Bs and III-As. "There was a definite indication that higher civil servants recruited on the basis of merit were increasing in number."[12] As a part of the government's "rejuvenation" programs, in-service training was established and vigorously pushed by the leadership, demonstrating its "positive conviction on the merits of systematic training for functional organization."[13]

By the end of 1961, all personnel of both central and local governments completed the one-week training progam, and in the following two years a reenforcement course was offered to all civil servants, including the mobilized physicians serving in doctorless towns. The military government ordered all bureaucrats from Grade II-A down to participate in such in-service training programs in order to counter the tendency among them to view the training order as a form of embarrassment. The in-service training emphasized two main themes, moral and technical. The first phase reiterated the moral corruption in the bureaucracy during the Rhee era and the spiritual meaning of the military coup in May 1961 in the national administration. The second phase reinforced technical training in which professionals, especially professors in public administration, participated as instructors. Experts from overseas were invited as lecturers to strengthen the program. The SCNR members, the dominant power elite, themselves often participated in graduation ceremonies to lift the morale of the trainees and stress the seriousness of their training. English terms like "category," "organization," and "budget" were introduced into such in-service sessions as part of their daily usage.

The military leadership demanded that all bureaucratic tasks be completed within designated time limits. While a few old civil servants demurred, the intermediary and high-level members were encouraged to be innovative and reform minded. Negative/routine attitudes toward initiatives among the high-ranking bureaucrats declined from 50 percent under Rhee to 27 percent under the military government. Positive/innovative attitudes increased to 36 percent. The positive/innovative attitude among them under Rhee had been zero.[14] The junta leadership took technical qualification as the most important criterion in bureaucratic appointments, especially at the cabinet level, and downplayed political implications. Thus, more than 80 percent of cabinet members in the ministries of Finance, Education, and Public Information during the military government period, for instance, were civilians. The Economic Planning Board (EPB), soon to play the central role in Korea's economic development, was headed by civilians from the time of its inception following the coup, and the EPB minister's position was subsequently elevated to vice premiership to emphasize the importance of its tasks. On the other hand, the ministries of Foreign Affairs, Interior, Justice, Defense, Agriculture, Construction, Communication, and Transportation were occupied by the managerial officers who had been adequately trained in their respective areas in the military. Between 1960 and 1967, the economy-related ministries alone underwent forty-seven upgrading reorganizations, while such had occurred only eight times between 1955 and 1959.[15] The reorganizations aimed at achieving the following purposes: (1) enlarging adaptive function in the economic sector to reflect social changes and demands; (2) professionalizing the bureaucracy to solicit "public acceptance of the legitimacy of political decisions and thus to bring the effective action of the bureaucracy"; and (3) "enhancing managerial coordination among different administrative sectors."[16] Salaries were also raised substantially to minimize opportunities for corruption and irregularity, accompanied by a stern warning that no such corruption and irregularity would be tolerated by the new government.

Governmental reorganization was conspicuous in the growth of overall structure and in the differentiation of task distribution along specialities. In 1960, the Korean bureaucracy employed 237,476 (including school teachers, police and fire officers, and central and local judges); by 1965 the number grew to 305,416, and eventually to 425,000 in 1970, almost doubling the size within ten years of the coup. For the Ministry of Agriculture, for instance, the number of workers increased from 13,497 to 28,118 between 1960 and 1966, the First Five-Year Economic Plan period. Within the ministry, the newly established Office of Rural Development increased the number of its rural extension workers sixfold, a majority with college degrees in agriculture, so that the number of households served by rural extension workers dropped from 2,100 to 375 per worker in the same period.

The evolution of an organization toward greater rationalization normally accompanies the multiplication and differentiation of substructures within it. A low-level organizational structure can handle only low-level, simplistic work tasks. Organizational elaboration is thus essential to task performance when the external demands exceed the existing capacities. The changes that the junta force imposed upon the Korean bureaucracy most dramatically demonstrated this organizational adaptation to the ideology and demand of the leadership, and to the external social conditions as well.

The greatest structural differention, via reorganization, naturally took place in the economy-related ministries and agencies. In 1959, for instance, the Bureau of Finance managed three separate tasks: treasury management, banking policies, and foreign exchange management. By 1963, however, three separate bureaus were established to handle the tasks. In 1959 the Division of Export within the Bureau of Commerce handled matters relating to export, which were differentiated into six separate divisions for specialized task performance.

The following table reveals some of the more startling structural differentiations in economy-related ministries under the new government:

Changes in Organizational Structure

Organization	As of 1959	As of July 1967
Exports and Exports Promotion	1 division	6 divisions 15 subdivisions
Treasury	2 divisions	1 bureau 4 divisions 11 subdivisions
Banking	2 divisions	1 bureau 4 divisions 11 subdivisions
Foreign Exchange Management	1 division	1 bureau 3 divisions 6 subdivisions
Taxation	1 bureau 7 divisions	5 bureaus 14 divisions 7 subdivisions 1 office
Industrial Development	1 bureau 7 divisions	2 bureaus 12 divisions 39 subdivisions
Fishery	1 bureau 5 divisions	3 bureaus 10 divisions 29 subdivisions 1 office
Forestry	1 bureau 3 divisions	3 bureaus 9 divisions 24 subdivisions 1 office
Highway	1 division	1 bureau 3 divisions 10 subdivisions
Aviation	1 division	1 bureau 4 divisions 12 subdivisions
Tourism	1 division	1 bureau 2 divisions 6 subdivisions
Agricultural Development	1 bureau 5 divisions	2 bureaus 7 divisions 23 subdivisions[17]

At the same time, tasks relating to foreign aid and property management (of the Japanese period) were consolidated into fewer compartments because of their relatively diminished relevance and task load in the 1959-1967 period.

New offices were established according to the expanded governmental purposes, among which were the Central Intelligence Agency, the Economic Planning Board, and the Office of Planning and Coordination. The EPB was elevated to a ministry soon after its establishment as the Bureau of Overall Planning in June 1961, to coordinate long-range economic plans. In 1963 the EPB was further upgraded when its minister was concurrently given vice premiership, making the EPB the most powerful of all economy-related ministries in Korea. For overall coordination and information feedback for the prime minister, the Office of Planning and Control was established in 1961. On the ministerial level, the Unit of Planning and Management was established for each ministry to "oversee planning, coordination of programs and policies, the legal process of program operations, review and analysis of progress, and performance of programs to facilitate the feedback information, and public relations."[18] The Economic Planning Board alone underwent ten reorganizations during the 1960-1967 period. The structural differentiation was also accompanied by expanded hierarchies: the economy-related ministries had three levels and six ranks in 1959, which increased to five levels and nine ranks by 1967. The "functional implication" of these governmental reorganizations represented, according to Whang,

the *adaptive function* of the bureaucracy to a changing society. The emphasis on planning and research activities has been manifested in the form of reorganization of the government at various levels. Even at the bureau level, each bureau tends to have its own specialized planning and research function conducted by a planning and/or research division or subdivision. Furthermore, beyond this formal manifestation, long-term planning and research became the predominant value of the post-1960 bureaucratic system. . . . The adaptive function of bureaucracy, through research and planning, can strive to attain control over society.[19]

The emphasis on organizational efficiency and technical qualification in management was also pronounced in the upper echelon of political leadership, notably the selection and maintenance of cabinet members. Guided by the principle of organizational rationality alone, the military leadership viewed the cabinet essentially as a "technical and professional instrument." While the real policy-making political powers of the cabinet posts were quite limited, they were given considerable autonomy and stable tenure to encourage professional continuity and performance. "The accent on achievement, technical proficiency, and Western

methods of organization and administration that had been features of
the military Government Cabinet" was now the political commitment of
the top leadership. Thus, "by 1967, vice-ministerial, presidential secretariat, and even Assembly ranks began to be filled by men who had
come to the top of the bureaucracy under the new program-oriented
emphasis of the administration and who served to institutionalize in the
political-administrative structure the emphasis on development, professionalism, and program achievement."[20]

Henderson noted that with the managerial emphasis of the new leadership in the government the "decisiveness and leadership" of the
individualist sort that had characterized the "flamboyant days of
factional leaders" were replaced by "quieter professionalism and
stability."[21] One survey reflects this trend among cabinet members who
gave "administrative competency" as the most important leadership
quality over "political confidence from the cabinet head," "the party's
support," "good relationships with subordinates," and the like.[22]
According to a contemporary observation,

The implications of these functional changes [were] that such adaptive managerial and institutionally supportive functions became specialized. The emphasis on
the adaptive function by the post-1960 bureaucracy implies that the new bureaucracy is becoming aware of the environment, sensitive to the social changes, and
is thus tending to bring either internal or external changes or both. Additionally
the elaboration of managerial and supportive functions implies that the post-1960
bureaucracy is becoming more positive toward changing society, as well as more
change-oriented and innovative.[23]

The "ritualistic" and "bureaucratistic" tendency of the Rhee bureaucracy thus declined gradually, to be replaced by the new emphasis on
"technical competency" and "technocratic attitude." Professional
knowledge was now held to be of supreme importance. Part of this shift
came from the long-range economic development plans in effect, which
demanded experts and expertise. With the recognition of formal education as the central criterion, experts and expertise were now supplied by
higher educational institutions. After 1961 universities began establishing graduate schools of public administration to meet the plans-created
demand for specialists. Especially with the launching of the Second
Five-Year Economic Plan, most major universities in Korea developed
independent graduate facilities for administrative and managerial
training, thus establishing the rational basis of supplying trained personnel for the government. This input of new blood into the government created rivalry and tension between the old and new elements,
especially when such changes were introduced wholesale by the junta
government. The seniority-based bureaucrats and merit-based new-

comers who looked upon the bureaucracy with a long-term career commitment continued to form two different yet dynamic elements in the postcoup national administration.

The composite picture that emerged in this period was of an administrative apparatus experiencing a rapid transformation as a response to structural social change as well as dominant political ideology. To be sure, a corps of old time bureaucrats still remained within the system, but they were being challenged by two main forces: from within, the younger, more merit-oriented civil servants were pushing their way up the ladder; from without, the large influx of new personnel at the top, both military and civilian, changed the very complexion of bureaucratic psychology. "The crucial question," an observer commented, "is to what extent the more genuinely innovational elements in both groups can be identified and nourished in order for them to exert an ever greater influence upon the entire bureaucracy . . . [for] there are elements both of conflict and of stimulation."[24]

The Democratic Republican party (DRP), another theatre for a view of this organizational change, was formed—formally in 1963 with the lifting of the ban on political activity—by the same leadership (especially that of Jong-pil Kim) that profoundly affected the new trend in the professionalized bureaucracy. One major difference setting the DRP apart, deliberately designed, was its rather new structure orientation, avoiding the personality orientation that had been the general feature of older political parties in Korea.

Even the extensive pannational anti-Japanese movement had produced no nationalism-based political party enjoying popular support and identification. The political parties that had existed in Korea prior to the coup by and large centered around individuals and small cliques. There were, for instance, twenty-five "one-man" political parties in 1948 and eighteen in 1950, each presenting a single candidate in national elections. Nearly every election between 1948 and 1960 was dominated by "independents," those political personalities who had no organized parties. An article on Korean political parties written before the military coup noted that "the Korean party system looks as if it has been made in the United States and there is nothing Korean about the Korean party system." Further, it stated,

There are no major policy differences among the political parties in Korea. The same observations can be made also of their membership compositions. Most of the party leaders and their followers, regardless of differences in their party identification, share the same characteristics as to their occupational, religious, ideological, geographical, and class status backgrounds. . . . Each party is for all the people, and even the Progressive party denies its class bias. When the Progressive party professes being a party of the farmers, it really means all the people in a country which still is largely agrarian. . . . All the parties in Korea have been baptized in the 20th century sea of democracy. As a result, each party, at least in its policy pronouncement, is as progressive as the others.[25]

From the junta government's standpoint, the major defects of Korean political parties had been the remnants of Japanese colonialism in their organizational format and in their political mentality. Their organizational format, or lack of it, symbolized their habits of backwardness and incompetence.[26] Conscious mass participation based on political ideology and the modern concept of instrumental organization was largely absent from the older parties. They continued to be either one-man or one-clique dominated, commonly around a prominent personality or personalities. The New Democratic party, born of the old Democratic party's split, for example, was at a disadvantage in the 1972 general election against the upstart Democratic Republican party, for it could not "shake off its origins in a once-landed elite," and was "more tradition-oriented, and more elitist, and less progressive" than even the old Liberal and Democratic parties.[27] Henderson at the time observed that while the Communist party in the North "has been a classic organization for presiding over a mass society, directing, coordinating, and supporting all governmental and non-governmental organizational activity under a unified chain of command," the Liberal party in the South failed to maintain itself as the political and social coordinating body.[28] It was this historical experience that set the course for the organizers of the Democratic Republic party, and their military organizational skills were put to good use in forming a "modern" political party along functional and structural lines. The organizational success of the Communist party in the North must have had a significant role in the structure of the DRP, for critics subsequently pointed out the similarities in the structural format of both parties.[29]

"Ours is an ideological party," declared a DRP pamphlet. "Ours is not a boss party which emphasizes the role of some specific people but an organizational one firmly founded on ideology."[30] To prove its point, the DRP took a giant step in its organizational format and separated politicans from party functionaries. Rhee's Liberal party's charter specified, for example, that the party president also occupy the top positions at the national convention and on the executive council, the managing committee, the central standing committee, and the central political council, giving the top politician total control of the party.[31] The DRP, it claimed, on the other hand, "operates around its secretariat." The structural innovation within the DRP (the secrtariat as the manager of party functions) can be observed in its emphasis on efficient organizational control, and its bureaucratic and structural format. As the DRP elaborated,

Our party has established a firm leadership by unifying the command channels for effective and powerful realization of party policies. Our party also has established the Secretariat as an executive branch of the party in order to expedite the management of the party. The party Secretariat shall handle party affairs and the management of the party funds. The raison d'être of the party secretariat can be found in the elimination of factionalism as well as in the realization of a genuine party politics system by emphasizing the non-parliamentary role of the party. The secretariat of our party has adopted a bureaucratic organization formula for the accomplishment of its mission and conscientious young men and women are mobilized for its operation.[32]

Although the DRP was subject to much scorn and criticism from its opposition, there was a unanimous if only grudgingly expressed recognition of its effectiveness and efficiency given by the opposition leaders and the general public alike. The DRP's party unity was also maintained, at least structurally, by discouraging inner party circles or cliques, another reactive recognition of the ineffective opposition parties historically torn by internal strife. The establishment of a secretariat was a genuine new invention in the political party system in Korea, which assigned its operational responsibility to a professional staff of functionaries, rather than politicians. This arrangement naturally drew heavy opposition, especially from the Assembly-based politicians, for a secretariat was basically nonpolitical leadership in party management, and a potent rival.

The origin of the "dual system," in which the "representative" and "functioning" committees formed the DRP's main party structure, had much to do with the previous political pattern of National Assembly-men. The junta leadership viewed the pattern of old politics as inherently inefficient and the cause of political corruption and public alienation. Such a view had its deep historical roots. First, National Assembly–based politicians, while nominally leading the district constituencies, had conducted their election campaigns helter-skelter, relying mostly on their personal appeals and acquaintances rather than on effectively managed organizational support. Second, without ongoing organizational support, the Assembly candidates seeking reelection easily succumbed to local pressure, compromise, and corruption. Third, and perhaps more importantly, there existed no unified control of members within the National Assembly, resulting in frequent defections and disorganization when issues called for a united front.[33]

One consequent conclusion reached by the DRP's founding leadership was that members of the National Assembly had to be made more accountable by a nonpolitical counterbalancing organ within the party, which resulted in the establishment of the secretariat. Thus, opting for efficient and purposive coordination, the party format in fact considerably neutralized the very political process by sacrificing the individual integrity (more often, lack of it) of the assemblymember. Party defection, therefore, was methodically and often ruthlessly punished whenever detected. This, the party's organizational charter declared, was the basic purpose of the Democratic Republican party:

The Democratic Republican party, not its candidates, will play the leading role in elections at various levels, and successful candidates thus elected will be precluded from irregular practices. The DRP will also ensure its National Assembly members to engage in their legitimate activities. Political party politics in its genuine sense must mean the realization of the will of the people. In view of this, the National Assemblymen belonging to our party must remain faithful to their true mission through the implementation of party policies.[34]

Amid controversy and criticism, a general consensus appeared to converge in the recognition of the DRP as an organization committed to its collective goal: attaining and maintaining political power. By the early 1970s the DRP boasted nearly 1.6 million registered party members (more than 10 percent of all qualified voters) and controlled a network of 260,000 cell units throughout the nation.[35] One obviously impressed observer marvelled that ''no party in Korean history has ever organized such a tight party network throughout the country.''[36] During election campaigns, the DRP cell units extended their activities ''to villages and remote rice paddies.''[37] The centralized organizational structure made the DRP by 1964 ''the most effective political organization, but not necessarily the most popular party,'' for the 1963 election results ''reflected the fact that it had been organized from the top down, that its grass roots organization and constituency had to be manufactured, and its programs and ambitions were still clearly reflections of the leaders rather than of a popular movement or even of acceptance.''[38] Despite the shortcomings, the DRP was a singularly modern political institution, envied, feared, and quite new, especially in view of the extreme factionalism that had paralyzed the Chang regime, eventually ushering in the coup d'état.

The DRP's stress on organizational efficiency and pragmatism in its formal structure as well as in its political behavior was relentless. It was a party organized by a new generation of leaders and composed of new recruits as its representatives, both unprecedented in Korean history. The party demonstrated its exceptional organizational efficiency by overcoming internal disputes, assaults from the opposition, and serious political unrest. The DRP stood in every way as a ''modern'' political party.[39]

There is good empirical evidence to indicate that the DRP's structural innovation was matched with equal success by the types of new political activists it attracted. Among the seventy founding members of the DRP, only eight were professional politicians, the rest coming from the military (twenty), education (thirteen), press (seven), commerce (seven), bureaucracy (seven), legal profession (four), banking (two), medicine (one), and art (one). The high echelon party leaders of the DRP reflected a similar trend, in which 50 percent had been newcomers to politics, 26 percent from the military, 10 percent from the independents, and the rest from other political parties.[40] Of the 110 DRP members elected to the National Assembly, more than 50 percent had been recruited into politics only after the coup. In contrast to 57 percent of the opposition, 75 percent of the DRP Assemblymembers were born either in small towns or in rural areas. The opposition New Democratic party members in 1971 had a majority (72 percent) who had been in politics more than ten years, whereas 73 percent of the DRP members had less than ten years of experience in politics. The channels of recruitment also revealed their differences. While 55 percent of the DRP assembly-members had been recruited into the party through party recruitment efforts or had been local elites, 27 percent of the opposition had been so recruited. Similarly, when asked how they got into politics, 45 percent of the DRP and 73 percent of the opposition respectively gave "self" as the recruitment agent.[41]

One of the most significant indications of the effectiveness of the DRP as an organization is revealed in the way answers were given to the question of the "most important reason for [their] electoral success." Among the DRP members 53 percent gave various organizational support as the key reason to election success, whereas only 10 percent of the NDP members so indicated; "national mood" was given as the key reason by 63 percent of the opposition's members, and just 26 percent of the DRP's.[42] The appearance of solidarity characterized the leadership of the DRP, while the NDP was given the wide publicity of factionalism and internal strife that had significant influence on the voters' perception of the two contending parties. When the credibility of election pledges was examined, 46 percent of the respondents said most of the DRP's pledges would be realized, while 23 percent gave a 50-50 chance for realization, and 2 percent expressed "absolute distrust" of those election pledges. The opposition fared far worse: only 14 percent said that most would be realized, whle 25 percent gave 50-50, and 17 percent "absolute distrust."[43]

Although the Democratic Republican party remained a successful organization, established with new structural and human purposes, this very basis of success seemed to herald some future problems for the party. They were seen in (1) the problem of overcentralization, the central party having overwhelming control over regional headquarters; and (2) the tendency for the central steering board and the elite groups within the party to form an oligarchic power center.[44] Also, there loomed the stifling effect of a strong party on democratic development in Korean society, although the controversy between political development and the economy of national management continued to be a complex one.

On the cultural front, other signs of political functionalization attested to the strong direction of the new junta force. "Begging war veterans," whom Father Rutt had described as a "nuisance" to small businesses,[45] literally disappeared overnight through the enactment of the Veterans Administration Law soon after the coup. This was a great relief to those who had to endure the overbearing and at times threatening war veteran peddlers. The symbolic effect of an uncompromising government, however, was much more significant: it imprinted in the Korean mind a profound recognition of the new social order. The way the war veterans' problem was resolved was fairly typical of the junta government's methods. While subjecting the peddling veterans to stern law and order like any other ordinary citizens, the government at the same time alleviated their chronic problem of poverty with the new bill that promised financial relief.

The junta government also attacked some of the more revered and cherished Korean habits that the leadership considered backward and unbearably expensive—observance of many traditional customs in which "the waste of money was appalling."[46] Father Rutt reported that a well-educated army officer had confided to him that "the sooner we get rid of this Korean custom, the better." The excesses of traditional ancestor worship rituals, weddings, funerals, and so on were finally abolished by a government decree. Rutt had also noted the confusion and waste in cultural and administrative matters of maintaining two calendars in Korea, one solar and one lunar.[47] The government unified the confusing system by adopting the western solar calendar for public reference, but tactfully designated lunar New Year's Day (which had been traditionally observed throughout Korea) as "Farmers' Day" for more traditional celebration. The furious legislative activity within the first year under the junta government updated or abolished 609 archaic laws, as opposed to 48 such legislative changes during the previous two regimes' 1945-1960 period, which left no doubt about the reformist intentions of the new government.[48]

Traditional human factors still remained difficult to eradicate completely despite the structural and policy rationalization within the political sphere. But neither skepticism nor impediment slowed down the junta leadership in its determination to defy history.

NOTES

1. Henderson, *Korea: The Politics of the Vortex*, p. 106.
2. Lee, *Korea: Time, Change, and Administration*, p. 96.
3. Cole and Lyman, *Korean Development*, pp. 29-30.

4. Lee, *Korea*, p. 96.

5. Ibid., p. 106.

6. Ibid., pp. 106-7.

7. Whang, "Elite Change," p. 263.

8. Suk-choon Cho, "The Ability to Plan and to Administer: Recent Development in Korean Public Adminstration." *Korean Journal of Publication Administration*, Vol. IX, No. 1, 1971, p. 217.

9. Ibid., p. 224.

10. SCNR, 1963, p. 31.

11. Cole and Lyman, *Korean Development*, p. 43.

12. Lee, *Korea*, p. 171.

13. Cho, "The Ability," p. 226.

14. Whang, "Elite Change," p. 263.

15. In-joung Whang, "Political Elite and Organizational Change of the Korean Government." *Korean Observer*, Vol. 2, No. 1, 1969, p. 67.

16. Ibid., p. 66.

17. In-joung Whang, "Leadership and Organizational Development in the Economic Ministries of the Korean Government." *Asian Survey*, Vol. 11, No. 10, 1971, pp. 994-95.

18. Ibid., p. 995.

19. Ibid., p. 1000 (emphasis original).

20. Cole and Lyman, *Korean Development*, pp. 46-47. This change in the membership composition of the National Assembly is also verified by a North-backed piece of propaganda, which stated that since the First National Assembly the majority of landlords (42.4 percent) had been replaced by a new majority of "comprador capitalists" and "reactionary bureaucrats," 28 percent and 32 percent respectively, by 1967. Byong-sik Kim, *Modern Korea: The Socialist North, Revolutionary Perspectives in the South and Unification* (New York: International Publishers, 1970), pp. 208-9.

21. Henderson, *Korea*, p. 358.

22. Dong-suh Bark, "Policy Decision in the Korean Administration." *Korean Journal of Public Administration*, Vol. 4, No. 2, 1966, pp. 225-26.

23. Whang, "Leadership," p. 1002.

24. Lee, *Korea*, pp. 172-73.

25. Kyoung-il Yim, "Interest Aggregation: Political Parties," *A Pattern of Political Development: Korea*, pp. 88-89.

26. Han, "Political Parties," p. 130.

27. Kim, "Korean Voting Behavior," p. 99.

28. Henderson, *Korea*, pp. 326-27.

29. Cole and Lyman, *Korean Development*, p. 40; also Henderson, *Korea*, p. 305. Jong-pil Kim had been an intelligence officer while in the military, and it is widely believed that he had an intimate knowledge of the workings of the Communist government in the North.

30. *The Democratic Republican Party*, 1972, p. 58.

31. Gou-zea Yi, "Some Operational Characteristics of the Democratic Republican Party." *Koreana Quarterly*, Vol. 10, No. 1, 1968, p. 78.

32. *The Democratic Republican Party of the Republic of Korea* (Seoul: The Central Office, 1962), pp. 13-14.

33. Yi, "Operational Characteristics," p. 82.

34. *The Democratic Republican Party*, 1962, p. 13.

35. *Dong-A Daily*, March 27, 1971.

36. Henderson attributes the success of North Korea's modernization and political stability to its collective organizational efforts through "collectivization, propaganda, and state-controlled education-indoctrination." As a result, in comparing a "totalitarian society with a partially free one," in the North "professionalization has apparently been more quickly created . . . with more discipline and success." In view of South Korea's "mass society," it suggests, a tight-knit collective control may be preferred to loose individual competition for social mobility. Henderson, *Korea*, p. 331.

37. Soon-sung Cho, "Korea: Election Year." *Asian Survey*, Vol. 3, No. 1, 1968, p. 29.

38. Cole and Lyman, *Korean Development*, p. 51.

39. Ibid., pp. 51-52.

40. *Kyung-Hyang Daily*, November 1, 1963.

41. Woo and Kim, "Intra-Elite Cleavages," pp. 547-49.

42. Kim, "Korean Voting Behavior," p. 78.

43. Ibid.

44. Yi, "Operational Characteristics," p. 88.

45. Rutt, *Korean Works and Days*, p. 185, 205.

46. Ibid., p. 199.

47. Ibid., p. 206.

48. SCNR, 1963, p. 842.

10

Analysis and Conclusion to Part III

It is time to reflect and ask, Was the junta government justified in its intentions and methods to bring about such sweeping structural and policy changes in Korean society? If so, as history has undoubtedly attested to its justification, what is its theoretical rationale? To answer this question, it would now be beneficial for us to digress somewhat from our narration into the conceptual minefields of organizational sociology. Those who are impatient with such social science distractions may bypass this chapter and proceed to the next.

To accomplish our purpose, it is convenient to start with sociologist Amitai Etzioni, who has divided his "system model" into two basic subtypes: (1) the "survival" model and (2) the "effectiveness" model. The first is concerned with "maintenance" and the second with "operation." The survival model refers to "a set of requirements which, if fulfilled, allows the system to exist," and the effectiveness model to "a pattern of interrelations among the elements of the system which would make it most effective in the service of a given goal."[1]

Concerning our present analysis, it is easy to see that these two models tend to coincide with the two major varieties of modern organization, political and economic.[2] A political organization concerns itself with the goal of survival or maintenance, and an economic organization with the goal of productive operation, or more visible goal attainment. Hage, and Mahoney and Weitzel, have proposed two subtypes emphasizing behavioral adaptiveness and production efficiency. These are some of the organizational referents that can be applied to the changes in Korea's political sphere.[3] As Etzioni has observed, the foci of analysis go beyond the functional level of mere maintenance, but also involve the

level of human dynamics. We shall therefore recall some of the main
features described in political rationalization to give it a theoretical
explanation based on organizational principles.

On the level of personnel mobilization by the junta government, the
mechanism and principle by which the general human resources were
mobilized closely approximate the rational-functional model of organizational effectiveness. Eisenstadt has remarked on the importance of
"political flexibility" in the modernizing efforts made in emerging
nations, that "while impetus to political change and innovation can be
located in all the different types of political organizations and institutions, some form of political organizations seem to be especially likely to
become the force of such innovations and of the institutionalization of
political change." Institutionalization and absorption of social change
depend greatly on the executive and bureaucracy, and how diverse
social interests and talents are channeled and mobilized through the bureaucratic apparatus.[4]

Another theoretical support for human resource mobilization through
talent cooptation has been indicated by Price's theory of organizational
effectiveness, in which he identifies elite cooptation as one principle of
effective organization. Drawing from different types of organizations,
Price observed that cooptation ("the recruiting of members with the goal
of increasing institutionalization") of major and minor elites ("decision
makers in a social system") tends to increase the overall effectiveness
and reduce conflict within a system.[5] The junta's effort to recruit
talented exmilitary officers and civilians alike is thus seen as a reflection
of the rationalist-functionalist orientation, which had largely been
absent in the earlier regimes. The high degree of elite-talent cooptation
also resulted in two tangible benefits: (1) it eliminated or reduced the
cause of friction between the military power elite and the civil
bureaucracy (the seriousness and detriment of which, in the case of
Greece, has been reported by Riggs)[6] and (2) it contributed greatly to
channeling private differences of interest to the public interest by a
societywide talent mobilization.[7]

In the policy element, the Park regime's disposition was seen as consistently bent on rationality, a typical case of which has been described
in the Korea-Japan Treaty of 1965. In general analysis, it can be classified
as a confrontation between the nationalist-emotive opposition forces
and the ends-means conscious (or rationally-oriented) administration.
This confrontation followed the classic contrast in Weber's analysis
between "rational action" and its three nonrational counterparts: "traditional," "affectual," and "absolute value-oriented" action systems.[8]
Traditional behavior is based largely on traditional and habitual
reflection. Affectual behavior connotes "uncontrolled reaction," as in
severely emotional response. Absolute-value oriented behavior repre-

sents absolutely held reference points in the order of "duty, honor, a religous call." Rationality in action, on the other hand, refers to "rational consideration of alternative means to the end, of the relations of the end to other prospective results of employment of any given means, and finally of the relative importance of different possible ends."[9] The extent of rigid determination in both parties involved—opposition and government—may indicate the schism between two such diametrically opposed orientations toward their perceived goals and necessity.

The treaty crisis can also be seen as an attempt, in the rationally conceived sense, to secure a more favorable organizational environment or to better adjust to its changing environment, in the principle of what has been called "the ecological approach of administration." Esman has observed that "achieving a secure position in the international community" is one of the most important goals and tasks of the emerging nations. Further, "Nations exist and function within an international system which is both competitive and cooperative. Depending on their ideologies and power potentialities, governments seek protection, access to resources, and opportunities to spread their influence. These they seek by individual action or in concert with other nations or groups of nations. Much of the energy of national leadership must be devoted to securing and strengthening their position in the international community."[10] By contrast, Rhee's basic orientation was nonrational in balancing ends and means and national, not international, in his worldview. And committed irrevocably to this action referent, he tended to ignore the ecological circumstances that required adjustment and change.

Finally, through the crisis, the government was able to show its strength in maintaining law and order on its own terms without resorting to outright coercion. The government's adequate performance concerning law and order—"the effective monopoly . . . of the power of physical coercion and the use of this power in accordance with rules clearly laid down and generally applicable"—is considered one of the minimum requirements for stable development in emerging nations.[11] Administrative effectiveness so demonstrated clearly pointed to the leadership's commitment to rational-functional performance through structural and behavioral adjustment.

The characteristic differences between the junta government and the pre-junta regimes have been well documented. However, we should mention the relationship between leadership and organizational effectiveness as a prelude to a more extensive analysis of the changes in the bureaucratic structure. Bennis has observed that leadership is one of the most critical factors in organizational effectiveness and has suggested various mechanisms by which leadership can be understood and exercised to promote organizational effectiveness.[12] As noted, Adelman and

Morris consider leadership the single most important element, among noneconomic factors, to account for economic development in the emerging nations.[13] Brown has identified the absence of "administration mindedness" among the leaders of underdeveloped nations as the principal problem involved in program management.[14] Similarly, Etzioni has noted that authority structure and organizational goals must coincide to bring about organizational effectiveness, or else the pathological bureaucratic phenomenon of "goal replacement" will occur.

A major interest of the student of organization is to determine the conditions under which attainment of such goals is promoted or hindered. One important factor determining the degree of goal realization is the nature of the authority structure of the organization. If the orientation of this structure is compatible with the organizational goals, the probability that these goals will be achieved is greater than in organizations where this is not the case. In bureaucracies where goals and the authority structure are compatible, it is likely that the goals will be modified. Goals originally considered secondary may become of primary importance in the organization's activity; means may become ritualized, that is, conceived of as parts of the goals themselves; and activities which were considered illegitimate when the organization was established may become part of the goal structure.[15]

Weber postulated as another conceptual tool the distinction between "substantive rationality" and "formal rationality." The former type, both ancient and patriarchal-theocratic, is irrational in the sense that the basis of judgment is derived fundamentally from outside sources or personal insights basically uncontrollable by intellect. The latter type relies on "procedural and logical rationality," derived from "adherence to external characteristics of facts" and the "logical analysis" of their meaning.[16] From what we have observed, the Korean bureaucracy under the old regime was characterized predominantly by substantive rationality, whereas the junta's emphasis was much more oriented toward formal-rational development. As Milne has described the general characteristics of bureaucratic practice in underdeveloped countries, the pre-junta pattern in Korean bureaucracy in general revealed (1) no effective delegation of authority, (2) no effective centralization, while the appearance of centralization existed, (3) a tendency toward ritualism, and (4) the wide gap between formal and substantial power and authority by the central source.[17] In common with Groves's observation of the prereform bureaucracy in Venezuela in 1958, Rhee's bureaucracy more or less reflected the pattern of "personalism"—"essentially oriented toward personal prerogatives and personal loyalties."[18]

The personal predominance in organizational behavior in the pre-junta bureaucracy is also found in Weber's "traditional" and "charismatic" authority structures, as opposed to the "legal-rational" type.[19]

Weber on traditional domination as elaborated by Bendix: "The persons exercising the power of command generally are *masters* who enjoy personal authority by virtue of their inherited status. Their commands are legitimate in the sense that they are in accord with custom, but they also possess the prerogative of free personal decision, so that conformity with custom and personal arbitrariness are both characteristic of such rule."[20] And on charismatic domination: "Personal authority also may have its source in the very opposite of tradition. The power of command may be exercised by a *leader*—whether he is a prophet, hero, or demagogue—who can prove that he possesses *charisma* by virtue of magical powers, revelations, heroism, other extraordinary gifts."[21]

Unlike the above two types, which may be said to find a strong affinity with Rhee's bureaucratic pattern, Park's administrative apparatus—through both structural and behavioral applications of organizational principles—could be properly identified as legal-rationalistic in the sense that it was based on the concept of technical, rationalistic, and administrative procedure.[22]

Now, it is possible for us to assess the junta bureaucracy's reorganizational activities reflected in their expansion, differentiation, and intra-organizational "spatial mobility" of personnel, and so forth. To do so, we shall apply the rules of organizational effectiveness as proposed by Price.[23] He identified a certain number of variables, derived from empirical research findings, as factors contributing to effectiveness. Relating to the fundamental changes in the structure of Korean bureaucracy, we may apply Price's assertion that "organizations which primarily have a rational-legal type of decision making are more likely to have a high degree of effectivensss than organizations which primarily have charismatic type of decision making."[24]

Reflecting upon the general evolution of modern formal organizations, Park's rational-legal type of organizational structure must definitely be considered functionally superior to its counterparts before the junta. The increased size of the bureaucratic structure, although not ipso facto effective, indicates the increased size of tasks to perform and the types of goals to achieve. It reflects the changing environment and the bureaucracy's adjustment to the change, vital to development administration "in which continuity through varying interchange with a variety of environments, internal as well as external, will have to be anticipated, planned for, and confronted."[25] Applying this to the increased size of domestic bureaucracy and overseas units, we may also quote Price, who identifies size as one factor of organizational effectiveness: "Except where there is a high degree of professionalization, organizations which have a high degree of size are more likely to have a high degree of effectiveness than organizations which have a low degree of size."[26]

On the organizational front of the junta government, role differentiation came with the increase in size, in which numerous bureaus and divisions were expanded and augmented. Weber himself identified as one of the universal organizational phenomena "the differentiation of specifically delimited spheres of functional activity, in systems of authority in the concept of office, in others in spheres of technical competence, or of assigned function under authority."[27] Price has also mentioned that the high degree of division of labor and specialization contributes to organizational effectiveness.[28] We have also observed that increased communication among bureaucrats for new ideas and their implementation, which altered their mutual recognition from negative to positive, was something of a new phenomenon in Korean bureaucratic behavior; this is also confirmed by Price as favorable to organizational function.[29]

Among other structural features that at least theoretically contribute to organizational rationality and effectiveness, suggested by Price, are: (1) the rotation of personnel within and among organizations, as well as from the military to the civilian bureaucracy;[30] (2) the presence of ideological commitment to development;[31] (3) centralization for effective task performance;[32] (4) mechanization through updating techniques and equipment.[33] We have seen that the junta administration's structural, behavioral, and personnel adaptations and changes may be considered a textbook application of such principles to make government organizations ever more effective.

NOTES

1. Amitai Etzioni, "Two Approaches to Organizational Analysis: A Critique and a Suggestion." *Administrative Science Quarterly*, Vol. 5, No. 1, 1969, pp. 271-72.

2. Reinhard Bendix, "Bureaucracy: The Problem and Its Setting." *American Sociological Review*, Vol. 12 (October 1947), p. 493.

3. Jerald Hage, "An Axiomatic Theory of Organizations." *Administrative Science Quarterly*, Vol. 10, No. 3, 1965, pp. 304-7; also Thomas A. Mahoney and William Weitzel, "Managerial Models of Organizational Effectiveness." *Administrative Science Quarterly*, Vol. 14, 1969, pp. 362-64.

4. S. N. Eisenstadt, *Modernization: Protest and Change* (Englewood Cliffs, New Jersey: Prentice-Hall, 1966), pp. 149-55.

5. James L. Price, *Organizational Effectiveness: An Inventory of Propositions* (Homewood, Illinois: Richard D. Irwin, 1968), pp. 110-16.

6. Fred W. Riggs, "Administration and a Changing World Environment." *Public Administration Review*, Vol. XXVIII, 1968, pp. 348-50.

7. Bauer and Yamey, *The Economics of Under-Developed Countries*, p. 156.

8. Max Weber, *The Theory of Social and Economic Organization*, Talcott Parsons, ed. (New York: The Free Press, 1947), pp. 116-17.

9. Ibid. This is not to say that the treaty itself was based on purely rational consideration on the part of the power elite. However, that it is possible to consider extrarational motives for the treaty is not the same thing as saying that it *was* based on extrarational considerations.

10. Milton J. Esman, "The Politics of Development Administration," *Approaches to Development: Politics, Administration and Change*, John D. Montgomery and William J. Siffin, eds. (New York: McGraw-Hill, 1966), pp. 63-64.

11. Bauer and Yamey, *Economics*, pp. 163-64.

12. Warren G. Bennis, "Leadership Theory and Administrative Behavior: The Problem of Authority." *Administrative Science Quarterly*, Vol. 4, No. 3, 1959, pp. 287-301.

13. Adelman and Morris, *Society*, pp. 78-79.

14. David S. Brown, "The Key to Self-Help: Improving the Administrative Capabilities of the Aid-Receiving Countries." *Public Administration Review*, Vol. XXIV, No. 2, 1964, p. 72.

15. Amitai Etzioni, "Authority Structure and Organizational Structure." *Administrative Science Quarterly*, Vol. 4, 1959, pp. 43-44.

16. Reinhard Bendix, *Max Weber: An Intellectual Portrait* (Garden City, New York: Doubleday, 1962), pp. 398-99. We obviously cannot claim that the difference between Rhee's and Park's administrative styles followed this clear-cut dichotomy as postulated by Weber. However, a certain general tendency can be outlined that makes the contrast between the two styles more meaningful.

17. R. S. Milne, "Mechanistic and Organic Models of Public Administration in Developing Countries." *Administrative Science Quarterly*, Vol. 15, 1970, p. 58.

18. Roderick T. Groves, "Administrative Reform and the Politics of Reform: The Case of Venezuela." *Public Administration Review*, Vol. XXVII, No. 5, 1967, p. 439.

19. Max Weber, *Economy and Society*, Vol. I (New York: Bedminster Press, 1968), p. 439.

20. Bendix, *Max Weber*, p. 295 (emphasis original).

21. Ibid. (emphasis original).

22. We must remind ourselves that formality itself may or may not contribute to organizational effectiveness. The Weberian formal structure, of course, must be understood as a composite picture of modern formal organizations.

23. Two pertinent points may be mentioned in this. First, we may compare certain statistical indicators—GNP, income per capita—from two historical eras for a measure of their respective effectiveness or lack of it. Second, we may contrast the two styles of formal organization, following the broad outline of Weber and later theorists on organizational effectiveness. In this book, as reasonably expected, we have combined both approaches.

24. Price, *Organizational Effectiveness*, p. 55.

25. Samuel A. Culbert and Jerome Reisel, "Organizational Development: An Applied Philosophy for Managers of Public Enterprise." *Public Administration Quarterly*, Vol. XXXI (March/April 1971), pp. 159-60.

26. Price, *Organizational Effectiveness*, p. 185.

27. Weber, *The Theory of Social and Economic Organization*, pp. 80, 83.

28. Price, *Organizational Effectiveness*, pp. 16-30.

29. Ibid., pp. 163-75.
30. Ibid., pp. 192-200.
31. Ibid., pp. 104-10.
32. Ibid., pp. 60-92.
33. Ibid., pp. 30-90.

Part IV

RATIONALIZATION OF THE ECONOMIC SPHERE

11

Some Introductory Observations

All the changes and struggles in the political sphere have now set the stage for the main part of our story: rationalization in the economic sphere. Because the economic cannot be separated from the political, especially in an emerging society, political rationalization was absolutely necessary for any notion of economic development. After a brief introduction to the Korean economy in this chapter, which again highlights the forward-looking quality of the military leaders, the succeeding chapters will deal with the details of how the so-called "economic miracle" was first launched.

The following are, then, the subjects that will occupy our subsequent attention: (1) policy and structural changes under the junta government, preliminary to the coming economic activities; (2) the population control campaign as one example of the effect of a nationally committed and coordinated program administered by a determined leadership; (3) theory and practice of the planned economy and its role in Korean society; (4) some specific structural changes for promoting economic development, such as the increased domestic share of economic resources, inducement of foreign capital, market-determined foreign exchange rates, highly successful export drives, and the role of Vietnam earnings; and finally, (5) changes in agricultural policies to bring about modernization of the rural sector.

Let us assume, at the outset, the validity of the following two assertions: first, that economic growth reflected in the size of gross national product and income per capita is a good thing, which largely justifies any positive action taken by the governing authority to bring about this development; and, second, that where there exists no contrary evidence, the statistical data compiled by the government and other agencies are to be accepted as valid.

To validate the first point, Cole and Lyman have stated on the economy of the emerging nations, "We assume that economic structural change to provide long-term growth—economic development—is desirable for these nations, not only because it is necessary to provide growing populations with better living conditions but because it seems to be a goal of most of the peoples in these countries."[1] To validate the second point, statistics on the Korean economy, for example, the export-import figures or domestic savings rates, are generally accepted as accurate. Professor Breidenstein, a socialist economist not readily inclined to praise the southern regime, observed that the economic statistics in Korea cannot be distorted, if only because "international creditors watch the Korean economy carefully and cannot be deceived completely."[2] Adelman also remarked that Korea was "one of the best data bases in the underdeveloped world."[3]

As noted, the capitalist economic form in Korea did not emerge until Japanese rule in the early twentieth century.[4] By the time of the military coup in 1961, however, Korea had established a fairly solid infrastructure in the economic sector—for example, the high literacy rate, a reasonable start in industrial development (although the country was still predominantly agrarian), an adequately trained labor force, and the somewhat mature capacity for electric power to satisfy industrial needs.[5]

Human resources, one of the most vital factors in the Korean economy in the junta era, had been superbly prepared for their eventual role that far exceeded its per capita GNP. As it turned out, Korea's human resources had fortuitously been "overeducated" in the fifties when everyone scrambled to move up in society through education, and became the major source of productive power when production became the predominant feature of economic activity under the junta government.[6] Yet, even with such potential resources in labor and infrastructure the Korean economy was exceedingly poor and listless. Korean capitalism having solidified only after 1945, a majority of the major business owners were, without a deep-rooted historical experience, still a postliberation phenomenon. The economic system as such, although capitalist in form, continued to be a managed economy "with varying degrees and forms of government control over trade, banks, approval of foreign loans, agricultural price supports, and a large amount of direct investment."[7] The government owned and managed most of the financial institutions and major industries, including power, railroad, and coal.[8]

Adelman and Morris have observed that the absence of positive factors, such as a leadership committed to development, a taxation system, and a centralized authority, is more detrimental to economic development than the presence of some negative social features in the emerging nations.[9] In the Korean case, then, positive factors emerged with the new political leadership committed to reorganizing the economic sphere of society, while the inherited negative features of society, such as bribery, were not stamped out. The changes made to galvanize the economic sphere in Korea after the coup constituted the "presence" of positive factors. The forward-looking commitment of the military leaders in power compensated for the existence of other negative features, many of which still existed, in the final balance sheet. The junta leaders were action-oriented, "entrepreneurial" social forces necessary for social change,[10] and had been trained for their eventual role.

Certain factors in the training of military officers were obviously central not only to their eventual role but also the way they played it. Their forward-looking time orientation was a result of both the internal modernization through their military organization and the organizational skills and problem-solving managerial approaches that they had acquired specifically through training. This combination of experience and knowledge gave the officer corps its brand of developmentalist outlook and forward-looking habits of mind unique to Korean society and institutions as a whole.[11]

The "entrepreneurial" and "developmentalist" outlook with a managerial sense of organization also gave the junta leadership a uniquely futuristic perspective on matters economic, expressed especially in long-term planning and structural arrangement. The futurist orientation of the leadership was crucial to establishing many mechanisms and institutions that became the backbone of its economic development. Lee lists the following as instrumental agents that represented the leadership's future orientation and investment:

1. The multi-year economic development plan: The establishment of Korea's long-term economic plans reflected the decisions of the leadership committed to long-term developmental planning as inevitable in an economically backward nation. The leadership saw that increasing domestic resources and foreign capital, building infrastructure, and binding the entire national management under one direction and purpose were essential.

2. Futurist institutions: In order to "establish the standards for objectives and to define the quality of social life in the long-run" the leadership also created instrumental institutions (or, "institutionalization of instrumental mechanisms") for training "futurist" personnel and developing appropriate bases for knowledge and experience. As an example of this orientation, the Korean Institute of Science and Technology (KIST) was established under the junta government for coordinating science and management in futurist development.

3. Special development projects: For a future-oriented developmental plan, the government undertook major, and previously unthinkable, construction projects. Under the junta leadership, for example, the Seoul-Pusan superhighway (which had been quite controversial for its sheer technical difficul-

ties) was constructed in order to facilitate long-term transportation needs and to coordinate an overall developmental management covering widely disparate areas and regions. Such projects, daring in scope and staggering in technical obstacles, also served their symbolic purpose in demonstrating the new government's intention as well as ability.

4. Incorporation of civil talents into the governmental organizations: The junta leadership desired an ongoing process of cooptation involving civilian talents from the educational, business, and journalist sectors of society, primarily for managerial reasons and secondarily for political reasons, warding off alienation among the college educated by absorbing them into the new national purpose.[12]

Applying the idea of "the absence of positive factors," as opposed to "the presence of negative factors," the difference between the Rhee and Park leaderships was clearly in the latter's *establishment of positive factors without stamping out negative factors*, for instance, in the persistence of irregularities in and out of government. While many such negative factors that had been the hallmarks of Korea's economic-political habits continued to exist, they were now "fitted into a different set of priorities over the next few years." And "in contrast to the Rhee regime, the independent economic growth of Korea was rated as a major objective to which older forms of corruption, as well as many previously favored interests, were sacrificed."[13]

Most significantly, the new government was in a position free of its ties with the old order of society. Unlike any other political segment in Korea, its origins in the military gave the new governing elite not only the freedom to act according to its own design but also the *necessity* to act against the old ruling elite and its interest. Indeed, some elements of the traditional ruling elite were diametrically opposed to the military government's direction, which made it imperative for the new government to act against the old order. Hence, the junta felt greater incentive to "break down older governmental patterns." This was more evident in the radical economic programs initiated and pursued after 1963.[14]

Previously, the source of corruption as a "mutually profiting system of cooperation" was in the sharing of limited privileges in banking, import quotas, and foreign funds, a type of corruption with no productive benefit. It had existed within a rather small circle of government officials and businessmen, both far removed from the dynamics of developmental planning and long-term considerations in the Korean economy.

NOTES

1. Cole and Lyman, *Korean Development*, p. 2.
2. Breidenstein, "Capitalism," p. 3.
3. Irma Adelman, "Introduction" to *Practical Approach to Development Plan-*

ning, Irma Adelman, ed. (Baltimore, Maryland: Johns Hopkins University Press, 1969), p. 10.

4. For a brief history of Korean capitalism, see Moon-hwan Choi, "The Path to Democracy: A Historical Review of the Korean Economy." *Korean Quarterly,* Vol. 3, No. 1, 1961, pp. 52-70. More economically detailed accounts can be seen in Parvez Hasan, *Korea: Problems and Issues in a Rapidly Growing Economy* (Baltimore, Maryland: Johns Hopkins University Press, 1976), pp. 25-35; L. L. Wade and B. S. Kim, *Economic Development of South Korea: The Political Economy of Success* (New York: Praeger Publishers, 1978), pp. 1-91; Gilbert T. Brown, *Korean Pricing Policies and Economic Development in the 1960s* (Baltimore, Maryland: Johns Hopkins University Press, 1973), pp. 15-50; and for a more recent account of the Korean economy, the two-volume study by the World Bank, *Korea: Managing the Industrial Transition* (Washington, D.C.: 1987) is also available.

5. Princeton Lyman, "Economic Development in South Korea: Prospects and Problems," *Asian Survey,* Vol. VI, No. 7, 1966, p. 385.

6. Cole and Lyman, *Korean Development,* p. 138.

7. Ibid., p. 251.

8. Kim, "Economic Development of South Korea," p. 148.

9. Adelman and Morris, *Society,* p. 244.

10. Max F. Milikan and Donald L. Blackmer, *The Emerging Nations* (Boston: Little, Brown, 1961), p. 38.

11. Lee, *Korea,* p. 152. Developmental planning is defined by Katz as "the process involving the rational direction and acceleration of . . . social change toward the specific objectives. It includes both the formulation of a set of decisions and the efforts to implement them. These efforts result in a feedback of new information revealing estimating errors, unexpected events, and new possibilities." Saul Katz, "A Systems Approach to Development Administration," *Frontiers of Development Administration,* Fred Riggs, ed. (Durham, North Carolina: Duke University Press, 1970), p. 110.

12. Lee, "Use of the Future," pp. 19-22.

13. Cole and Lyman, *Korean Development,* pp. 93-94.

14. Ibid.

12

Changes in Policy and Structure

As noted, one of the more outstanding contrasts between the Rhee and the Park regimes was their respective time orientations regarding economic development. To state it simply, the older leaders took little notice of Korea's economic future. Rhee's economic policy, such as it was, had been irrevocably tied to maximizing foreign assistance, mainly from the United States, in which growth was identified in the increasing volume of foreign aid. Numerous short-run problems, such as national security, hunger, and survival, especially after the Korean War, commanded immediate attention and made a futurist outlook difficult to conceive. Yet, meager and precious resources were allocated without due regard for long-run effects—a "present-orientation" emphasizing enlarged consumption by the national administration. "Part of the failure of the Rhee government was that it did not adjust to this extension of the time horizon, whereas the military and successor governments, and even the Chang government, which seriously considered planning and future growth, responded to, and stimulated, popular expectations as to the future."[1]

The Combined Economic Board (CEB) was established in 1952, comprising both Korean and United Nations representatives, to coordinate Korea's economic policy and implementation in the war and the postwar periods. Although the CEB's initial objective was to stimulate a long-term economic development, the problem it encountered with the Korean officials was typical of such in the underdeveloped societies. Meetings between the CEB and the Korean government "began to degenerate into 'horse-trading' arrangements" in which both sides traded their projects to secure their own by approving the other's in exchange.

Because the CEB was only half-heartedly organized on its part, and because it received no political and administrative support from the Korean government, the CEB's was largely a record of failure. In addition, since the foreign resources that the Korean government received came as aid, their independent use was severely circumscribed by the conditions imposed by the donor government.[2]

This lack of central direction in economic activity under Rhee was coupled with the suffocating effect of government control over the entire economic sector. Historically, "property and the economy were oriented toward central power and politics. There was no real theory of private property. Indeed, as in many modernizing nations, privacy was regarded as virtually subversive. Economic status was based exclusively on political power."[3] During the Rhee regime, this unfortunate tradition continued. The economic sector, such as it was, became thoroughly stifled by the executive exercises of power in licensing control, foreign funds allocations, and preferential bank loans. While these practices, arising from short-run political interests, encouraged needless corruption without accompanying productive outcomes, the main national economic preoccupation was in making every concerted effort to secure more foreign aid.

The Rhee government regularly ordered its officials to understate harvests in order to increase the size of U.S. grain aid, thus sacrificing Korea's own long-term domestic development. Likewise, it maintained overvalued exchange rates, while making no effort to stimulate export, in order to strengthen its hand in increasing U.S. aid by presenting Korea in the poorest possible posture. In a more general but equally pernicious way, the regime habitually discouraged the advancement of those who had been trained abroad in economic development and ignored their innovative ideas.

Thus, subservient to politics with no life of its own, the economic sector was hopelessly tied to the fortunes of political whims in Korea. The modern concept of autonomous economic activity was virtually unrecognized, much less practiced. For the short-run benefits of welfare maximization, Rhee encouraged import substitution with intermediate goods, rather than either domestic production or export expansion. In place of light industrial investment for immediate use in manufacture, the regime emphasized heavy industrial investment mainly as a sovereign showcase for investment of scarce national resources. Rather than maintain a realistic foreign exchange rate to encourage export, it kept the rate low by force while the illegal market rate was several times higher. Shunning entrepreneurial competition and initiative from the civilian sector in the economy, the government controlled every major financial transaction, which not only stifled potential growth but also produced self-consuming corruption. Failing to effectively summon internal revenues that had been considerably underused (to be evidenced in the revenues and savings increases after the 1964-1965 structural changes), the government looked to foreign aid as the quickest and easiest source for capital. These contrasting structural limitations and policy intentions were to become the critical basis for the Rhee-Park comparison in the coming years of economic rationalization.

Under Park's leadership, the overriding objective in national development was always in the direction of *attaining maximum returns* from the resources invested through efficient and rational management, planning, formulating, and implementing specific economic policies. As a defining characteristic of the junta leadership in matters economic, *factual orientation* in planning and administration was notable for its intensity and consistency. (1) Unlike the Rhee regime's disdain for details, the junta leadership emphasized the "factual, quantitative data" and made great demands for accuracy in developmental trends and results. (2) Institutions specifically charged with collecting and analyzing data were established—for instance, the Computer Center at the Korean Institute of Science and Technology, the Science and Technology Information Center, and the Export Information Center, among other such facilities for information and resources. (3) As a result of these new emphases on data collection and factual analysis, high-level and intermediate bureaucrats developed a mental habit toward facts and long-term planning for more rational and efficient economic forecasts.[4] Prominent among the rationalizing policy changes was the removal of many of the old regime's structural impediments to development:

The new government permitted the operation of a free enterprise system, based upon market incentives rather than political favoritism. It liberalized quantitative import restrictions. Realistic market interest and foreign exchange rates were established in 1965. A new Foreign Capital Inducement Law was promulgated in 1966 to attract large-scale equity investment and private, as well as public, credits. In order to induce foreign capital, favorable treatment such as tax exemption and government guarantee of foreign loans were offered to foreign investors. Compensation was promised in case foreign capital is expropriated or requisitioned during a domestic crisis.[5]

The government, in enacting the Inducement Law, rejected the narrow-minded but popular view of foreign capital as "an economic exploitation" of the poor by the wealthy, but as a "catalyst" for generating and expanding domestic economic development. One of the principal reasons for a speedy conclusion of the Korea-Japan Treaty in 1965 was the inflow of new capital entailed in the reopening of relations with Japan. "By the 1965 Korea-Japan agreement, Japan provided Korea $800 million—$300 million in grants, $200 million in governmental loans, and additional private commercial loans of $300 million. The use of above funds was made in the areas of agriculture, fisheries, raw material purchase and acquisition, development of small and medium industries, railway and shipping industries and other construction areas."[6]

The junta leadership identified Japanese capital as positive and consistent with Korean economic objectives. With this essentially modern view of foreign capital, the leadership sought to assuage the public's obsessive fear of Japan's new economic inroads by stressing Korea's domestic economic confidence. As a result, Cole and Lyman reported at the time, "since the restoration of normal diplomatic and commercial relations in 1965, the Koreans have endeavored to increase the inflow of Japanese capital and to make greater use of Japanese resources, though still within a system of constraints."[7]

According to Strout's analysis,[8] Korea performed well in the economic sphere when compared with other selected countries. In GNP growth rates in the 1963-1967 period, Korea recorded 9.8 compared with the 4.9 sample average. In export in particular, Korea's achievement was spectacular, with 43.6 in the same period compared to the sample's 6.8. As Lyman observed, "what distinguishes the period [of high growth] from previous periods of growth is purposeful movement toward basic structural reform."[9]

One of the earliest economic commitments was the now-famous export drive, first as a means to a "self-reliant" economy and later, as its success became prodigious, as a "lead sector" in the overall scheme of economic development. The successful export drive made major changes in policies imperative. One such change was the 1964 devaluation of the won by almost 100 percent,[10] and another equally important was the 1965 "open, floating rate" of foreign exchange. Devaluation of the won suddenly became a powerful incentive for export, for the exporter could convert the foreign exchange profit into a larger sum in the Korean won, which through the floating rate system was set at a par with the market fluctuation. By this open system of foreign exchange, the hitherto profligate black market operations became unprofitable and were therefore greatly reduced. At the same time the entire export sector learned the valuable lesson of becoming more sensitive to international standards and market conditions. Restrictions on imports were also liberalized, which gave domestic products greater competitiveness and less retarding protection through high tariffs, as had been the case previously. By the end of 1965, over 80 percent of import items were on the "automatic approval" list.

The stifling bureaucratic bottleneck in allocating foreign capital was also lifted by allowing the newly established Korean Reconstruction Bank to manage loan applications to be worked out between foreign lenders and domestic borrowers. In this new commercial system of securing foreign loans, the government merely acted as the final overseer but not as a direct participant in the transaction, which made the process more expeditious and efficient. Special credit was extended to manufacture for export and export-related production. Domestic revenue sources were expanded first by rationalizing tax collection via the establishment of the Office of National Tax Administration, and by inducing the crucial domestic savings by offering an interest rate set as high as 35 percent per annum. With this increased interest rate the government sought to divert funds from private channels to public funding by becoming commercially more attractive to the saver. Amounts of capital circulated through private usurious practices had often been greater than those saved in public commercial banks. The raised interest rates gave the public an incentive to save more and rationalized the capital circulation by equalizing public and private interest rates. The policy was rewarded with the increasing shares of GNP by domestic savings, which continued its pattern of spectacular increase thereafter.

With such various structural and policy changes made to encourage rational management in the Korean economy, national defense gradually lost its preeminence among governmental budget priorities under the junta leadership, quite in contrast with the Rhee regime's preoccupation with military buildup. During the postwar period of 1954-1957, Korea's defense expenditures for the 600,000-person military were the highest in the world as a portion of the total government budget, an astounding 53 percent. Its share of national income in the same period averaged nearly 14 percent.[11] Under the junta government the American burden of Korean defense expenditures gradually declined, for instance, from 72 percent in 1962 to 27 percent in 1968.[12] By 1976, the end of the Third Five-Year Economic Plan period, the American share of Korea's defense disappeared.

As an astonishing change of national ideology and testimony to its rational outlook, the military establishment realized the importance of military expenditures in purely *economic* terms. The leadership recognized the essentially wasteful military spending as such and "thus defense needs were in the nature of a minimum constraint that had to be satisfied, rather than one of several objectives to be maximized."[13] By the end of the junta's first decade, South Korea was spending about 4 percent of its GNP for defense expenditures, as opposed to the North's 15.6 percent, estimated at $337 million and $700 million respectively; military expenditure per capita stood at the time at $49 in the North and $11 in the South.[14] Foreign economic aid, savior of impoverished Korea for many years, also began to decline in the First Plan period of 1961-1967, from over $200 million to $100 million, or from nearly 9 percent of Korea's GNP to 2.3 percent in the same period.[15] Foreign aid in the form of grants-in-aid, notably from the United States, gradually shifted to loans. In the 1961-1967 period alone, loan financing from foreign capital was sufficient to offset the trade deficit. The flow of foreign loans, as world confidence in South Korea's economy solidified, continued thereafter to become the backbone of Korean capital formation. In the meantime the "almost exclusive dependence on governmental grant assistance" disappeared.[16]

In July 1961, the Economic Planning Board was formally established as an independent ministry, reorganized and upgraded from the Council for Economic Development within the Ministry of Reconstruction under the Chang administration. The EPB was now charged with "national economic development planning and coordination, annual budgeting, statistical control and coordination, and cooperation with aid agencies."[17] The minister of the EPB was to act concurrently as vice prime minister to further strengthen its authority in economic coordination. Committing itself totally to efficient and functional economic development, the leadership made the EPB the most powerful of all economy-related ministries in Korea, and gave it full support in its policy formulation and implementation. Absorbing agencies from other ministries, such as the Bureau of Budget in the Ministry of Finance and the Bureau of Statistics in the Ministry of the Interior, in addition to the Council for Economic Development in the Ministry of Reconstruction, the EPB drafted the First Five-Year Economic Development Plan by the end of 1961.[18]

Emulating the successful Japanese model, the Korean Trade Agency (KOTRA) was inaugurated in 1962 as a semigovernment organ with worldwide branches aimed at bridging the gap between foreign buyers and domestic suppliers. The Korea Exchange Bank, formerly a department within the Bank of Korea dealing with foreign exchange, was established in 1967. Seoul National University was charged with research on foreign trade problems. Smaller technical centers were also established, devoted exclusively to helping the export sector. A contemporary observer described the activity this way:

The numerous policy measures undertaken in recent years in support of export expansion, reminiscent of the eighteenth century mercantilism in western Europe, were an expression of strong and effective government leadership. . . . The government's positive attitude toward foreign policies opened up a new vista for international economic cooperation in the interest of domestic economic growth and expansion of exports. . . . Frequently, trade missions were sent to remote countries as well as familiar ones. The overseas network of foreign service units was expanded and assigned a new task of "economic diplomacy" and of sales promotion for the private exporters.[19]

The junta leadership's determination to bring about economic development took on two major themes: (1) to establish and expand positive factors, both in policy and structural changes as noted, and (2) to campaign against those factors deemed detrimental to economic efficiency and growth. For the latter, there is no better example of the government's dogged determination than its massive national campaign to curb Korea's burgeoning population growth, which demonstrated "clearly the importance of sheer administration."[20] This campaign, one of the most dramatic shows of collective effort under a determined leadership, will be the main subject of the following chapter.

NOTES

1. Cole and Lyman, *Korean Development*, p. 168.
2. Nahm, "Korea's Search for New Status," pp. 42-43.
3. Henderson, *Korea*, pp. 32-33.
4. Cho, "The Ability to Plan and to Administer," pp. 124-25.
5. Kim, "Economic Development," pp. 152-53.
6. T. C. Rhee, "South Korea's Economic Development and Its Socio-Political Impact." *Asian Survey*, Vol. 13, No. 7, 1973, p. 679.
7. Cole and Lyman, *Korean Development*, p. 166.
8. Alan M. Strout, "Korea's Use of Foreign and Domestic Resources: A Cross Country Comparison," *Practical Approach to Development Planning*, Irma Adelman, ed. (Baltimore, Maryland: Johns Hopkins University Press, 1969), p. 278.
9. Lyman, "Economic Development," p. 382.
10. Some of these policy and structural changes will be dealt with in greater detail in Chapter 15.
11. *Economic Statistics Yearbook*, 1957 (Seoul: Bank of Korea, 1957), pp. 1-21.
12. *Korea Annual*, 1969 (Seoul: Hapdong News Agency, 1969), p. 109.
13. Cole and Lyman, *Korean Development*, p. 167.
14. Clemens, "GRIT at Panmunjom," p. 535.
15. Jong-chul Lim, "Korean Economic Development and the Role of Foreign Capital." *Korean Observer*, Vol. 1, No. 1, 1968, p. 93.
16. Cole and Lyman, *Korean Development*, p. 185.
17. Nahm, "Korea's Search," p. 41.
18. Lee, *Korea*, pp. 157-58.
19. Song, "A Case Study," p. 86.
20. Taek-il Kim, John A. Ross, and George C. Worth, *The Korean National Family Planning Program* (New York: The Population Council, 1972), p. 3. (The following chapter on the population control campaign is heavily drawn from Kim and his coauthors.) It is possible to consider population control under the subject of "political sphere" via mass mobilization. However, the obvious intention of the campaign was more economic than political, for the campaign itself had little political implications and its results had no immediate bearing on the leadership's political advantages. Hence our decision to include it in the economic sphere.

13

Population Control: Case of a Functional Government

The population problem in Korea had been well known. By the early sixties Korea was one of the most densely populated nations in the world. Historically the population had grown phenomenally without an influx of immigrants, increasing about 18 times between 1395 and 1904, and doubling between 1910 and 1944. Between 1945 and the time of the military takeover in 1961, there had been a 65 percent increase in Korea's teeming demographic scene. Korea's population density was world ranking, registering at 59.4 persons per square mile in 1910, 113.7 in 1944, 161.3 in 1945, and 267 by 1962. Each year over one million new persons had to be added to the already crowded peninsula's population. The increase in GNP was seriously offset by the increasing population. Despite the considerable increase in GNP in 1962, for example, although greater than that of the previous five years, income per capita fell during that period because of the growing population. Simply stated, the "population growth rate was greater than the growth of GNP. This resulted in a decrease in per capita income."[1]

Clear and imminent as its negative implication was for any effective economic development, the population problem had been given little positive treatment. Not only had there been little government action to curb it, the growing population was even considered a national asset of strength, thanks to the continuing postwar North-South tension during the Rhee administration. Very little policy formulation and implementation was considered under "Rhee's anti-birth control policy,"[2] although "in spite of the unfavorable attitude of the president, several efforts were made within the government to get activities started."[3] By 1961, however, the population growth rate of 2.9 was ahead of the 2.6 GNP growth rate.

It became clear that, without some check on population growth, Korea's economy would actually be moving backward while seeming to move forward. Under these circumstances, what little stride was made in the economic sector would be self-defeating. It was with this background of factors and perspectives that the junta leaders committed themselves to a national campaign to curb the soaring population in Korea. Not only did the leadership make it an instrumental government policy for its obvious economic necessity, but also, reminiscent of the drought-fighting campaign, they took it as a showcase of national will and administrative powers.

Renamed "family planning" to erase the negative implication of population control practiced under Japanese rule, a new massive national campaign on the problem immediately faced many and varied difficulties, not the least of which was the fact that it had to be imposed on the public by the government. Other questions were public acceptance or rejection of the proposed idea, its complex implications for sexual morality, the degree of cooperation within various administrative agencies and its long-term significance for the South's sovereign strength with a smaller population. With these potential problems and difficulties in the background, the Supreme Council for National Reconstruction announced its decisive and sweeping commitment in October 1961, within five months of the coup d'état, to execute the following policies:

1. Enacting a new law and promulgating policies to implement family planning.
2. Abrogating the law prohibiting importation of contraceptives and permitting such importation of all types.
3. Promoting the domestic production of contraceptives and controlling their quality.
4. Entrusting to the National Reconstruction Movement (NRM), in cooperation with other government and nongovernment agencies, the implementation of the family planning information and education program.
5. Training family planning workers.
6. Seeking foreign aid and using this aid appropriately.
7. Establishing family planning clinics.
8. Organizing a family planning advisory council.
9. Supporting private agencies interested in the family planning program.[4]

In November of the same year, the family planning activities got under way. Between November 20 and 29, a total of 1,250 physicians, nurses, and midwives were trained in nine separate cities as the initial technical core; the NRM headquarters printed 8,000 copies of *The Ideal Family*, a booklet explaining family planning, to be distributed nationwide; 181 "lead members" were trained and, in turn, instructed 7,310 local family planning workers.[5] In the following year, 700 new workers were trained and over half of them were assigned to 183 local clinics to carry out the program; 1.2 million contraceptives were distributed; and vasectomy was introduced in November. Also in the same year, the Family Planning Advisory Council was established (Cabinet order No. 375) to oversee the campaign; 6,600 schoolteachers were trained in family planning; and 90,000 social workers in the NRM were also instructed.[6] About 4,000 vasectomy operations were performed in the year in which the Planned Parenthood Federation of Korea (PPFK) "acted as the broker for this hospital work, making the contacts, developing doctors' training, and channeling payments for the work done."[7] Experts from the U.S. Population Council were invited in November 1962 and, after a month's investigation, they suggested the following structural changes:

1. The creation of a largely autonomous family planning unit with relation to several ministries.

2. The expansion of publicity and education and the appointment of specific officers for this purpose in the Ministry of Public Information and in the NRM.

3. The expansion of family planning training and the placement of several family planning workers in each health center.

4. The initiation of investigations into the suitability of the IUD (a very recent innovation at that time and not tested in any national programs); a study of the incidences of induced abortion; expansion of the use of vasectomies; the monitoring of the development of oral contraceptives; and continuation of traditional contraceptives.

5. A national survey and a large-scale demonstration project.

6. An increase in the proportion of the Ministry of Health's budget earmarked for the plan from 5 percent to 10-15 percent.

7. An expanded search for extra technical aid funds from overseas.[8]

These suggestions were adopted well within one year. More experts were invited from Japan in early 1963 to compare notes on each other's experiences. In June 1963, the Ministry of Health was reorganized to create a unit exclusively charged with family planning, and an advisory committee made up of members of the PPFK and other agencies was established. The minister of the Economic Planing Board in 1962-1963 was convinced of the importance of population control, and as a result he decided to throw his full support at upgrading the program to a top priority national project. In December 1963, the Minister of Health made two sweeping decisions: to assign family planning workers to each of 1,473 townships in Korea, and to vastly increase the IUD program, as a result of which over 100,000 IUDs were implanted in the following year.

The year 1963 became the point of major departure for the program: the family planning budget rose from 42 million won in 1962 to 77 million in 1963. By July the government printed 2 million instructional pamphlets, 25 million pregnancy calendars, and 1.3 million family planning posters. A total of 3.3 million home visits by the workers were made by July, and local clinics were visited by 2.5 million clients; further, over 19 million persons participated in various meetings on the subject. In the same year, three key specialists were sent to the U.S. Population Council for a year to study population control methods. A four-person team was sent on a thirty-five-day tour overseas, and another group of four was also sent to overseas seminars on family planning. In December, the EPB established a Family Planning Policy Council to strengthen the program.[9]

A ten-year family planning program covering the 1962-1971 period was drawn. In that span 780,000 loop insertions and 2 million vasectomies were performed, 150,000 condom distributions made, and 355,000 continuing pill users enrolled. The family planning budgets rose accordingly as the importance of population control became well recognized by the leadership: 77 million won in 1963, 158 million in 1964, 423 million in 1966, 526 million in 1969, and finally 644 million in 1971, a fifteen-fold increase in the ten-year period. In the 1961-1969 period, a total of 13,045 physicians, field workers, health center nurses, township level workers, and PPFK local administrators received preservice training; a total of 8,865 instructors, designated doctors, county pill administrators, supervising nurses, midwives, health educators, mobile clinic staff, members of industrial and social groups, and army reserve instructors received in-service training; and a total of 18,376 persons attended seminars on different levels in the same period.[10]

Aside from the official figures and results, the field workers experienced varying degrees of personal challenges and hardships in carrying out the campaign on the grass roots level, quite unprecedented in Korea's history. The workers often met with one another to compare their experiences and to exchange moral support.

The rural population received particular attention in the campaign. In addition to the mobilized physicians for doctorless towns, the government organized "mobile teams," equipped with army ambulances and foreign-donated modern vehicles, that toured "isolated rural areas." In many of these villages modern medicine had rarely been available before.

Each unit was staffed by a physician, a nurse-midwife, a health educator, and a driver. Sometimes local doctors would work with the team for a period as part of their training in family planning. The mobile unit's schedule was developed by the provincial health officials in cooperation with county health center directors and township workers. Areas without doctors, or low achievement rates, or high

incidence of side effects were given priority. Another scheduling system used by
several teams focused on special market days: large crowds are available then
for movie showings; many women regularly come to these places from remote
villages for shopping. This makes them available to the mobile clinic for either
insertion or follow-up services. Villagers were informed at least three weeks
before the visit by the village chief, a social worker, or a family planning field
worker. If a field worker was in the area, she would attempt to recruit IUD and
vasectomy candidates to be waiting for the unit's arrival.[11]

In the 1966-1969 period alone, the ten mobile units made 6,452 township
visits, spending 7,242 days in the field, performing 112,00 IUD insertions and follow-up services and 5,320 vasectomies and follow-ups, and
holding 4,305 meetings on family planning, at a total cost of $325,000.[12]
    Public relations campaigns played a significant role in overcoming the
initial public reluctance and bringing about positive attitudes. In 1964,
1.5 million instructional pamphlets, 45,000 family planning posters, 88,000
pregnancy calendars, and 400,000 counter cards for restaurants were
distributed. In 1965, gifts for participants and acceptors of the program,
memo plates for teahouses, and mirrors with loop messages for beauty
parlors were prepared. By 1968, 17,000 "mothers' clubs" were organized by the PPFK and the government, with the monthly magazine
Happy Home published for their use. Initial messages were exploratory:
basic questions like "What is family planning?" and "Why do we need
family planning?" were raised and answered. Soon they were more
direct and positive: "Practice family planning"; "Do it for better education" (or "opportunity," "health," etc.); "Do it for your children";
"Visit your doctor"; or "Ask about the loop, the modern way of
practicing family planning that's so simple."[13] Four varieties of dramatic
series divided into 25 installments were broadcast over the radio, which
was a popular medium for dramatization; talk shows and small group
discussions were also heard on the radio. A survey indicated that 50
percent of married women under 45 admitted that radio programs made
them aware of family planning. In 1970 alone, a total of 520 articles
dealing with population control appeared in newspapers and journals.
In the same year, family planning movies reached over 1.5 million
persons, in addition to the 500,000 who saw a total of 12 different films
made available by the mobile units. *Happy Home* magazine, inaugurated
in 1968, reached a circulation of 60,000 copies per edition to become a
major voice on family planning. Television networks were also enlisted
to televise drama and public information programs.
    A month in the spring of every year was designated "Family Planning
Month," set aside to reemphasize the program. The month saturated
the public with radio and television spot announcements, films, exhibitions, "Family Planning Song," special dramas, and cartoon shows,

and the Ministry of Public Information's 118 mobile vans were in full use with films for the local residents. Newspapers stressed the importance of family planning, magazines put out special sections on the issue, and contraceptives manufacturers sponsored meetings and seminars on the subject. During the month, taxis and buses carried family planning stickers, train speakers broadcast topical jokes and skits, the family planning theme was performed by well-known entertainers, agricultural extension workers made special visits to rural families, commemorative stamps on family planning were issued, and military troops received lectures on vasectomy and literature for their reading rooms. Countless meetings were held to bestow awards on outstanding persons in the program; in 1970, for instance, they took place in 140 counties.

Results of this intensive information campaign were encouraging; a survey comparing 1962 and 1966 in public awareness showed that those who were aware of the "family planning" program rose from 68 to 88 percent in the rural areas, and those who knew at least one contraceptive method increased from 46 to 72 percent in the rural areas and from 67 to 73 percent in the urban areas. National surveys taken in the 1965-1967 period showed that over 90 percent of married women, twenty to forty-four years, approved of family planning, while the approval rate for rural areas was a slightly lower 85 percent.[14]

The overall result was a sharply reduced population growth rate in Korea, from the annual 2.9 percent in the 1960-1961 period to 1.9 percent in 1970,[15] and to 1.8 in 1971.[16] The government's goal was to achieve 1 percent by 1976, the end of the revised Ten-Year Family Planning period of 1967-1976.[17] Demographer Ralph Thomlinson observed that "Korea stands a good chance of being one of the first nations to bring down its birth rate quickly by official action."[18] More tangibly, the ratio of children, birth to 4 years, to eligible women, 15 to 44 years, declined from 764 per thousand in 1962 to 567 in 1968, in urban areas, from 687 to 422; and in rural areas, from 851 to 675.[19]

The most telling reason for this success in the national administration's effort to curb the population cannot be overemphasized—it is obvious: the leadership was committed to the task, overcoming the "public displeasure by using extensive public education."[20] The leadership had no doubt that "rapid population growth tends to negate other efforts to promote economic growth and raise living standards."[21] Other factors unique to Korea, such as negligible religious opposition and a high literacy rate, for instance, favored positive results.

But the most important of all factors still remained the "understanding and forceful leadership shown by the government in including population planning as an aspect of national planning."[22] Essential to its success and evident in abundance were "coordination and hard work from the highest level—the president and the legislators—to the lowest—the field workers and the participating couples themselves."[23] Together they were eventually responsible for establishing "one of the most effective programs in the world."[24] South Korea's national family planning campaign, unequivocally, was a triumph of planning present action in anticipation of long-term future returns—in short, economic planning.

NOTES

1. Ik-soon Im, "Population Growth and Economic Development," *Patterns of Economic Development: Korea*, pp. 32-44.

2. Kim, Ross, and Worth, *Family Planning*, p. 16.

3. Ibid., p. 39.

4. Ibid., p. 44.

5. *Korea Annual*, 1962 (Seoul: Hapdong News Agency), p. 427.

6. *Korea Annual*, 1963 (Seoul: Hapdong News Agency), p. 392.

7. Kim, Ross, and Worth, *Family Planning*, p. 45.

8. Ibid., p. 46.

9. *Korea Annual*, 1964 (Seoul: Hapdong News Agency), p. 355.

10. Kim, Ross, and Worth, *Family Planning*, pp. 65, 72, 101.

11. Ibid., pp. 143-44.

12. Ibid., pp. 147, 151.

13. Paul Hartman, "Korea: Medical Referral System and Mobile Services," *Studies in Family Planning* (No. 13) (New York: The Population Council, 1966), pp. 10-12.

14. Kim, Ross, and Worth, *Family Planning*, pp. 87-95.

15. Patricia Bartz, *South Korea* (Oxford: Oxford University Press at Clarendon, 1972), p. 55.

16. Rhee, "South Korea's Economic Development," p. 683.

17. *Korea Annual*, 1970 (Seoul: Hapdong News Agency), p. 218.

18. Ralph Thomlinson, *Demographic Problems: Controversy over Population Control* (Belmont, California: Dickenson Publishing Co., 1967), p. 109.

19. Kim, Ross, and Worth, *Family Planning*, p. 168.

20. Ibid., p. 94.

21. Bartz, *South Korea*, p. 55.

22. Tae-bin Im, "Population Projection in Korea." *Koreana Quarterly*, Vol. 3, No. 2, 1964, p. 163.

23. Panos D. Bardis, "Modernization and Birth Control." *Journal of Asiatic Studies*, Vol. VXIII, No. 2, 1970, p. 114.

24. S. M. Keeny, "Family Planning Programs: What They Cost and How They Work," *Family Planning and Population Programs*, Bernard Berelson, ed. (Chicago: University of Chicago Press, 1966), p. 224. The 1976 target was variously reported: 1.5 by Kim et al., p. 177; 1.3 by Bartz, p. 57; 1.1 by Hapdong 1970, p. 218; and 1.5 by Whang 1970, p. 479.

14

Ideology and Planned Economy

The junta leadership's future-oriented outlook made the planning mentality the most outstanding characteristic of the new leadership. From an organizational perspective, long-term planning is undoubtedly far more effective for goal attainment than short-term management. It was this future-orientation of the new leadership, in contrast to the old regimes, that encouraged factual habits and developmentalist outlook in the administration.

Under Rhee and Chang, ideological biases and circumstances had worked against long-range plans for the Korean economy. Rhee's basic "economic policy" was maximizing foreign aid, showcasing heavy industrial investment with little immediate returns, and overlooking the abundant surplus labor force for light manufacture. In view of his basic economic policy, Rhee had disdained a governmental commitment to a planned and fairly fixed economic position that would bind the leadership and the government. Such a commitment would have deprived them of their arbitration power in the politics of economic resource allocations. The Nathan Plan, the first such plan ever devised in Korea, never drew much attention from Rhee and the Liberal party. A revised plan was also drawn under the Chang administration, which had realized the positive aspects of a planned economy. But political pressure, not economic plans, commanded the regime's full attention. The 1962 First Five-Year Economic Development Plan inaugurated under the junta government was, thus, an outgrowth of the two preceding plans, this time with the leadership's full commitment.[1]

Introducing the plan, the EPB declared that "the ultimate course of the Korean economy lies in industrialization." This is how it was described by the EPB:

During the plan period, the period of preparation for industrialization, emphasis will be placed on development of power, coal, and other energy sources, increase in the earnings of farm households by raising agricultural productivity, expansion of key industrial facilities and adequate provision of social overhead capital, utilization of idle resources, some improvement in the balance of international payments, primarily through increased exports, and technological advancement.[2]

The plan audaciously projected a GNP increase of 140.7 percent for the 1962-1966 plan period, and an increase of 141.8 percent in government investment, 234.5 percent in private investment, 131 percent in government consumption, and 118.2 percent in private consumption.[3] The emphasis on the "lead sectors," that is, electric power, agriculture, and social overhead capital, aimed at providing "a basis of essential inputs for growth of industrial production which would be carried out mainly by the private sector."[4] Export was viewed early on to be the sector that would lead Korea out of its trade gap—from the then $316.1 million to $41 million by the end of the plan period—by maximizing the use of Korea's surplus labor force for relatively quick returns in light industrial investments. During the plan period export was to rise from $61 million to $117 million,[5] and, as we have seen, the leadership made it known that it had committed itself to promoting export by altering structural arrangements and creating special impetus to stimulate export trade. (The export target was, it turned out, underestimated, actually reaching $250 million in 1966.)

The GNP growth rate projected at 7.1 percent per annum, set in the plan, was much higher than the average of 4.7 percent in the preceding seven years, and called for "a highly efficient political leadership and administrative management." The plan also placed a heavy demand on public austerity by imposing a high rate of investment in the period. This "implied a great sacrifice on the part of the public, which would mean either a high degree of political persuasion or coercion."[6] (The main source of investment actually came from domestic savings, which, after the 1964-1965 structural changes in the tax administration and the savings interest rate, greatly increased.) The plan asked for extensive participation by the private sector, 66 percent of the total capital formation. This meant the increasing role of the Korean entrepreneurial class and their increasing influence, despite the fact that the government still owned and operated a large number of main enterprises.[7] With the increased role placed upon the private sector, internal savings became the most crucial factor in capital formation, which reflected the junta regime's judgment in its ultimate outcome.

However, the real significance of the plan, both real and symbolic, was the fact that the military administration took the planning and planned economy seriously. This in itself was a remarkable development in Korea's political history, for a major administrative instrument to bring about social change had been actively adopted by the government. The military administration took the important step of adopting the program that had been germinating in the previous regimes. The economic plan was by no means an easy project to implement, but the military regime made the plan its central theme. The fact that the government committed itself to a major plan gave substance to its subsequent action programs.[8]

The implementation of the plan was admittedly hasty and at times confused. Although the plan succeeded in achieving its overall effect, it was not until after the 1964-1965 structural changes that boosted the export sector that the plan achieved (and overachieved in some areas) its general targets. The net result was a GNP growth of 43.9 percent in the 1962-1966 plan period, which was above the 33.3 percent set in the plan, averaging 8.3 percent annually as opposed to the planned 7.1 percent, while the investment plan of 22.6 percent annual increase in the plan period fell short, at 16.4 percent.[9] The family planning campaign, as part of the First Five-Year Plan, succeeded in halting the runaway population expansion. The actual achievement of the economic plan by the junta leadership can easily be overstated, but the main significance, aside from the statistical results, was that the government was now actively committed to what it considered a more rational and programmatic management of the economic sphere. In it long-term planning became its most telling characteristic and most potent instrument.

By the time the Second Plan for the 1967-1971 period began to be drafted in 1965, "the planning function and the planners became integral parts of the government's decision-making process," thanks to more accurate statistical projections, the effective leadership firmly consolidated in the EPB, and better coordination among governmental and overseas agencies that partook in the planning phase.[10]

In the summer of 1966 the Second Five-Year Economic Development Plan was unveiled. Prior to that, however, a great deal of advance publicity had been created through press conferences given by the officials of the Economic Planning Board who explained its main features. Thus, even though few surprises were unveiled, the plan attracted much media attention and stirred much public awareness. The government, in anticipation of questions and criticisms, organized a program to answer questions and deflect criticisms regarding the new plan. The plan was formally endorsed by the cabinet and approved by the president, who vowed his commitment to moving forward with the goals. Unlike the First Plan, the Second Economic Plan was conceived with greater knowledge and experience, presented with greater unity from the government, and perceived in general with greater confidence for its success.[11]

Th growth of GNP per annum was set at 7 percent in the Second Plan period despite the World Bank's opposition to it as being too high to be realistic. The actual result, however, was 11.4 percent. The United Nations Commission for the Unification and Rehabilitation of Korea (UNCURK) reported that "all main objectives in the Plan were achieved, and the projected growth rates for investment, industrial production, exports, social overhead and services were exceeded."[12] The obviously symbolic and at times helter-skelter nature of the First Plan was meticulously revamped by the time the Second Plan was formulated. The planners now commanded "a thorough review of the entire economy and the collection of a detailed, up-to-date mass of economic data . . . [which] provided the government with a basis for rational policy decisions in the economic sphere."[13] Notable for the more "scientific" and "fact-oriented" basis of the plan, the government created a series of industry committees to provide the planners with accurately detailed technological and demand information.

These committees, composed of engineers, business experts, economists, ministry officials, and technical experts, soon transcended their original technical function and became vehicles for consensus building for plan formulation and implementation. They also served to disseminate information pertaining to industrial implementation and to industrial prospects, thus performing the "indicative planning" function so necessary for plan implementation in a mixed (public—private) economy.[14]

The junta leadership's commitment to planning was as far-reaching in time as it was wide-ranging in scope. Whang found that over 40 percent of the plans under the junta regime, as compared with fewer than 10 percent prior to it, were long-term projects ranging five years or more: the First Five-Year Economic Plan, the Seven-Year Plan for Food Production, the Five-Year Technical Development Plan, the Long-Term Economic Projection for 1967-1981, the Ten-Year Population Control Plan, and others.[15] The scope of 26 percent of these plans was extraterritorial, involving international concerns, compared with 8 percent with such a scope prior to the junta government.[16]

Independent of the EPB's flagship Economic Development Plans, however, other ministries developed their own five- to thirty-year plans on various projects. The mushrooming of long-range plans became so pervasive under the junta government that an observer lamented that "what

Korea currently needs is the plan of plans, in which the plans of each agency are mutually coordinated and all of these are in turn geared to the Five Year Economic Development Plan."[17] At the time, accordingly, the Ministry of Agriculture had nine such plans, the Office of Forestry five, the Ministry of Construction three, the Ministry of Public Health two, the Ministry of Education one, the Ministry of Science and Technology three, and the Ministry of Commerce and Industry six.

The implementation of the First Plan had necessitated many ad hoc policy alterations, as much as it required sustaining structural changes on the administrative level. Among the governmental efforts toward efficient and rational economic development were the policy changes inaugurated in 1964-1965 to give solutions that many of the plan projects demanded. Among them antiinflation policy, savings interest rate reform, floating exchange rates, and other policy reforms for export promotion were most notable, and we will now turn to them.

NOTES

1. For comments on various aspects of the First Five-Year Economic Development Plan, see Charles Wolf, "Economic Planning in Korea." *Asian Survey*, Vol. 11, No. 10, 1962, pp. 22-28; and the articles by Song; Choi; Paik; Youk; and Kim in *Korean Affairs*, Vol. 1, No. 1, 1962, pp. 4-43. There is also the EPB's *Summary of the First Five-Year Economic Plan*, Economic Planning Board, Republic of Korea, 1962.

2. EPB's *Summary*, p. 29.

3. Ibid., p. 31.

4. David Cole and Young-woo Nam, "The Pattern and Significance of Economic Planning in Korea," *Practical Approach to Development Planning*, p. 24.

5. EPB's *Summary*, p. 68.

6. Lee, *Korea*, pp. 158-59.

7. The list of government-owned and operated public corporations at the time included the following: Bank of Korea; Korea Development Bank; Medium Industry Bank; Citizens Bank; Housing Bank; Korea Power Corporation; Korea Coal Corporation; Korea Highway Corporation; Chungju Fertilizer Co.; Naju Fertilizer Co.; Korea Salt Co.; Korea Mint Corporation; Korea Trade Promotion Corporation; Korea Mining Promotion Corporation; Korea Irrigation; Korea Water Resource Promotion Corporation; Korea Agricultural Promotion Corporation; Korea Tourism Promotion Corporation; and Korea Insurance Guarantee Corporation. (Reported in Cho, "Bureaucracy and Local Government in South Korea," *Government and Politics of Korea*, pp. 95-96). In addition, the government owned and managed the railroads and tobacco manufacture and sales in monopoly.

8. Lee, *Korea*, pp. 160-61.

9. Kie B. Lee and San O. Park, "Foreign Investment and Korea's First Five-Year Economic Development Plan, 1962-1966." *The Korean Economist*, Vol. 4, No. 1, 1969, pp. 15-18.

10. Cole and Lyman, *Korean Development*, pp. 218-19.

11. Ibid., p. 220.

12. UNCURK's *Report to the General Assembly*, p. 27.

13. Irma Adelman, "Introduction," *Practical Approach to Development Planning*, p. 8.

14. Ibid., p. 9.

15. Whang, "Elite Change," pp. 256-57.

16. Ibid., p. 258.

17. Cho, "The Ability to Plan and to Administer," p. 123.

15

Specific Policies for Economic Rationalization

The Five-Year Plan called for heavy domestic as well as foreign capital investment. In response, certain changes were adopted by the government: (1) inducement of foreign capital through favorable governmental action in policy and structural adaptations; and (2) greater mobilization of domestic resources through more efficient taxation and savings policies. Both actions required heavy government involvement, and in consequence they produced unprecedented results.

The circumstantial factors for the decision to induce foreign capital were both internal and external. Economic self-sufficiency was one of the professed goals of the junta leadership, and at the same time foreign aid, notably from the United States, was rapidly declining, for example, from $383 million in 1957 eventually to $82.6 million in 1970. In the same period foreign savings among the sources for investment declined from 64 percent to 36.5 percent. By 1961, foreign aid had been cut in half by the donors. Another avenue for foreign capital had to be sought. This was when the military government made the decision to seek capital from private foreign lenders as an alternative source. New laws—the Foreign Capital Inducement Act and the Foreign Investment Act, for example—were enacted to encourage foreign investors by guaranteeing repayments. The Korean Reconstruction Bank and the Bank of Korea were authorized to handle the loan business on a case-by-case basis. This new approach was quite in contrast to that of previous regimes, which had relied almost exclusively on gratuitous aid from donor nations.

Many positive factors made Korea's call for foreign capital attractive: (1) the junta government's clearly defined economic goals sufficiently offset the negative impression of Korean performance created in the fifties and even in the early sixties; (2) the geopolitical importance of South Korea was not lost on foreign investors as Korea's strategic location was seen as a significant political and economic asset; (3) skilled and abundant labor in Korean light manufacture made foreign investments a highly feasible and profitable venture; (4) political stability was provided by the junta government firmly in control; (5) there had been no previous foreign debt obligation on the part of Korea; and finally (6) the tacit understanding was that despite the decreasing amount of direct aid, the United States "would not for the foreseeable future allow Korea to fall into default on debt repayments."[1]

The new laws greatly facilitated private firms that dealt directly with foreign investors, the final government authorization pending. The foreign investor's confidence in Korean investment was specifically enhanced by (1) government guarantees on almost 95 percent of all medium- and long-term foreign loans; (2) a thorough advance investigation by the EPB into the "feasibility of projects, interindustry linkage, and—in particular—the availability of satisfactory infrastructure facilities"; and (3) the liberal terms offered to equity capital, through favorable tax treatment, transfer of profits and capital, and so forth.[2]

Under Rhee, foreign capital, mainly from grants-in-aid, had been tightly controlled for political leverage. This political practice not only encouraged bribery and corruption in the government, with many competing for the few resources; it was also responsible for the indulgent consumption habits in which the foreign fund allocations favored consumer goods and import substitution. This misallocation of funds was contrary to the widely held belief among economists that efficient use of funds through productive allocations of capital was as important as the volume of the investment itself. Rhee's policy of resource use had been generally oriented toward heavy industry and import substitution. As a result, the former neglected the value and potential of the then-abundant surplus labor force that could be mobilized in labor-intensive rather than capital-intensive industry. The latter stifled the domestic development and competitiveness of manufacturing industry by imposing favorable tariffs or exemption on imported goods. In addition to breeding corruption, "the system gave the greatest rewards to those who were most competent at obtaining favorable government actions with the least sharing of the resulting profits."[3]

Realizing the potential of the well-educated labor force in Korea, the junta leadership shifted the policy from heavy to light industry. Nearly half of the foreign investments approved through 1968 were allocated to light manufactures, with a special emphasis on export items, without much "partisan consideration" in the pattern of allocation.[4]

Capital formation and investment are the two central factors in the economic development of the emerging nations.[5] The First Five-Year

Plan had rather heavily relied on foreign capital. In the plan period, 1962-1966, the foreign to domestic resources ratio was to decline from 81.7:18.3 to 43.1:56.9 in favor of increased domestic share. It turned out, however, that the actual sharing of foreign capital in the plan period declined from 83 percent to 39.9 percent and domestic savings rose from 11.4 percent to 54.4 percent in the same period, due to the induced increase in private savings.[6] Many were concerned about the negative implications of foreign loans, for example, that foreign lenders—especially the Japanese—were gaining control over the Korean economy. However, the structural and policy innovations to induce foreign capital to finance the plan were enormously successful, especially after 1965, to more than offset the trade deficit. By 1970, foreign loans reached a total of nearly $3 billion in both public and private loans, without which the growth rate of GNP in the plan period would have been less than half.[7] Foreign loans, private or public, had been practically nonexistent prior to 1962, but with the structural accommodations offered by the government, including the lifting of the inefficient process of government-National Assembly control over foreign funds, the privately procured loans began to exceed those of the government after 1963.

The government used various fiscal techniques to control inflation, which had been rampant especially in the fifties under Rhee and in the first two years of the junta government. In the decade that had preceded 1963, the average annual new money supply stood near 38 percent, and wholesale prices increased 21 percent. In the same period consumer prices increased by an average of 23 percent. Government spending accounted for over 80 percent of the new money supply, causing the fiscal deficits responsible for inflation in the immediately preceding years.[8]

The first major step that the junta government took to counter inflation was the reduction of capital investments and administrative expenditures. Wages of civil bureaucrats were held down without increase despite the rise in consumer prices. Bank credit policy also changed after 1964 toward "preferential interest rates" used in credit allocation, which had proved to be ineffective. Despite the quarterly loan ceilings, the preferential terms were often extended beyond the ceilings to many sectors, and the use of bank credit could not be effectively checked by the government. The 1964 credit policy placed all bank credit under the ceilings, and the private sector's loan credit was heavily restrained and reduced despite the higher demand for more credit due to the devaluation of won in May 1964. "Other techniques used to check credit expansion were the issue of central bank bonds and short-term treasury bonds to commercial banks and the requirement that commercial banks maintain interest-earning blocked deposits with the central bank in excess of the required reserves against deposits."[9]

By the end of 1964, much of the cash deficit was eliminated by such changes in the government's fiscal policy. But the most significant factor in offsetting government deficits at first, and then building surplus capital for expenditures and investments later, was the reformed national revenue system beginning in the same year. The positive relationship between an effective taxation system and economic development had been well established. As Adelman and Morris observed, "the contributions that an effective tax system can make to the economic growth of underdeveloped countries are varied." These varied factors include government controlling national resources for capital allocations and investments, making the revenue resources an instrument of more equitable income distribution, and checking inflation by collecting potentially inflation-creating surplus resources.[10] A domestic revenue share of GNP around 15 percent is considered "adequate," according to Adelman and Morris, but in 1964, before the taxation reform was put into effect, the share stood at a pitiful 6 percent.

It was believed in some circles that Korea had been grossly undertaxed, and the junta leadership agreed. The first step the government took toward overhauling the revenue system was reorganizing and expanding the structure of tax collection. Under Rhee, the Bureau of Taxation had dealt with both policy formulation and its administration. The junta government upgraded it into the Bureau of Tax System exclusively in charge of policy formulation, while creating a four-bureau Office of National Tax Administration for policy administration only. This change was accompanied by the introduction of "speedy techniques of assessment and collection" and "the strong personal support given to the tax drive" by the top echelons of the leadership.[11] Every conceivable revenue source was searched out. Included in it, for instance, were the writer's fees that had been overlooked in deference to the subsistence-level incomes of many intellectuals and writers, to which the principal beneficiaries raised vocal objections.

The reform in taxation policy and implementation became one of the major developments in the government's effort to increase domestic revenues for economic investment. The president took personal interest in the new reform in domestic revenue collection by appointing one of the original junta members head of the Office of National Tax Administration, by waging a public persuasion campaign stressing the importance of revenue collection, and by publicly praising high-bracket taxpayers. The general economic expansion in the period also made it possible to maintain a high level of taxation without causing undue resistance from taxpayers.

With the leadership's full commitment and the structural changes instituted to accommodate the new purpose, the revenue resources climbed phenomenally, reaching 10.3 percent as domestic revenue's share of GNP by the end of the First Plan period in 1967, which was to increase to 14.3 percent by 1971, the end of the Second Plan period. The increased domestic revenue is also revealing in sheer numerical terms: in 1962, a grand total of 18.5 billion won was estimated for collection, which rose to 88.4 billion won in 1966, 473.5 billion in 1970, and finally 683.2 billion won by 1972.[12] Thus the pessimistic view on "the capability of the Korean revenue system to expand revenues mainly by stronger administrative action" was dispelled.[13] The increased revenue from state-owned enterprises whose efficiency had significantly improved was enough to enlarge government expenditure 150 percent between 1964 and 1967, and subsequently helped finance some of the governmental development outlays.[14]

Concurrent with the tax reform to rationalize the Korean economy were also the policy changes aimed at inducing private savings, which had almost been abandoned by the previous governments despite their enormous importance in domestic capital formation. There had been many justifiable sociopolitical factors to discourage private savings on a massive scale: inefficiently managed savings institutions; the generally low income per capita; constant threats of inflation; and most important and deep-seated, lack of confidence in political stability and continuity. As an indicator of economic development in the emerging nations, Adelman and Morris observed the crucial importance of domestic savings institutions. According to their view, one that is generally shared by other development specialists, the proportion of "total domestic resources available for investment" is crucial for national development. They argue for increasing domestic resources through increasing the rate of domestic savings, as well as for channeling such domestic savings into investment for maximum productivity. In both of these functions—increasing domestic savings and investing them effectively— various financial institutions must play a central role. Institutions and banks—"such as central banks, commercial savings, and specialized development banks, and where they exist, developed monetary exchanges"—emerge at the forefront in the execution of these crucial functions.[15]

This importance of domestic savings had been recognized earlier by the junta leadership, which, in June 1962, startled the nation with a currency reform, in order to: (1) induce idle cash holdings into long-term deposits at banking institutions and channel them toward long-range economic development purposes; (2) prevent the possible resurgence of an open inflation by curbing excess consumption and speculative expenditures; and (3) finance investment outlays under the Five-Year Plan within the framework of monetary stability, thus laying a sound foundation for future economic growth.[16]

The circulation of private loans had been pervasive through noninstitutionalized usurious circles called the "gye" and "mujin." The private lenders not only evaded taxes on the interest they collected but also stifled other public banking organizations whose viability depended very much on the circulation and expansion of monetary transactions through them. The 1962 currency reform, conducted in utter secrecy by the junta government, aimed at "freezing" this circulation and turning it into long-term investment in government projects, especially those in the First Plan. There had been a widespread belief that there was an enormous surplus of capital in Korea that was kept out of public circulation. The 1962 currency reform proved nothing of this sort; there was, it turned out, no hidden capital to surface through the reform that would come under public accounting. In some ways, this abortive attempt to increase domestic savings "was typical of government efforts for most of the postwar period, which were based on coercion and exhortation rather than on creating a structure of incentives and conditions to encourage voluntary savings."[17]

Through 1963 and 1964, demand for capital investment increased as the plan was put into full effect. Hard pressed, it was in this period of high capital demand that the government instituted "undoubtedly the most significant change effected in monetary policy": the September 1965 enactment of new banking interest rates on time and savings deposits.

The general level of interest rates was sharply increased to reflect the true scarcity value of capital, to encourage savers by providing an adequately attractive "real" interest rate (i.e., the nominal interest rate adjusted for the rate of price increase), and to help the shift in credit policy from quantitative rationing toward indirect regulation. The interest-rate reform was also intended to serve a clearcut demonstration of the government's determination to curb inflation. Other objectives were to attract funds from the "curb market" into the banking system in order to strengthen the influence of the monetary authorities and to promote the use of owned capital (in preference to borrowed capital) by the business sector.[18]

Through the reform, the government brought the commercial banks' interest rates up to a par with (or even higher than) those of private monetary markets and as a result "a substantial amount of money was transferred to the banking system from the curb market" by private savers.[19] The interest rate reform act increased the time deposit rate from 9.0 percent per annum to 19.6 percent; for three months' deposits, from 12.0 percent to 26.8 percent; for six months' deposits, from 15 percent to 30 percent; for over-one-year deposits, from 18 percent to 34.5 percent. The results prompted Cole and Lyman to remark that "it seems fair to say, however, that no one involved in the so called interest rate reform anticipated anything like the response that did occur."[20]

The total of time and savings deposits at all banking institutions stood at 12.7 billion won in 1963 and 14.4 billion in 1964, a slight increase but in reality no increase at all as it was offset by the increase in wholesale price. A year after the reform, in 1966, however, the total deposits soared to 70 billion won, and rose to 128.5 billion in 1967, 255.5 billion in 1968, 451.5 billion in 1969, 569.1 billion in 1970, and finally 701.5 billion in 1971.[21] Savings originating from individuals and households were mainly responsible for the large increase; otherwise they would have continued their monetary transactions in curb markets.

Corresponding to the interest rate increase on savings, loan rates were also raised, from 14 to 26 percent per annum. At the same time, ''by increasing the volume of savings flowing through the banking system, the interest-rate reform allowed the government to free the banking system from some of its more severe control, as well as from its dependence on nonmarket rationing devices for the allocation of loans.''[22] With the large inflow of new capital into the banking institutions the pervasive private market system lost its leverage in competition with the government's new policy. As Adelman noted above, the junta government was then able to relax its loan ceilings and restrictions by instituting a wide range of "preferential rates." Interest rates on loans for purchase of aid goods, for instance, increased by the reform act from 14 percent to 26 percent per annum, from 20 percent to 36.5 percent on overdue loans, and from 12 percent to 22 percent on call loans, but the preferential rates covered the loans for export and rice liens, which remained at 6.5 percent and 11 percent respectively. Approximately one-third of commercial loans came under the protection of preferential rates, which dealt with export and export-related raw material purchase.[23] These preferential rates extended to specialized banking institutions, that is, the Korean Reconstruction Bank, the Medium Industry Bank, and the National Agricultural Cooperative Federation, which ultimately reduced the business sector's dependence on the curb market, thus rationalizing the economic sphere in general.[24]

In order to relieve the strain on profit margins at commercial banks, due to the discrepancy between interest rates on deposits and preferential rates on loans, the monetary authorities utilized the profits created by the payment of interest on special deposits that commercial banks were required to maintain with the central bank. In addition, the central bank issued a bond with 10 percent interest. Since the prolonged inflationary rate prevented any significant securities trade in Korea, furthermore, the increased interest rate did not result in heavy loss for the security holders.

The interest rate reform brought two notable political effects. First, in a dramatic way the reform involved the public more intimately in the process of economic development. Private savings more than tripled in the first year of the reform, indicating the extent to which Korean citizens were willing to respond to financial incentives. They were delighted to earn higher interest rates at safe commercial banks rather than at the risky "curb" market that most small savers had used before the reform. Second, the reform increased banking resources that made loan allocations less strained and contributed to eliminating the chief cause of favoritism and corruption in bank lending, many competing for small resources. Previously, the banks had been forced to lend their limited capital well below the market rates because of the government-imposed rates that had been kept artifically low.[25]

The series of structural reforms in the economic sphere included the March 1965 "floating exchange rate system" instituted following the May 1964 devaluation of the Korean won by approximately 50 percent to conform to the real market value. In the fifties, a low, fixed foreign exchange rate was considered a matter of sovereign dignity, and the rate was maintained by the government with much rigidity. The chief obstacle to active export under the Rhee administration had been the constantly rising wholesale price, registering almost 370 percent in the 1955-1960 period in contrast to about 21 percent for Korea's six trading nations—Japan, Taiwan, Thailand, the Philippines, Vietnam, and India. As such Korean commodities could not command competitive advantages in the export market. However, the Rhee government in the fifties was "reluctant to promptly devalue the won and instead kept the currency continuously overvalued." In spite of the wholesale price rise in the 1955-1960 period, the exchange rate remained unchanged in the same period, forcing a won overvaluation that had discouraged export.[26]

In addition to sovereign dignity that the government had associated with a low, fixed rate of foreign exchange, there were more legitimate reasons to keep the won deliberately overvalued: (1) the overvalued won helped the tendency of import substitution in the fifties by keeping the import costs low, and the licensed importers "who made easy profits importing raw materials with the overvalued local currency" strongly supported the overvaluation policy; (2) the overvaluation temporarily increased the dollar earnings from the sale of goods and services to the United States troops stationed in Korea, which in the 1958-1960 period, for instance, was far greater than Korea's entire export earnings; (3) it was reasoned that devaluation would not cause any drastic export increase, for the main commodities in Korean export were marine products and mineral ores whose prices were generally fixed in the international market; and finally (4) it was feared that devaluation of the won would simply increase inflation, for Korea would have to pay higher prices on import items upon which it heavily depended for domestic consumption.[27]

The extent to which the won had been overvalued can be seen in the subsequent changes in the won to dollar ratio. The ratio remained at 50:1 in the 1955-1960 period, but rose to 130:1 in early 1961. With the 1964 devaluation, the ratio increased to 257:1 in May 1964, but by the end of 1969 the ratio stayed close to 300:1, with fluctuations not more than 30 after 1965.[28] Devaluation of the won caused the rise of some prices, especially on commodities based on import material, but the 10 percent price rise was easily offset by the 100 percent devaluation of the won in 1964. "Devaluation of the won discouraged any importers who wanted to import foreign commodities simply because they were cheap due to the overvalued domestic currency."[29] The habits in the fifties of importing intermediate and substitution commodities for quick domestic consumption had been merely raising the consumption level without creating domestic productivity or capital investment. The junta government's emphasis on light industry for manufactures on the other hand encouraged an increase in production capacity, and the relaxed import restrictions on raw materials not only satisfied domestic demand but also provided Korea with goods for export. At the same time, the government stressed the importance of efficiency and competitiveness in foreign trade.

The Korean government announced that it would not permit new firms to be established through foreign investment or foreign loans if output prices by the firms were expected to be higher than world prices. This new policy intended to discourage the establishment of economically inefficient small firms. The economies of large-scale operation and the adoption of modern technology were stressed in organizing new firms. . . . In view of the need for strengthening the competitive position of export industries, the government suggested that within a certain planned period, already existing firms should also be required to meet the international standards in terms of both price and quality; otherwise the imports of similar products would be allowed.[30]

With the devaluation of the won and adoption of a unitary, fluctuating exchange rate, the Korean economy was made more realistic and open to the international market. The raised won to dollar ratio certainly encouraged the export sector to promote export trade, undermining at the same time the curb market in which the dollar had been exchanged at a much higher rate than the fixed official rate. With these incentives, it took little time for export to emerge as Korea's new mania.

The national commitment to foreign trade, designated as the lead sector in the First and Second Economic Plans, has been recognized as the single most significant economic thrust of the junta government. The many changes in monetary and investment policies were adopted and pushed with their bearing on the export sector in mind. Undoubtedly, Korea's economic development was most pronounced in export performance, which was enormously and immediately boosted by the series of governmental actions.

Adelman and Morris have considered both positive and negative implications in foreign trade for the emerging nations: it can be extremely positive in that it helps stimulate the economy and raise the general living standards; it can have negative impacts in that it may produce income discrepancies in the population, create a dependency on one or two major items for export, and contribute to ineffective infrastructures for high productivity and elasticities in production. On balance, however, they see little doubt about the "importance of foreign trade sector in many, if not most contemporary developing countries."[31] Korea's junta leaders had obviously seen export as the only way out of backwardness and impoverishment.

At the outset of the First Economic Plan, the export sector was designed as top priority under the junta government, reversing the Rhee administration's traditional policy. The junta government's determination to increase foreign trade called for a combination of strong-arm tactics by the administration and the more individualistic lures of economic incentives. It exerted political pressure on the business sector whenever necessary, mixing it with financial rewards and gains to enlarge export trade and with policy and structural changes favoring the sector. In addition, the initial devaluation of the won encouraged export for higher earnings in won, and resulted in lower interest rates for commercial loans on export and export-related industries. As the exchange rate became stabilized after the initial jump following the floating-rate policy, the government resorted to other measures for incentives, such as favored credit access and tax preference.

Export industries were virtually exempted from business tax, and domestic productions of material related to export were freed from indirect taxes in addition to the 50 percent reduction in income tax. Imported goods for export purposes, raw material and intermediate goods to be used in producing export items, were also free from custom duties. When the initial import for domestic purpose was later transformed into export production the government duly refunded levied duties. On new investments for export, the government's tax concession was often as large as 12 percent of the entire investment. A special system of depreciation charges was allowed when the export proceeds ratio exceeded 50 percent, and 15 percent for the ratio exceeding 20, but less than 50, percent.[32]

Included in the incentives for promoting export was the direct won subsidy, as high as 25 won for each dollar earned in export, and the special import license to the exporter on restricted items that meant greater profits, therefore greater incentives. These subsidy and export-import linkage policies were responsible for the initial surge in exports in the 1963-1964 period, but were discontinued as other more indirect incentive measures, such as credit and tax measures, were substituted. With the devaluation of the won came the liberalization of import. But this new liberal import policy with the devalued won made the import of raw material for domestic consumption quite expensive, unable at times to compete with similar goods directly imported by the privileged export producer. This nonprotective measure on domestic consumption, con-current with the open exchange rate, forced the domestic producers to be more realistic and competitive, with special emphases on cost-cutting efficient management. In countless other ways, the entire administrative apparatus acted as if it existed only for pushing export drives.

The nature of incentives gradually changed as the export sector's per-formance became more solid. Direct and indirect incentives in import substitutes were soon replaced by those for greater exports during the years 1965 and 1966. At the same time a major policy decision was set in motion: a decision to enlist the entire government apparatus to promote exports. The government resolved to commit its entire political and ad-ministrative resources in an all-out campaign to expand exports. Typically, the government would set targets nearly impossible to attain. Then, upon attaining them, it would set still higher targets even more impossible to attain. The president himself was the locomotive of this gigantic export promotion machine. He held monthly meetings to re-view the export sector's growth and progress, and constantly empha-sized that no administrative obstacle should ever impede export prog-ress. Administrative and procedural rules were simplified to facilitate the export sector. Every conceivable help was given to exporters facing difficulty in filling their orders. The entire overseas staff, including the ambassador himself, was enlisted in promoting Korean exports. At home and abroad, every government segment with any usefulness at all was converted to the virtually single-minded service of the export drive. The political leadership made it known in no uncertain terms that every government agency's and official's performance would be almost wholly judged by export promotion and little else.[33]

"The incentives and encouragement given to exports were sizable and effective," making export performance the most pronounced highlight of the junta government's achievements.[34] A simplified quantitative description attests to Korea's phenomenal export growth: total export, which in 1961 was a meager $40.9 million, rose to $119.1 million in 1964, $250.3 million in 1966, $455.4 million in 1968, and by 1971 the total exceeded $1 billion.[35] The number of nations to which Korea exported rose from 60 to 104 in the 1965-1970 period, while the number of export commodities rose from 350 to 952 in the same period.[36]

For the most effective use of Korean labor for labor-intensive goods, the government stressed the export of manufactured goods rather than primary goods that embodied relatively small labor costs. By 1960, the ratio of primary to manufactured goods in export had stood at 80:20, in which food (chiefly sold to the U.S. troops stationed in Korea) and mineral ores occupied the majority of export items. By 1971, however, the ratio was thoroughly reversed in favor of manufactured goods.[37] No single commodity dominated Korean export as its major item, as it protected itself against a sudden drop in price in the single-item world market, and the diversified export items in the secondary sector contributed to the stability of export drives.[38] Clothing, footwear, wigs, veneer and plywood, and engineering products continued to be evenly represented among the manufactured goods for export. By 1968, however, high-technology, non-labor-intensive goods, such as heavy machinery and chemical products, emerged as major items for export, which were expected to increase in the future.[39]

With growth in the export sector, import also increased to make the trade deficit much larger than it was in the sixties. Between 1961 and 1971, the military government's first decade of rule in Korea, the total amount of export rose from $40.9 million to $1 billion, while the imports rose from $316 million to $2.4 billion in the same period, a rise in deficit from $266 million to about $1.3 billion. Viewed as the export-import ratio, however, the increase in export actually narrowed the deficit from roughly 1:7.8 in 1961 to 1:2.4 in 1971, improving the traditionally crippling trade gap. The authorities were confident that, with the rise of export, the gap would eventually be narrowed, for export increased faster than import in the long run.[40]

Included in the phenomenal rise of Korean export in the sixties were the fortuitous earnings from Vietnam. Although the Vietnam earnings had not been anticipated for the 1967-1971 Second Economic Plan, and the plan's target was reached well ahead of schedule, the Vietnam earnings were not inconsequential, beginning with 1963's $12 million. Fluctuating somewhat, they brought $6.3 million in 1964, $14.7 million in 1965, $13.8 million in 1966, $7.3 million in 1967, $4.6 million in 1968, $12.8 million in 1969, $12.7 million in 1970, and $14.4 million in 1971.[41] The export total, however, did not represent a major portion of the entire earnings from Vietnam. Including service and labor, military allowance from ROKA troops, technicians' wages, construction earnings, commodity supplies to the allied forces, and other miscellaneous items, the entire Vietnam earnings in the 1966-1968 period, for example, were far greater: $60.4 million in 1966, $139.2 million in 1967, and $180 million by 1968.[42] The 1968 earnings of $180 million alone represented 16 percent of these total earnings from "invisible trade" that could be transferred without having to import costly raw materials or intermediate goods, which substantially increased Korea's holdings of international liquidity. The total Vietnam earnings in 1966 amounted to 2.4 percent of GNP, 4 percent in 1967, and 2.8 percent in 1968.

Fortuitous as the role of Vietnam in the Korean economy was, the Vietnam earnings as a whole contributed little to Korea's export expansion and subsequently enlarged GNP. South Korean involvement in Vietnam, over opposition from political opponents, was an insignificant event from a purely economic standpoint. However, many Koreans compared Korea's involvement in Vietnam with Japan's profits from the Korean War, which had spurred *its* postwar economic recovery. With the phenomenal increase in Korea's GNP and export, as it turned out, the entire Vietnam earnings figured much less than they might have under the previous regimes because of their small-scale economy. Vietnam certainly did not hurt the Korean economy, but its total effect was much less than many analysts claimed. Transfer payments from Koreans in Vietnam, soldiers and civilians, were too small to offset the then-decreasing foreign aid. During the peak 1966-1968 period, for example, payments from Vietnam constituted a small portion of foreign capital that entered Korea, and the 1967 export of $7.3 million to Vietnam accounted for less than 3 percent of Korea's total export that year. "Of course, had there been r.o Vietnam War participation, total transfer payments in Korea might have been smaller than actually occurred. But transfer payments from South Vietnam were hardly the major factor affecting economic development in Korea, and they were short-run economic phenomena."[43]

According to Cole and Lyman, the main contribution of Vietnam was in foreign exchange earnings, in which the Vietnam transfers constituted nearly 20 percent of all foreign receipts in 1967, for instance. But since the Vietnam market was "transitory" for certain types of manufactured goods, it was not a major factor in the expansion of commodity exports.[44] As for Vietnam's contribution to domestic savings, one observer noted that the remittances from Vietnam could not be "expected to remain a major factor."[45] Since the Korean economy had been taking its independent course of action through international markets before the Vietnam buildup began, the ending of war in Vietnam left no discernible economic impact on Korea. The government had been quietly preparing for such an eventuality, including a ceiling on the importation of foreign loans so as not to overburden Korea's payment capacity.[46] What could be potentially significant was the future economic participation by those soldiers and civilians who had toured in Vietnam, bringing home sizable savings of $5,000 to $10,000, sufficient to initiate a small business in Korea. Close to 50,000 civilians and 100,000 soldiers returned from Vietnam after 1966.[47]

Many remarkable changes took place in the first decade of the military government's new leadership. The sources of financing for domestic economic development reversed the foreign to domestic capital ratio from 78:22 to 37:63 by 1969, thus relying mostly on domestic revenues and savings rather than on foreign loans. Manufacturing became a prominent feature of Korea's economic composition, rising from 13.7 percent of total GNP in 1960 to over 35 percent in 1971. Both trends continued to grow: greater domestic resources were mobilized and manufacturing increased among the Korean economic sectors.[48] Consequently, manufactured goods became dominant among export items, replacing primary goods, reversing the secondary to primary ratio of 20:80 in 1960 to 85:15 by 1971. There were criticisms on Korea's export drive, for instance, that the increased size of export was not coinciding with real profits, or that the emphasis on "unbalanced growth" that had spurred the export expansion might be ignoring the parallel development in other sectors of Korean industry.[49] Viewed within a detached historical perspective, however, the export drive—the locomotive of the "economic miracle"—was nothing short of an astounding success. Export elevated Korea from a perennially backward society to a middle-rank power, permanently altering Korean society.

NOTES

1. Kim, "Economic Development," p. 157; also Cole and Lyman, *Korean Development*, p. 182.

2. S. Kanesa Thasan, "Stabilizing an Economy: The Korean Experience," *Practical Approach to Development Planning*, p. 273.

3. Cole and Lyman, *Korean Development*, p. 187.

4. Young-whan Kihl, "Urban Political Competition and the Allocation of National Resources: The Case of Korea." *Asian Survey*, Vol. 13, No. 1, 1973, p. 379.

5. Seung-hee Kim, *Foreign Capital for Economic Development: A Korean Case Study* (New York: Praeger Publishers, 1970), p. 42.

6. Lee and Park, "Foreign Investment," p. 20.

7. Kim, "Economic Development," pp. 157-58.

8. Thasan, "Stabilizing," pp. 258-60.

9. Ibid., p. 263.

10. Adelman and Morris, *Society*, p. 113.

11. Thasan, "Stabilizing," p. 261.

12. *Monthly Statistics of Korea (MSOK)*, November-December 1962 (Seoul: The Economic Planning Board), p. 67; also *MSOK*, September 1972, p. 100.

13. Cole and Lyman, *Korean Development*, p. 117.

14. Thasan, "Stabilizing," p. 260.

15. Adelman and Morris, *Society*, p. 118.

16. EPB's *Summary*, 1962, p. 5.

17. Cole and Lyman, *Korean Development*, p. 178.

18. Thasan, "Stabilizing," p. 264.

19. Ibid.

20. Cole and Lyman, *Korean Development*, p. 180.

21. *MSOK*, May 1970, p. 95; September 1972, p. 110.

22. Adelman, "Introduction," pp. 5-6.

23. Thasan, "Stabilizing," p. 265.

24. Despite the competitiveness created by the interest rate reform, the curb market was not entirely eliminated. The August 1972 emergency decree, which fixed the private interest rate at two-thirds below the going rate for three years, revealed that 40,000 industrial organizations owed 350 billion won to 200,000 private lenders. (Reported in Lee, "South Korea," 1972, p. 97).

25. Cole and Lyman, *Korean Development*, p. 89.

26. Cheul W. Kang, "Emergence of Korea's Foreign Trade: A Positive Response to Expanding International Trade and Development." *The Korean Economist*, Vol. 4, No. 1, 1969, pp. 29-31.

27. Ibid., p. 32.

28. *The Review of Korean Economy* (Seoul: The Bank of Korea, 1969), p. 138.

29. Kang, "Emergence," p. 37.

30. Ibid.

31. Adelman and Morris, *Society*, p. 126.

32. Song, "A Case Study," p. 86.

33. Cole and Lyman, *Korean Development*, pp. 189-91.

34. Ibid., p. 131.

35. *Korea Annual*, 1972 (Seoul: Hapdong News Agency, 1972), p. 153.

36. Nak-kwan Kim, "Is Korea's Export Promotion Scheme Consistent with Her Industrialization?" *Koreana Quarterly*, Vol. 14, No. 3, 1972, p. 53. Toward the decade's end, the United States gradually replaced Japan as the largest buyer of Korean goods, purchasing about 50 percent of Korea's total export, while Japan maintained 25 percent and other nations in Europe, Asia, and Latin America shared the rest.

37. *Korea Annual*, 1972, p. 156.

38. Lyman, "Economic Development," p. 384.

39. Bartz, *South Korea*, p. 98.

40. The Third Five-Year Economic Plan's export-import ratio was projected at 24.3:12.9.

41. *MSOK*, August 1966, p. 75; September 1972, p. 91.

42. Kwan S. Kim, "The Economic Impact of the Vietnam War in South East and East Asia, With Special Reference to Balance-of-Payment Effects." *Asian Forum*, Vol. 2, Nos. 1-4, 1970, p. 520.

43. Kim, "Economic Development," p. 161.

44. Cole and Lyman, *Korean Development*, p. 135.

45. P. W. Kuznets, "Korea's Five-Year Plans," *Practical Approach to Development Planning*, p. 61.

46. Kim, "The Economic Impact of the Vietnam War," p. 523.

47. Ibid., p. 522.

48. *MSOK*, September 1972, p. 35.

49. Kim, "Is Korea's Export Promotion Scheme," p. 57.

16

Changes in Agricultural Policy

As a solid industrial basis had been secured, the military leadership turned its attention to the agricultural sector. Critics of the Korean economy had often said that in the first two plan periods rural needs had received less than their full share of attention, and correctly so. By the end of the Second Plan period in 1971, the agricultural sector had grown only 4 percent per annum, unlike the 20-25 percent in the industrial sectors. Production of grain for the grain self-sufficiency program launched by the government not only failed to achieve its target in the sixties but worsened. The 93 percent sufficiency rate in the 1965-1966 period, for example, slipped to 75 percent in the 1968-1969 period. To compensate, imported grain supplies increased from 525,000 metric tons to 2.2 million metric tons in the same two periods, mainly due to the farmer's diversion to cash crops. Without inserting modern technology into farming, the limited arable land area in Korea was constantly outpaced by the growing farm population in spite of the family planning program that cut down the growth rate to about 1.8 percent per annum.[1]

It was widely acknowledged that "the first two economic development plans concentrated on industry, infrastructure, and exports for quick capital buildup, and agriculture was given only secondary priority in the allocation of available resources."[2] As a result of this shift in emphasis, agriculture's share of GNP declined in the sixties from nearly 40 percent to 28.4 percent. Considering the developmental conditions in Korea, the socialist economist Breidenstein recognized the validity of this policy: "This shift from agricultural to manufacturing production is a necessary step in the process of modernization. The setting up of new and basic industries, such as fertilizer plants, oil refineries, cement factories and power plants, which were successfully established in South Korea during the First and Second Five Year Economic Development Plans, as well as infrastructure investment in roads, railways, water and electricity supply, communication, etc., are inevitable conditions of development in any economic system."[3]

While there was no denying the agricultural sector's secondary role, the commitment of the junta government to modernizing the general economy had profoundly affected the farming population in Korea as well. By the end of the junta's first decade, the agricultural legacy inherited from the Rhee administration, largely traditional and backward, virtually disappeared. In the fifties under Rhee, for instance, the 40 percent share of GNP by the primary sector was produced by the 62 percent of the national population that belonged to farming. Due to this low productivity, the per capita income of farmers was about 58 percent below that of their nonfarming compatriots. In the 1948-57 period, the Rhee regime had invested only 4.8 percent of total government expenditures in the agricultural sector, while heavily relying on foreign aid to make up for the deficit. In the meantime, farmers were subject to heavy taxes; over 20 percent of national revenue came from the agricultural sector's land income tax alone. Moreover, farmers were forced to pay governmental taxes and land debts to the government for the going market price, which doubled pressure on farmers.[4] As for agricultural policy, "it proved to be much easier and vastly more profitable for the people involved to import huge quantities of relief grain from the United States rather than use scarce administrative skills and resources in an effort to promote agricultural productivity and rural prosperity."[5]

The junta government began its overhaul of the agricultural sector through a series of legislative enactments for policy and structural changes. The laws established in the first year alone included the Agricultural Cooperative Law, which aimed at forming a nationwide agricultural cooperative organization for integrated marketing and purchasing with credit service through the Irrigation Associations, the National Federation of Fishery Cooperatives, and the Office of Farm Extension (a Japanese system demolished under Rhee as a part of his anti-Japanese campaign); the Land Improvement Law; the Land Reclamation Law; the Plant Disease Control Law; the Sericultural Law; the Major Crop Seeds Law; the Saplings and Seedlings Law; the Fertilizer Control Law; the Farm Warehouse Law; the Agricultural Products Inspection Law; the Raw Silk Price Stabilization Law; and the Farm Usury Debt Settlement Law.[6] The Office of Farm Extension was later reorganized into the Office of Rural Development "so that agricultural development projects could actually be carried out and the funds effectively allocated in accordance with the original purpose." The fundamentally antiagricultural habits of the Rhee regime had been such that "it was eventually necessary to circumvent these institutions entirely in order to accomplish anything."[7]

The Irrigation Association, later reorganized into the Land Improvement Association, increased the rice output through various irrigation projects by 50,000 metric tons per annum in the First Plan period, consuming nearly 9 billion won and covering 219,733 hectares. The "all-weather" farming project was adopted by the government in 1965, which began to finance farm consolidation and paddy rearrangements for higher productivity, including the installation of drainage facilities for double-cropping.[8]

Through the Land Reclamation Law, the government subsidized the expenses of reclaiming hills and tidelands to enlarge arable land, and allocated specific targets to local provinces. This labor-intensive project, aiming at adding up to 15 percent of arable land for increased agricultural output, employed hundreds of thousands of rural workers as a spectacular show of coordinated human efforts. By flattening hills and stopping tides, every conceivable piece of land was cleared for agriculture. Between 1962 and 1968, for example, a total of 138,775 land reclamation projects were carried out in nine provinces and two special cities. In 1963 alone, 14,970 chungbo (1 chungbo = 2.45 acres) of land was reclaimed, adding the new productive capacity for up to 17,000 metric tons of grain. For 1964, 22,357 chungbo was reclaimed for an additional production capacity of 143,000 metric tons of grain, in which much of the terrace-type reclamation was government financed.[9]

The Usury Debt Settlement Law of 1961 was aimed at relieving the farmer and fisherman of their chronic high interest rate debts to private lenders (at an interest rate as high as 60-80 percent per annum). The law provided 70 million won in government funds, in which 30 million was allocated to the farmer-fisher group (but not including the urban industrial sector).[10] Some 45 million won—an amount thirty times greater than similar funds had ever been under Rhee—was provided as low interest rate loans to the agricultural sector. Loans to farmers and fishers by commercial banks alone rose from 11.5 billion won in 1960 to 34 billion won in 1967.[11] By the end of 1961, a total of 4.8 billon won in usurious private loans was reported to the government according to the provisions of the Settlement Law. By the time of its close in 1968, 2.5 billion won in principal and 1.6 billion in interest were settled by the provisions in the law. Debtors were to repay the government in installments at an interest rate of 12 percent per annum. By the end of 1968, however, only 45 percent of the total amount was collected by the government, and the rest was invalidated by a decree for deceased or otherwise incapable debtors.[12]

The Rural Development Law established the Office of Rural Development (ORD) in March 1962, under which came the Office of Agricultural Extension, established in 1957 for agricultural and technological services, and the Bureau of Community Development, which "brought about very substantial improvement and strengthened the farm exten-

186 Th e Economic Sphere

sion system." With branches in the provinces and rural guidance stations established on the city-county level, the ORD "took charge of
research and experimentation, rural enlightenment and guidance, dis-
semination of technology, and the training of guidance workers."[13]

The number of extension workers—over half college-educated—
increased sixfold within five years of the military coup, and "became
one of the more popular elements of government representation in the
rural area."[14] The National Reconstruction Movement (NRM), organized nationwide in 1961, was also mobilized in land reclamation, construction of farm roads, natural disaster counteraction, and town-village
brotherhood formation for mutual help. As a semi- and later nongovern-
mental organization, the NRM provided an alternative approach to rural
guidance to complement the ORD, although there were areas in which
the agencies overlapped. In November 1964, a pact was signed by the
ORD, the National Agricultural Cooperative Federation, and the Union
of Land Improvement Association (ULIA), by which the ULIA joined
the ORD in rural guidance work.

The vast organization of the Office of Rural Development performed
vital functions in the rural areas. During the First Plan period, 1962-1967,
1.3 billion won was earmarked for over 1,000 research projects involving
600 researchers for the development of more efficient production techniques, the improvement of agricultural varieties, and the standardiza-
tion of farm equipment and supplies. The number of extension workers,
which rose from 1,110 in 1957 to 6,500 in 1966, made it possible to assign
40-50 workers to each county. During the First Plan period, 1.1 billion
won was spent on guidance services, about 500 won on each farm
household. Over 125,000 metric tons of improved seeds were distributed to the farmers, costing the government 618 million won, which
was managed through local agricultural cooperatives, the ULIA, and
contracts with private farmers. A 622 million won joint project on
demonstration communities by the government and the private sector
was carried out in the plan period. For the project, the Six-Year Rural
Village Development Program involving 407,000 projects, 33,100 villages, and a cost of 31.9 billion won was established. More than 100,500
areas throughout the nation were selected for high rice yield demonstration farms, and 14,600 farms were chosen for improved farming methods on other crops. The ORD in the plan period also inspected 1.7
million soil and fertilizer test items; controlled plant disease and pests at
724 locations; carried out management analysis and farm planning for
20,000 farm households; devised better methods for utilizing paddy
cropland in 2,500 areas; demonstrated livestock production techniques
in 8,578 cities; guided community development in 33,100 rural villages;
assisted in the organization and operation of 17,575 women's clubs; and
taught home economics to 19,552 voluntary leaders.[15]

One of the most significant factors in the increased farm output, rising by 50 percent in the first five years of the junta government, was the enlarged use, and availability through added production, of fertilizer. Between 1961 and 1969, total sales of fertilizer rose from 2.5 million won to 26,589 million won, while credit sales gradually declined from 77 percent to 41 percent in the same period. The supply of chemical fertilizer per hectare rose from 143 kilograms in 1962 to 229 kilograms in 1969, while the total area of farmland increased by 270,000 hectares in the same period. Improved technology also increased use of farming machinery: between 1961 and 1969, the number of power threshers rose from 4,794 to 33,878, power pumps from 3,736 to 49,534, and pumps from 27,331 to 62,157, thanks to the intensive drought-fighting program.[16]

The extensive modernizing efforts of the government through organizational and technological management resulted in some concrete quantitative results for the agricultural sector, although by no means as phenomenal as its counterpart in the industrial sector. The total agricultural production more than doubled in the 1960-1969 period, from 72 to 165.6, using the 1964-1966 index of 100; value in the farm sector increased from 244 billion won to 366.2 billion won, or 150 percent in the same period, a 140 percent increase in value per capita with population growth accounted for; among the 18 rice-growing-yielding nations, the 1966 rice yield per hectare placed Korea (at 43 kilograms) below only Japan (50), the United States (48.5), and Italy (46.9), revealing the extent of improved farm technology and use of fertilizer and pesticides. Although the farm-industrial sector gap remained considerable, it narrowed significantly, from 58 percent in the fifties to 34.7 percent in 1967, thanks mainly to improved techniques and diversification of cash crops. As another sign of overall improvement, the wholesale price index for rice fluctuated by only 23.3 percent in the sixties compared with 53 percent in the fifties.[17]

The third Five-Year Economic Development Plan was now prepared to address the problem of balance between the agricultural and manufacturing sectors. A contemporary observer described this intention:

The most ambitious project of the Plan is the one geared to modernize agriculture—including scientific farming techniques (utilization of mechanized farm tools, hybrid and other improved seeds, better breed stock, and education in modern methods of farming), and the development of the four major river basins. The government also plans to encourage the development of cash crops for industrial and/or export use (oil-yielding beans, fruits for canning, modernization of the fishing fleet and equipment) and the combining of small excessively sub-divided paddy-fields into larger tracts, irrigated from a central source.[18]

The New Village Movement as part of the Third Plan, the most celebrated rural development spectacle in Korea, called for an investment of 642 billion won out of a total agricultural budget of 1,642 billion won, in addition to Japan's governmental loan of over 300 billion won.[19] Upon the successful completion of the New Village Movement, many heads of state and rural specialists from other emerging nations visited Korea for the purpose of replicating the program's success in their own societies.

Some expressed doubts whether the performance of the first two plans could be equally effective in the ambitious Third Plan period (1972-1976). But history proved them wrong. For the agricultural sector in Korea, as for the other sectors of Korean society before it, dramatic changes in its economic life, eventually surpassing the urban area in income per capita, were ahead.

NOTES

1. Sang-Chul Suh, *The Strategy for Agricultural Development in Korea* (Seoul: Samwha Corp., Publishers, 1971), pp. 77-80. Much of the following description on South Korea's agricultural changes is drawn from Suh's study.

2. Rhee, "South Korea's Economic Development," p. 682.

3. Breidenstein, "Capitalism in Korea," p. 4.

4. Jyung-han Rhi, "Farm Management and Economic Development in Korea." *Koreana Quarterly*, Vol. 2, No. 1, 1960, pp. 66-67.

5. Vincent Brandt, "Mass Migration and Urbanization in Contemporary Korea." *Asia (Asia Society)*, No. 20, 1970-71, p. 35.

6. Suh, *Strategy*, p. 26.

7. Brandt, *Mass Migration*, p. 35.

8. Suh, *Strategy*, pp. 27-28.

9. *Korea Annual*, 1965. (Seoul: Hapdong News Agency), p. 185.

10. SCNR, 1963, pp. 1068-69.

11. Cole and Lyman, *Korean Development*, pp. 147-48.

12. Suh, *Strategy*, pp. 55-56.

13. Ibid., p. 47.

14. Cole and Lyman, *Korean Development*, pp. 91, 149.

15. Suh, *Strategy*, pp. 47-51. See Alice Y. Chai, *Community Development in Korea* (Hawaii: The East-West Center, 1968), for a detailed description of major rural development programs.

16. Ibid., pp. 30-31, 57.

17. Ibid., pp. 42, 63-67.

18. Rhee, "South Korea's Economic Development," p. 683.

19. Lee, "South Korea," pp. 97-99.

17

Analysis and Conclusion
to Part IV

The story of Korea has been—and continues to be—the story of government action. The leadership-orientation of the government in the emerging nations in general has enormous bearing upon the "functioning of the economic system which is profoundly influenced by the institutional framework within which it takes place; and in turn, the framework is necessarily affected by government action . . . even where it is not the object to magnify its role in economic life."[1] Active participation by the government is necessary, in general, because the government represents "institutions suitable for the efficient operation of the system itself."[2] We have seen in the story of Korea's most arresting decade the active role of the administrative bureaucracy, and the determined leadership behind it, to promote rapid socioeconomic changes.

There were of course other factors in society that made the leadership appropriate and its accomplishments possible. Many Korean observers have marvelled at the receptiveness of Korean society to the varied and numerous measures undertaken by the junta government, many of them quite radical in nature and sweeping in scope, as well as at the effectiveness of the way such changes actually worked. These observers have agreed on certain general attributes of Korean society as responsible for its amazing receptiveness and effectiveness:

First, there had been virtually no monolithic, dominant religious doctrine prior to 1961 that might have come into conflict with the junta leadership's efforts to change Korea's political and economic life. Nothing like the Islamic faith in the Middle East, for instance, which often collides with the central authority's intentions, ever existed in Korea. Although a great number of Koreans still claim to be Buddhists, they are usually removed from political life. Christianity had pioneered the modernizing effort via education during Japanese rule, and the junta government's progressive aims appealed to the Christians in general. While some observers have noted that this lack of homogenizing religious unity in Korea was rsponsible for the age-old factionalism at all levels of social organizations, it certainly did not hamper the junta government's new drives.

Second, there was no serious traditional element in conflict with the general tone of the political and economic changes put into effect by the military. Not only was there no tradition-based objection. The population also agreed with the need for an efficient government, and actively supported the leadership in carrying out its major programs, for example, the family planning program. This modernistic outlook was largely a reaction to the Japanese colonial experience, which most Koreans attributed to their nation's traditional backwardness. Korea's past ills were generally attributed to the Yi dynasty's "Hermit Kingdom" policies and the aversion of the landed aristocracy to the ways and means of modern technology.

Third, the United States became the major western power upon which Korea relied heavily for its survival and development. As such, Korea was ideologically inclined toward westernization and open minded in its overall worldview. When the western-influenced structural changes were introduced by the junta leadership for greater efficiency and productivity, even the moderately educated Koreans saw no conflict in their implementation.

Fourth, for centuries Korea had been under one centralized governmental authority with very little, if any, local autonomy in the provinces. The central authority had rarely experienced difficulties in effectively administering its designs on the population. In addition, the absence of local dialects, of ethnic diversities, and of cultural variations, among other factors, also helped. (Henderson has argued, however, that this very characteristic of homogeneity and class fluidity without local autonomy has been the major detriment to Korea's political development.[3])

And last but not least, due to such national homogeneity and class fluidity with no traditional barrier to social mobility, Koreans had been a fiercely upward-moving people. The predominance of the American capitalist creed bound personal success within the sphere of the individual, rather than through class consciousness or collective identities. This population, ever-eager for upward mobility, given the high level of educational attainment that was the product of this very goal, became explosive resources for high productivity and innovation. The junta government effectively exploited this potential by offering profit incentives in business and merit-oriented promotions in the bureaucracy for the productive and innovative. The junta leadership never failed to appeal to this individualistic element in the Korean psyche for profit, mobility, and status. It expanded international politics, trade, and communication with open diplomacy; it normalized Korea-Japan relations to extract the needed capital for economic investment; and it took part in the Vietnam conflict for military and economic advantages. In doing so, the junta government warded off the explosiveness of the Korean situation, releasing the pent-up frustration of a narrowly defined but overly eager society to reach out and accomplish.

Corruption and bribery, two of the means by which individuals had traditionally sought social mobility under the previous regimes, were never stamped out by the junta government. Yet with the establishment of more positive goals in productivity and efficiency, the old forms of corruption and bribery were channeled into different ends. Inasmuch as the combination of managerial and political leadership gave a developmentalist direction and outlook in politics and economics, these fortuitous factors in Korean society provided the right chemical mixture to be ignited by the military leadership.

At the end of the decade 1961-1971, Korea had become a rather different society, more confident, prosperous, and promising than it had ever been. There would be much turmoil ahead—both political and economic. President Park would be assassinated by his bodyguard; a worldwide oil crisis would slow down Korea's economy; students would once again challenge the military establishment for political hegemony.

Through it all, however, Korea's thriving economic machine would never look back.

NOTES

1. Bauer and Yamey, *The Economics of Under-Developed Countries*, pp. 171-72.
2. Ibid., p. 172.
3. It is the general thesis of his book, *Korea: The Politics of the Vortex*.

Part V

THE KOREAN MODEL

18

Korea and the Emerging Nations: An Analysis of the Role of the Military in National Development

Let us now pause for one last analytic look at Korean development from the viewpoint of organizational sociology.

We have seen the way the military leadership intervened in Korean society and, using its superior managerial skill and functional outlook, altered the very foundations of Korea. Politically and economically, Korea after 1961 was never the same. Even with the fortuitous historical circumstances and social resources, which favored massive social change, it was military intervention in the hitherto predominantly civil system that made the Korean story possible. The final question then logically arises: Can the Korean experience be duplicated in other emerging nations? It is this question to which we must now turn.

MILITARY RATIONALITY AS A SOCIAL RESOURCE

The question requires a brief but critical examination of the issues and controversies bearing upon the idea of the military's role in emerging nations. The general support for the military as a positive force in social development can be summarized as follows:

1. The military is often the most technologically advanced of all groups in society.[1]
2. The military is the most "rational" of all social organizations, and the military organization can contribute to the modernizing role in social development.[2]
3. The rational aspects of military organizations promote "modern" outlooks among officers and soldiers.[3]

4. The military is the ultimate alternative when the civil regime is unable to function for maintenance and survival.[4]

5. The class origin of military personnel that closely approximates the masses further facilitates its capacity for national development.[5]

6. The military's rational disposition can exercise a powerful modernizing influence upon the whole society.[6]

These students of the military's role in the emerging nations have attributed to the military the presumed qualities of rationality as legitimate components of military organization: pannational, cross-sectional conscription; personnel's background in lower classes; efficiency-oriented organizational management; modern technology and equipment; functional-rational outlooks and perspectives, and so forth. Further, these presumed qualities are interpreted as contributory to national development, both political and economic. Here the general consensus indicates that the military is thought of primarily as a stationary and structural component of society, rather than a dynamic force in the process of its utility. Unlike some other social indicators of rationality—for example, high literacy, technological resources—the rational and efficient qualities of the military as a modern organization do not automatically become developmental assets without a dynamic process in which they may be utilized.

On the theoretical level at least, the military both in developed and developing societies is considered an autonomous tool of violence to be maintained independent of the social and political context of society. The primary purpose of any military organization, analytically speaking, is not its function in direct social development through its use in administrative and economic rationalization. Rather, using the military in national development is considered a sign of weakness even by underdeveloped societies. Other than in cases of emergency in domestic disorder or natural disaster, it is considered desirable to keep the military separate from its nonmilitary social functions. Given this assumption, it can be stated that military resources (where they exist) remain only a contingent possibility. The transformation of this contingent possibility into a functional reality, in which the resources are actually put to use in national development, is thus necessarily a dynamic process. This process may take a direct military takeover through a coup d'état as in the case of Korea, or active participation in national administration through a traditional process of civil-military cooperation, as in the case of Thailand. At any rate, the military is almost never an ipso facto agent of modernization in any given society.

This theoretical contention can be further substantiated by reexamining the South Korean military organization as a presumably rational social force. Following the stabilization of the postwar armament, the

Korean Army regularly trained and discharged five full-size companies a week, some with highly modern technical skills acquired during the service. One out of every twenty persons in Korea served in the modern armed forces for a mandatory period ranging from two to three years. Virtually all physically eligible males at one time or another belonged to the military organization for various duties. However, contrary to Pye's contention that the military contributes to modernization by virtue of its modernistic resources and organizational effectiveness, the military establishment in Korea before the 1961 coup had no visible effects on modernization.[7] Not even during the peak of military buildup after the Korean War until 1961 did GNP or income per capita show any significant change. Nor did those who served in the military in various ranks and capacity play a vital role as local or central leaders, either in or out of government. The pre-junta leadership had not tapped the enormous potential qualities of the Korean military (as manifest in the aftermaths of the 1961 coup). The military establishment before the coup provided the ruling regimes with political funds and votes, but was hardly called upon to provide organizational skills and managerial talents in the political and economic spheres.

Even after the coup, the military organization's contribution to national development was generally limited to the managerially trained high-ranking officers and the idealistic political officers. The number of both managerial and political officers who performed the vital role remained rather limited, both in the military government and in the military-civilian coalition phases. A handful of generals and colonels represented the entire 600,000-member military organization, as they were the ones most directly involved in national development.

The role of the military in Korea's political and economic development required an effective combination of (1) the ideolgy of rationality and development held by the political officers; (2) the availability of organizational skills of the managerial officers; and (3) the circumstances—political, social, and economic—under which these ideological and managerial resources were put to effective use. The combination of these three aspects, a theory originally proposed by Lovell,[8] is the key to understanding military behavior in civil politics in the emerging nations.

Let us examine, then, the military coup d'état as a mechanism by which military resources and skills can be structurally integrated into the total social resources for national development.

THE MILITARY COUP AS A MECHANISM FOR MILITARY-CIVIL INTEGRATION

On the role and prospect of the military coup in emerging nations, Henry Bienen has observed that "the case studies show that a unified military can take power with relative ease in Asia, Africa, and Latin America. The military is thus a 'heavy institution' in underdeveloped countries and can act with authority because it is first and foremost an institution of force with organizational features that give it the capacity to be effective in intervening against a civilian regime."[9]

Finer has presented four types of military intervention, the strongest of which is a coup d'état: (1) constitutional influence; (2) intimidation of civilian authorities; (3) threats of violence or noncooperation with civilian authorities; and (4) the direct use of violence—coup d'état.[10] Military intervention may take any of these forms at any given time. Varying sociopolitical conditions—for example, the degree of democratic practice, education, military capability—determine which of these forms the military-civil interaction may take. The military coup, from the sheer efficiency point of view in political changes, may perhaps be "a more efficient method (and certainly a less painful one) than that of classic revolution" to seize power.[11] The propensity for coup shown by the military element lies, ultimately, in the ease and speed with which a small group can overthrow a civilian government. In regions where coups have been more prevalent, "most new states have granted the military a disproportionately weighty place" in terms of human resource, technology, hardware, and status.[12]

While underdeveloped societies in general may lag centuries behind the more developed nations, the military establishment in the former societies commands unique status in advanced material and technology that are denied to the larger society. This parallel existence of a lagging political culture that breeds discontent and frustration on one hand, and the highly advanced military forces with the compelling means of violence on the other, summarizes the familiar historical and cultural setting for a military coup. As a means of swift political ascent, the following is more or less the general pattern of military coup:

1. The new military leaders now in power drop all pretenses of "democratic" efforts.

2. They tend to consolidate the existing single mass-party (where such is available) into a national organization.

3. They face, then, the double task of "supplying national leadership" and "developing mass support" for the political and economic programs that are the new leadership's creation or adoption.

4. They develop a civilian-military alliance but under strict military dominance.[13]

As we noted above, there are varying degrees of military intervention in civil politics, and the different types of intervention are primarily determined by the types of leadership in the military, its ideological and technical resources, and the general political and social climate. One primary factor to encourage the view of military coups as an acceptable pattern of power succession (where other objective conditions for coup are present) is the frequency with which it occurs, especially in Africa and in Latin America. Observing the coup phenomenon in Africa and Latin America, First reported that

Africa was becoming another Latin America, where political instability has long been chronic. There, modern political history is a chaotic account of coups and counter-coups, of precipitate but meaningless changes of president, minister, cabinet, government and army chief. One professional soldier replaced another at the head of government. Sometimes the military unmade the very power formation they had themselves installed. A coup every eight months, or twelve, in some states; elsewhere, a breathing space, before another spurt of barracks-room-revolt, or coup d'état, or some combination of the two. . . . [In Africa] it has proved infectious, this seizure of government by armed men, and so effortless. Get the keys of the armoury; turn out the barracks; take the radio station, the post office and the airport; arrest the person of the president, and you arrest the state.[14]

However, that military coups take place rather frequently in those continents and elsewhere in the eighties does not necessarily mean that the coup is the only (or the most desirable) mechanism by which the military's capacity and commitment can be channeled into civil use for national development. Viewing the Korean experience, one might conclude that had the Rhee regime committed itself to a more rational view of society and utilized the military's managerial talents in the process, the May coup might have been avoided as unnecessary. The civil-military integration in Korea might have taken the more integral mode of Thailand, in which the national bureaucracy regularly draws talents from the military as a long-standing practice. For the emerging nations where civil talents are in short supply, and the military possesses the needed resource in large-scale management, the civil-military coalition may take the Thai pattern of gradual integration rather than a military coup.

As we argued above, a military coup (and the military itself) is no guarantee to political and economic rationalization; nor is the coup inevitable in the emerging nations as a mechanism enlisting military resources. Each society has a set of unique variables that account for the conditions of military intervention, civil-military coalition, or military coups in its own sociopolitical and economic structure. The Korean model shows its similarities with, and differences from, other emerging nations facing political and economic backwardness. To what extent the Korean case study can be a common model of analysis is suggested in the following section.

A MODEL OF ANALYSIS FOR
MILITARY-CIVIL INTEGRATION

A model of analysis utilizing the three conceptual elements suggested by Lovell—support and demand in society, resources of the military, and ideological commitment—is helpful.[15]

Lovell proposes that these three factors determine how military intervention in civilian society may bring about positive results. To elaborate, the positive-negative results of military intervention can be anticipated by: (1) whether the sociopolitical circumstances are in need of the military as an intervening agent; (2) whether the military is capable of fulfilling the sociopolitical needs; and (3) whether the military is willing to act and carry out the commitment. Results can be measured either on the structural-analytical level or on the empirical-cultural level, the former by analyzing structural changes and the latter by measuring individual attitudes. Both levels are mutually complementary. In an ideal situation they are expected to show similar trends, that is, structural changes accompanied by individual perception recognizing and responding to the changes, and vice versa.

Military coups are a controversial issue, mainly because of their ethical and political meaning, as a form of radical social transformation. It is partly for this reason that military coups have been considered only one of the various mechanisms by which military talents and commitment, where they exist, can be enlisted to fulfill the needs, where they are present, of the emerging nations. The success of analysis, therefore, depends ultimately on how well and accurately the observer determines the degree to which the needs, the talents, and the willingness are present. It is not only a methodological issue, but also a requirement of comprehensive historical understanding, upon which the welfare of millions and the future of a nation may depend.

NOTES

1. Henry Bienen, "Introduction," *The Military Intervenes*, Henry Bienen, ed. (New York: Russell Sage Foundation, 1968), p. xv.

2. Lucian Pye, *Armies in the Process of Political Modernization* (Cambridge, Mass.: Center for International Studies, MIT, 1959), p. 16; also Lucian Pye, "Armies in the Process of Political Modernization," *The Role of the Military in the Underdeveloped Countries*, John J. Johnson, ed. (Princeton, New Jersey: Princeton University Press, 1962), pp. 73-82.

3. Janowitz, *The Military*, p. 28.

4. Edward Shils, "The Military in the Political Development of the New States," *The Role of the Military in Underdeveloped Countries*, p. 9.

5. Elie Salem, "Emerging Government in the Arab World," *Orbis*, Vol. 6, 1962.

6. Milikan and Blackmer, *The Emerging Nations*, p. 31.

7. If anything, the institutions of higher learning, mushrooming after the 1945 liberation, contributed to the general habits of "modernization" in Korea more than any other factors. American influence, which thoroughly dominated the post–World War II Korean consciousness, had a significant role in fostering the superficially westernized attitudes in the educated population.

8. Lovell, *The Military and Politics*.

9. Bienen, "Introduction," p. xv.

10. S. E. Finer, *The Man on Horseback: The Role of the Military in Politics* (New York: Praeger, 1962), p. 168.

11. Edward Luttwak, *Coup d'état: A Practical Handbook* (London: Allen Lane, Penguin Press, 1968), p. 54.

12. William G. Andrews and Uri Ra'anan, "Introduction," *The Politics of the Coup d'état,* William G. Andrews and Uri Ra'anan, eds. (New York: Van Nostrand Reinhold Co., 1969), p. 3.

13. Janowitz, *The Military*, p. 29.

14. Ruth First, *The Barrel of a Gun: Political Power in African Coup d'état* (London: Penguin Press, 1970), pp. 3-4.

15. Lovell, *The Military and Politics*, pp. 7-13.

Appendix: Significant Social and Economic Changes, 1961–1971

Table 1
GNP and Population Growth Rate

	GNP in won	Population in thousands	Growth Rate in percentage
1955	116.06	21,424	1.6
1957	197.78	22,677	1.6
1959	221.00	24,003	1.6
1961	296.82	25,402	
i963	487.96	26,863	2.8
1965	1,805.85	28,377	2.7
1968	1,575.65	30,469	2.3
1970	2,561.95	31,898	1.9

Source: Korea Annual (KA) 1971: 136, 407; Korea Statistics Yearbook (KSY) 1971: 37.

Table 2
Growth Rate and Composition of Sectors of GNP

	1961	1964	1966	1968	1970
GROWTH RATE OF SECTORS AT 1965 CONSTANT MARKET VALUE					
Agriculture, fishery, forestry	10.1	16.2	11.0	1.2	-0.8
Mining and manufacturing	3.2	5.4	15.2	25.9	17.7
Social overhead capital and other services	-1.1	2.3	14.8	15.9	9.9
COMPOSITION OF GNP IN PERCENT					
Agriculture, fishery, forestry	43.8	41.9	37.9	29.4	25.8
Mining and manufacturing	14.9	17.3	19.8	24.8	28.0
Social overhead capital and other services	41.3	40.8	42.3	45.8	46.2

Source: (KSY) 1971: 104.

Table 3
National Taxes and Their Share in GNP

	National Taxes in million won	Sharing in GNP in percent
1961	25,633	9.5
1966	103,798	10.8
1967	143,340	12.3
1968	213,645	14.6
1969	289,407	15.3
1970	367,955	15.8

Source: (KSY) 1962: 313;. (KSY) 1971: 303.

Table 4
Savings Deposits at Deposit Money Banks in Billion Won, and
Time and Savings Deposits Considered Alone in Million Won

	Savings Deposits Total	Time and Savings
1961	24.7	5,419
1962	39.1	12,163
1964	43.1	14,496
1965	78.5	30,573
1966	120.9	70,085
1967	205.9	128,901
1968	373.1	255,538
1969	619.2	451,527
1970	784.0	573,300

Source: (KSY) 1971: 311, 324.

Table 5
Exports by Commodity Groups in Million Dollars

	1960	1963	1965	1967	1970
TOTAL	32,827	86,802	175,082	320,229	835,185
Food & animals	9,701	18,059	28,190	37,928	65,573
Beverages & tobacco	451	250	898	7,019	14,231
Inedible crude materials	15,816	26,187	37,033	58,005	99,973
Mineral fuels, lubricants & re-lated materials	1,147	2,579	1,899	1,772	8,761
Animal & vege-table oils & fats	199	92	71	119	59
Chemicals	401	904	380	2,359	11,413
Manufactured goods	3,937	28,119	66,414	101,382	220,887
Machinery & trans-port equipment	88	4,067	5,501	14,185	61,469
Misc. Manufactured articles	93	6,401	34,487	97,239	352,497
Not classified elsewhere	995	146	209	219	357

Source: (KSY) 1971: 351.

Table 6
Exports of Fishery

	Quantity in tons	Value in thousand won
1955	5,065	
1957	9,837	
1960	15,008	
1961	16,962	
1962	24,884	12,341
1964	38,781	23,666
1966	67,622	42,036
1968	76,439	57,323
1969	112,312	73,916
1970	130,165	90,052

Source: (KSY) 1962: 137; (KSY) 1971: 142.

Table 7
Foreign Loans and Exchange Rates

	Loans in thousand dollars	Exchange Rates in won per dollar
1953		18.0
1955		50.0
1960		65.0
1961		130.0
1964	34,600	255.51
1965	31,500	271.50
1966	108,400	270.90
1967	167,300	268.39
1968	299,600	281.50
1969	475,700	304.45
1970	400,200	316.65

Source: (KSY) 1971: 351, 391.

Table 8
Electric Power Production and Number of Customers

	Production in million kwh	Number of Customers
1955	879.2	604,760
1957	1,323.0	660,402
1959	1,686.2	724,415
1961	1,772.9	797,252
1962	2,208.7	847,703
1964	2,699.8	1,043,563
1966	3,885.8	1,298,394
1967	4,910.9	1,487,997
1968	6,000.1	1,594,872
1969	7,700.0	1,735,381
1970	9,167.4	1,969,618

Source: (KSY) 1962: 186, 192; (KSY) 1971: 200, 204.

Table 9
Mechanization of Farms (Major Items Owned by Farmers)

	1961	1968	1969
Power tillers	30	6,225	8,832
Power threshers	4,794	26,675	33,878
Power duster-sprayers	310	11,568	24,721
Power pumps	3,736	37,796	49,534
Plows	617,766	1,022,861	1,013,509

Source: Bong-kyun Suh, The Strategy for Agricultural Development in Korea
(Seoul: Samwha Corporation, Publishers, 1971) p. 31.

Table 10
Indicators of Agricultural Productivity per Farm Household

	Agricultural Income in won	Agricultural Capital in won	Labor hours
1962	54,026	90,602	2,536.4
1963	76,542	120,198	2,076.4
1964	103,745	102,707	2,116.9
1965	88,812	79,831	2,086.6
1966	101,430	126,525	2,064.1
1967	116,359	146,500	2,015.8
1968	139,936	181,861	1,883.2
1969	167,128	226,759	1,843.7
1970	194,037	260,768	1,810.3

Source: (KSY) 1971: 148.

Table 11
Index Number of Industrial Production

	Total	Mining	Manufacturing	Electricity
1955	28.9	17.0	32.7	27.0
1957	40.8	29.7	44.4	40.7
1959	51.6	43.3	54.7	51.9
1961	59.4	64.6	60.0	54.5
1963	78.6	87.4	79.3	67.9
1965	100.0	100.0	100.0	100.0
1967	155.7	113.1	161.8	151.2
1969	245.6	104.1	265.3	236.9
1970	286.7	119.1	309.6	282.1

Source: (KSY) 1971: 184.

Table 12
Monthly Income and Expenditure of Households in Won

	1963	1965	1967	1969
Income	6,680	9,300	20,720	27,800
Expenditure	7,010	9,560	19,980	27,020
Balance	-330	-180	740	780

Source: (KA) 1971: 219.

Table 13
Yearly Income and Expenditure of Farm Households in Won

	1963	1965	1967	1969
Income	93,179	112,201	149,470	217,874
Expenditure	82,111	107,439	135,311	180,532
Balance	11,068	4,762	14,159	37,342

Source: (KA) 1971: 219.

Table 14
Living Expenditure of Average Household in Won and Percent

	Urban Workers				Farm Households			
	1968		1969		1968		1969	
	won	%	won	%	won	%	won	%
Total	23,190	100.0	26,070	100.0	11,925	100.0	14,281	100.0
Food	9,840	42.4	10,670	40.9	5,651	47.4	6,628	46.4
Housing	3,980	17.2	4,820	18.5	580	4.9	615	4.3
Fuel/light	1,200	5.2	1,330	5.1	972	8.1	1,292	8.1
Clothing	2,510	10.8	2,800	10.7	1,072	9.0	1,292	9.1
Misc.	5,660	24.4	6,450	24.8	3,650	30.6	4,588	32.1

Source: (KA) 1971: 219.

Table 15
Annual Crude Rate of Birth and Death, and Number of Cases
and Deaths by Contagious Diseases

	Birth	Death	No. of Cases	No. of Deaths
1955			3,209	909
1957			1,963	197
1959			5,531	961
·1960	42.0	13.0	5,074	640
1962	41.0	13.0		
1964	39.0	11.0		
1965	37.0	10.0	6,016	513
1966	35.0	10.0	8,473	1,151
1968	31.9	8.9	6,001	485
1969	30.6	8.6	7,453	232
1970	29.5	8.5	5,867	87

Source: (KA) 1971: 409; (KSY) 1962: 373; (KSY) 1971: 419.

Table 16
Amount of Mail Handled, and Number of Telephones

	Mail Handled in thousands	Telephones
1957	98,146	49,417
1959	128,696	72,552
1961	147,094	97,016
1965	367,623	220,635
1967	440,438	339,280
1969	522,382	442,452
1970	540,269	481,207

Source: (KSY) 1962: 181, 183; (KSY) 1971: 215, 217.

Table 17
Number of Government Employees

1955	236,148
1957	233,861
1959	246,857
1961	235,456
1965	304,416
1970	425,000

Source: (KSY) 1962: 330; Chang-hyun Cho, "Bureaucracy and Local Government in South Korea," Government and Politics of Korea, Se-jin Kim and Chang-hyun Cho, eds. (Silver Spring, Maryland: The Research Institute on Korean Affairs, 1972), p. 93.

Bibliographical Note

In writing this book I wanted to convey the dynamics and the flavor of social change in Korea during the decade 1961-1971. Therefore, I have concentrated more on the actions and reactions that took place during that period rather than on a chronological and technical analysis. For the latter, especially with economics as the central theme, I found the following titles to be of adequate quality: Parvez Hasan, *Korea: Problems and Issues in a Rapidly Growing Economy* (Baltimore, Maryland: Johns Hopkins University Press, 1976); L. L. Wade and B. S. Kim, *Economic Development of South Korea: The Political Economy of Success* (New York: Praeger Publishers, 1978); Gilbert T. Brown, *Korean Pricing Policies and Economic Development in the 1960s* (Baltimore, Maryland: Johns Hopkins University Press, 1973); and the two-volume study prepared by the World Bank, *Korea: Managing the Industrial Transition* (Washington, D.C.: The World Bank, 1987).

Of the numerous sources I have examined or quoted in this book concerning South Korea in general and the decade of 1961-1971 in particular, the following may be considered for special mention. Standard Korean history up to 1961 available in English can be found in Bong-youn Choy, *Korea: A History* (Rutland, Vermont: Charles E. Tuttle Co., 1971), and Pow-key Sohn, et al., *The History of Korea* (Seoul: Korean National Commission for UNESCO, 1970); Kyung-cho Chung, *New Korea* (New York: Macmillan, 1962), which takes the military takeover into consideration; Chung's more extensive assessment of the junta's first decade is in his *Korea: The Third Republic* (New York: Macmillan, 1971); Keun-woo Han, *The History of Korea* (Seoul: Eul-yoo Publishing Co., 1967), with particular attention to the "transitional period" on pp. 361-509; John Cope Caldwell, *The Korea Story* (Chicago: H. Regnery Co., 1950), and E. Grant Meade, *American Military Government in Korea* (New York: King's Crown Press, 1951) for the U.S. military government period. For discussion on the beginning of Korea's "modernization" in world historical perspective, see C. E. Black, *The Dynamics of Modernization: A Study in Comparative History* (New York: Harper & Row, 1961), and Irving Louis Horowitz, *The Three Worlds of Development* (New York: Oxford University Press, 1966). Chong-sik Lee's *The Politics of Korean Nationalism* (Berkeley, California: University of California Press, 1963) also contains good historical backgrounds. An anecdotal and literate introduction to Korean culture is in Richard Rutt, *Korean Works and Days: Notes from the Diary of a Country Priest* (Rutland, Vermont: Charles E. Tuttle, 1964).

Insightful and refreshing discussion of Korea's political and social dynamics, especially concerning the military junta, has been offered by Gregory Henderson in *Korea: The Politics of the Vortex* (Cambridge, Mass.: Harvard University Press, 1968), and by David Cole and Princeton Lyman in their book *Korean Development: The Interplay of Politics and Economics* (Cambridge, Mass.: Harvard University Press, 1971), both of which have been used extensively in this book. Their critical yet sympathetic discussion of Korea's potentials and problems have been of great value to my own task in this volume. John Oh's *Democracy on Trial* (Ithaca, New York: Cornell University Press, 1968), a critical look at the military government in Korea, is also an important source on Korea's military-civil coalition. Kwan-bong Kim's *The Korea-Japan Treaty Crisis and the Instability of the Korean Political System* (New York: Praeger Publishers, 1971) is important both for its historical description of the crisis and for its analytical insight into the problems of legitimacy in Korea's political structure.

Of the literature attempting to shed some sociological light on the military government in Korea, the many research articles contained in the following anthologies are also helpful: Eugene Kim, ed., *A Pattern of Political Development: Korea* (Detroit: The Korean Research and Publications, Inc., 1964); Se-jin Kim and Chang-hyun Cho, eds., *Government and Politics of Korea* (Silver Spring, Maryland: The Research Institute of Korean Affairs, 1972); Byung-chul Koh, ed., *Aspects of Administrative Development in South Korea* (Kalamazoo, Michigan: The Korean Research and Publications, Inc., 1967); and Andre Nahm, ed., *Studies in the Developmental Aspects of Korea* (Kalamazoo, Michigan: Western Michigan University Press, 1969).

Of particular interest today, William A. Douglas's research on student activities in Korea is excellent. See his "Korean Students and Politics." *Asian Survey* Vol. 3, No. 12, 1963, and "The Current Status of Korean Society." *Koreana Quarterly* Vol. 1, No. 4, 1962.

The development of the Korean military and its political involvement is best described in Se-jin Kim, *The Politics of Military Revolution in Korea* (Chapel Hill, North Carolina: University of North Carolina Press, 1970); the military's modernizing orientation is insightfully dealt with in Hahn-been Lee, *Korea: Time, Change, and Administration* (Hawaii: The East-West Center Press, 1968). I have used these two sources liberally and benefited much from their analysis.

On a more technical level, I have found a wealth of information in the following sources: Taek-il Kim, John A. Ross, and George C. Worth, *The Korean National Family Planning Program* (New York: The Population Council, 1972) for the family planning campaign in Korea; Sang-chul Suh, *The Strategy for Agricultural Development in Korea* (Seoul: Samwha Corp., Publishers, 1971) for all the statistical information concerning Korea's agricultural development in that period; and In-joung Whang's fine studies comparing the two leadership styles, "Political Elite and Organizational Change of the Korean Government." *Korean*

Observer Vol. 2, No. 1, 1969, and "Leadership and Organizational Development in the Economic Ministries of the Korean Government." *Asian Survey* Vol. 11, No. 10, 1971.

For the analysis of organizational effectiveness, I used the definitively comprehensive work of James L. Price, *Organizational Effectiveness: An Inventory of Propositions* (Homewood, Illinois: Richard D. Irwin, 1968).

The following volumes provide fairly standard factual information (although mostly published in Korean) dealing with the decade, from which I extracted abundant statistical data: *Korea Annual* (Seoul: Hapdong News Agency); *History of Korean Military Revolutionary Tribune* (Seoul: Publications Committee, The Supreme Council for Military Revolutionary Tribune, 1961-1963); *Monthly Statistics of Korea* (Seoul: The Economic Planning Board); and *History of the Republic of Korea Army* (Seoul: Ministry of Defense, Republic of Korea, 1968).

Of course, there are a number of professional journals that bear upon the chronicle of Korea's development. The ones I quoted more frequently in this book are *Koreana Quarterly, Journal of Asiatic Studies, Korean Journal of Public Administration, Korea Focus, Asian Survey, Asian Forum, Korean Observer,* and *The Korean Economist.*

Index

Adelman, Irma, 65, 85, 140, 171, 176
Agriculture: extension services performed, 186; in first two economic plans, 183-84; land reclamation, 185; New Village Movement, 187-88; overall changes in, 184-88; productivity in, 183; rice yield, 187; rural organizations, 94; share in GNP, 184; structural changes, 184-85; in Third Economic Plan, 187; use of fertilizer, 187; usury debt settlement for farmers, 185

Breidenstein, Gerhard, 140
Bureaucracy: "adaptive function" of, 119; aims of, 117; attitude changes in, 116; budget increase in, 97; as a contrasting theme under Rhee and Park, 64; enlargement of, 116-18; "entrepreneurial outlook" in, 68, 141; factual orientation in, 147; infusion of military personnel in, 115, 121; inadequate qualifications of personnel in, 114; in-service training, 116; long-term orientation in, 141-42; mental outlook in, 115; procedural changes, 116; professionalism in, 119-20; "ritualistic," 120; structural changes in, 116-17,

141-42; wholesale dismissal of personnel in, 97, 115

Central Election Committee, 14
Central Intelligence Agency (Korean), 119
Chang, John: administration of, 17-20, 33-34; dilemma of in power, 18, 32-33; economic conditions under, 21-22; election of, 18-19; factionalism and, 17-20, 32-34, 105-6; history of Democratic party, 17; military and, 33; rural economy under, 22; social unrest under, 20; students and, 20-21
Chun, Doo Hwan, xiii
Cole, David, xi, 89, 140, 148
Combined Economic Board (CEB), 145-46
Communism in Korea: Chang and, 40; Communist party (in North), 122; Marxism and, 43; North-South relations and, 40; origin of anti-Communism in South, 40-41; as political ideology, 39-40; as radical theory, 43; Rhee's policy toward, 41
Currency reform, 171-72. See also Domestic savings

About the Author

JON HUER is Associate Professor in the Department of Sociology and Anthropology at the University of North Carolina at Wilmington. His previous publications include *Art, Beauty and Pornography* and *The Dead End* as well as numerous articles.